Also by Lauren St John

The White Giraffe
Hardcore Troubadour: The Life and Near Death of Steve Earle
Walkin' After Midnight: A Journey to the Heart of Nashville
Greg Norman: The Biography
Seve: Ryder Cup Hero

rainbow's end

A Memoir of Childhood, War and an African Farm

LAUREN ST JOHN

SCRIBNER

New York London Toronto Sydney

SCRIBNER
1230 Avenue of the Americas
New York, NY 10020

SCRIBNER and design are trademarks of
Macmillan Library Reference USA, Inc., used under license
by Simon & Schuster, the publisher of this work.

For information about special discounts for bulk purchases,
please contact Simon & Schuster Special Sales:
1-800-456-6798 or business@simonandschuster.com

Designed by Davina Mock
Text set in Berling Roman

Maps by Paul J. Pugliese

Manufactured in the United States of America

1   2   3   4   5   6   7   8   9   10

Library of Congress Cataloging-in-Publication Data

St John, Lauren, [date]
Rainbow's end: a memoir of childhood, war and an African farm/Lauren St John.
p. cm.
1. St John, Lauren, [date]—Childhood and youth. 2. St John, Lauren, [date]—Family.
3. Zimbabwe—History—1965–1980—Biography. 4. Zimbabwe—History—
Chimurenga War, 1966–1980—Personal narratives. 5. Farm life—Zimbabwe—
History—20th Century. 6. Zimbabwe—Social life and customs—20th century. I. Title.
DT2984.S725A3 2007
968.91'04092—dc22
[B]   2006050620

ISBN-13: 978-0-7432-8679-4
ISBN-10:   0-7432-8679-0

For the safety and protection of the individuals concerned, some names and identifying characteristics have been altered.

For Miss Zeederberg, wherever she is . . .

And for my father, who I finally understood

The barb in the arrow of childhood's suffering is this: its intense loneliness, its intense ignorance.

Olive Schreiner, *The Story of an African Farm*

contents

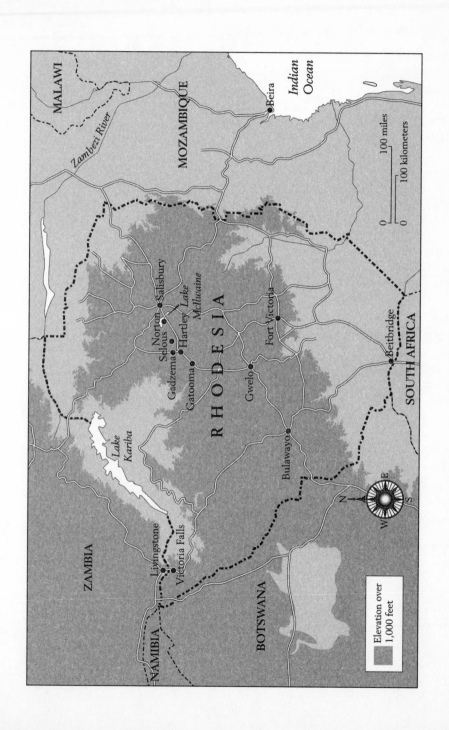

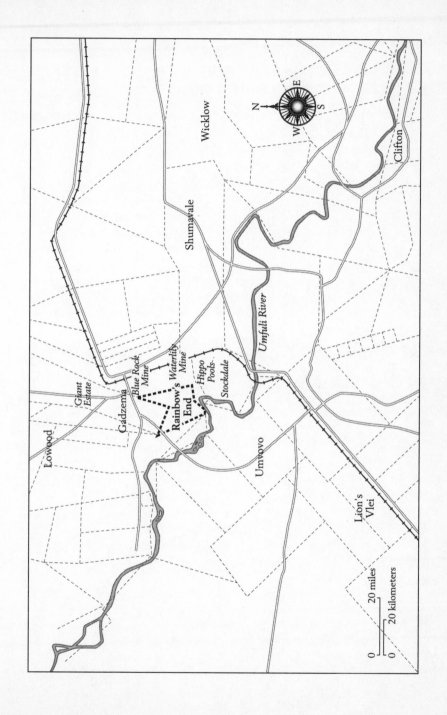

Lowood

Giant
Estate

Gadzema

Blue Rock
Mine

**Rainbow's
End**

Waterlily
Mine

Hippo
Pools

Stockdale

Umvovo

Shumavale

Wicklow

Umfuli River

Clifton

Lion's
Vlei

N
W   E
S

0   20 miles
0   20 kilometers

rainbow's end

prologue

They weren't supposed to be there. That was how Camilla always remembered it.

They had only gone because her mother-in-law, a year and a half ill with cancer, had taken a turn for the worse, and because the farm store that had been so many months in the planning was opening the next day, and because they had a house full of kids—the Lawson boy, Brian, and his stepbrother, Alan, up from Salisbury; and their own brood, Nigel, aged nine, Julie, eight in three weeks' time, and Bruce, eleven years old and already so like his father in his quietness and passion for wildlife. And where better to take them than Rainbow's End.

It was 1978, and the Rhodesian Bush War was at its height. For the past two years, the Communist-trained forces of the Zimbabwe African National Liberation Army (ZANLA) and the Zimbabwe People's Revolutionary Army (ZIPRA), terrorists or nationalists, depending on your point of view, had been pouring over the Rhodesian border from their bases in Zambia and Mozambique, and the struggle that had started in the mid-sixties with a few minor skirmishes, easily crushed, had become a brutal and bloody war. The focus of the attacks was the white-owned farms. To Camilla, it seemed that almost every night now there was some grisly killing on the news, and every week brought fresh reports of land mines and ambushes in nearby rural areas.

Not that any of that had stopped Ben Forrester from following his dream of owning a game farm. At Wicklow Estate, they already had all that they needed. Camilla came from a farming family of considerable success and renown, and her husband had an excellent job running her brother's tobacco and cattle operation out in Selous. But Ben had an independent streak. *He* wanted to be the one to build a beautiful future for his family. *He* wanted to help them fulfill their vision of a life spent in harmony with nature and Africa.

In 1976 he'd bought Rainbow's End, a pretty, thousand-acre farm, five miles from Hartley. They had continued to live on Shumavale, one of three farms that came under the banner of Wicklow Estate, some twenty minutes' drive away, but Ben's heart was at Rainbow's End. He'd grown his own crops and sectioned off a hundred prime acres on the banks of the Umfuli River for use as a game reserve. He'd moved his elderly parents into the sprawling thatched house, where they could sit in their lounge and watch the wildlife drift down to the water hole at sunset: fifty impala, a wildebeest, two ostriches, a troop of monkeys, and a giraffe, her legs splayed in a graceful triangle as she drank from the coppery dam.

For the most part Camilla stayed at Rainbow's End only when Ben was away fighting in the War. Like most other able-bodied white, Asian, or colored men in Rhodesia, he was on compulsory "call-up" with the Army for periods that varied from unit to unit but could be anything up to six weeks at a stretch. At those times Camilla would take the kids and they would spend a month or so with his parents, where Ben felt there was safety in numbers and where her nurse's training meant she could help his father care for her gravely ill mother-in-law, Sheila. Camilla loved Rainbow's End as much as Ben did, but the terrorists were known to use the weir on the farm as a crossing place and she had come to dread the opening of the game park gate that led to the house, particularly when they had to wrestle with its lock after nightfall. It was the perfect place for an ambush. Once, when Bruce had climbed out in the darkness to open it, their extreme vulnerability—an anxious mother and a small, careful boy—had smacked her in the chest like a physical force and she had cried out to him to hurry.

More recently, too, something else had happened to make her think differently about the place. She had awoken one night with the overwhelming sense that an evil presence was in the house. The feeling was so intense and she was so distressed by it that she shook the children from their sleep. They'd all held hands and said a prayer. Over the weeks, the feeling had faded, but she'd never totally dismissed it. It was gone but definitely not forgotten.

On Monday, January 9, the Forresters rose to the hiss of crickets and fierce singing of birds—Africa's fervent celebration of life after a bout of heavy rain. Before long, the echoey old passages of Rainbow's End rang with the laughter of their sons and the husky, fresh-broken voices of the visiting boys. Julie, the lone girl, was sick in bed. So was Sheila, for whom they had just taken on a black nurse's aide. Camilla did her best to keep them from feeling left out, particularly because old Mr. Forrester was away in the Eastern Highlands. Ben was to spend the day procuring the last of the supplies for the farm store, and the bare-chested boys were already on their way down to the rushing brown river in front of the house, the summer sun warm on their skin.

Later that morning Camilla had to drive to Wicklow on an errand. By then Bruce had had his fill of splashing and diving with the others in the foaming pools below the weir, and he dried himself off and told her that he'd like to come with her and fly his falcon. On the airstrip at Wicklow, they stood together and watched the falcon's freedom flight. It soared in the haze above the crop sprayers' ragged runway. Bruce had never been a particularly demonstrative child; he had something of his father's shy reserve. But in the thrill of the moment he turned to his mother and gave her a hug. Camilla squeezed him hard and felt elated.

Yesterday it had come home to her how precious, and brief, life is. They'd gone to church as usual. During the service the minister had told them of an attack the previous day on a farming family in the rural community of Norton, which lay between Hartley and Salisbury. The congregation winced audibly. Most of them were farmers, well aware that at any given hour it could happen to them. Many were friends with the family involved.

Billy Miller had been on patrol with his Army unit in the valleys around Lake McIllwaine, coincidentally close to his own farm. His wife and two daughters waited alone at home. When a fuel delivery driver knocked on their door asking for directions to the house on the farm's second section, usually occupied by Billy's brother and his wife, now away on holiday, they offered to show him the way. And walked into an ambush. Sheila Miller and fifteen-year-old Sarah were killed outright. The other daughter, Victoria, was left for dead. Down in the valley, Billy heard the shots.

Camilla had found it difficult to come to terms with the realization that an entire family, bonded tight by love and memories, could be devastated at the speed of a bullet. Or the notion that no one in the tragedy was where they should have been—or could have been—had circumstances been different. She was quite shaken by the story.

Back at Rainbow's End she spent time with Julie, who was still in bed, and read her *The Snow Goose*, the Paul Gallico story of a lonely hunchback lighthouse keeper and a bird wounded by a gunshot. When she finished, Ben took her aside and explained to her in detail how the store would work. Camilla sat in the shelter of his green eyes, as she had done for the thirteen and a half short years of their marriage, and allowed herself to be carried along on the rush of his enthusiasm. A lot of people considered Ben dour, but all were agreed that he was a true gentleman, the highest accolade Rhodesians could give. He was totally devoted to his family. Ben was not a liberal, but he had a vision of making life better for the Africans in his employ. He was good to them. He had already built a farm school for their children, and the store was just another step toward his goal of creating better conditions for his workers. His truck was loaded with goods, and tomorrow they'd have a grand opening.

At seven, dinner was ready to be served. The nurse's aide had taken Sheila her tray in the main bedroom to the left of the hallway, and Camilla, Ben, and the boys were in the lounge. In the house, the air was noisy with good-natured banter. Outside, the frogs were in competition with the weir's ocean roar. Camilla debated whether to collect the back door key and lock the front door. The same key fitted both locks. But the sun had only just set. Through the window it was already profoundly dark, but it was still early.

Julie called from the back bedroom. Camilla went down the passage to check on her. That's when she heard it—a discordant noise in the garden. Something about it was threatening.

"What was that?" she shouted through to Ben.

"Stay where you are, Cammy," he yelled, and then the world exploded.

Afterward Camilla would ask herself time and time again whether she should have picked up the shotgun in the bedroom and gone out with both barrels blazing. But it was over so quickly. There was just a shout and the earsplitting jackhammer of machine-gun fire, and then Camilla heard the most terrible sound of her life: a deathly hush.

The minutes passed. More gunshots. Then footsteps whispered on the concrete floor of the passage. Two bloody apparitions appeared at the bedroom door: Brian Lawson, wounded but alive, and Nigel, eyes wet with tears, his leg shot to pieces.

"Daddy's dead," he burst out. Then: "Bruce was so brave."

Afterward she'd never know what he had meant by that. Frantically she began to hunt through the bags, discarded swimming things, and school uniforms—ready for the start of the new term the following morning—for the first aid kit. Blood was bubbling like a spring from Nigel's leg, and she didn't want to lose him, too. Finally she just grabbed an eiderdown and bound it around the jagged hole. She tended to Brian. She comforted Julie. Then she left the room in a trance.

The lounge was crimson, the floor slick with gore. Ben had died with his hand curled around his son's foot. Half of Bruce's face had been shot off. Camilla stood gazing down at her boy, thinking, irrationally, *tenderly*, how healthy his exposed young bones were, so clean and new. Alan was slumped bloodily in a chair. He groaned. Camilla started mouth-to-mouth resuscitation on him before coming to the agonizing conclusion that what she'd heard was not a living breath but air escaping from his dying lungs. Numbly she moved into the main bedroom. The old lady was slumped over her tray in a spreading pool of scarlet.

Everywhere there was the smell of death and food and the intolerable sound of silence. The kitchen was empty. The cook and nurse's aide had fled into the night. Mechanically, Camilla locked the back and front doors, as she'd meant to do earlier. She had no idea where the terrorists were or if they were regrouping for another attack. She returned to the bedroom where the children were huddled and dug out the revolver. Her hands shook so much that it accidentally discharged. The bullet missed Julie by inches.

Into the shocked room blasted the telephone's defiant ring. Camilla walked back down the passage and through the puddles of blood to pick it up. As if through a time warp she heard loud, jovial Richard Etheridge, their neighboring farmer on the river, boom down the line: "Are you all right? We heard shots."

"No," Camilla said. "No, we certainly are not all right."

Someone, she could never remember who, drove them to the clinic in Hartley that night. And even that was fraught with risk because the Umfuli River was in flood and the truck bobbed on the torrent as they crossed and Camilla found herself thinking: That would just be our luck. To now be swept away. She put her arms around Julie, who was just as white as the boys because the security forces, who'd come to their rescue thirty-five minutes after Richard had called them, had failed to cover up the bodies, and the little girl had witnessed the horror for herself.

"I saw Daddy dead," she told her mother.

At the clinic, Dr. Bouwer wanted to give Camilla something that would knock her out, at least until the morning, when she'd wake up in an antiseptic Salisbury hospital, but she refused to take anything until the ambulance men arrived to take care of the children. "Then you can hit me over the back of the head for all I care," she told him.

She never returned to Rainbow's End. Instead it was her brother and his wife, heavily pregnant with their first child, who mopped, scrubbed, and wept over the blood-splattered walls and floors. After that the house stood empty. The trees, which had always crowded too close for comfort, giving the place a gloomy air, seemed to crowd closer still, the yellow grass grew right up to the windows, the thatch turned gray and sagged and fell in, and the antelope and monkeys tripped through the silent rooms. That's how it was the day I first saw it.

The day we decided to move to Rainbow's End.

Giant Estate, Gadzema
1975–1978

Fishing trip, 1971

Errol　　　　May　　　　Lauren　　　　Lisa

1

Most people left Rhodesia to get away from the War. *We* came back for it.

It was April 1975. One year after moving to South Africa to start a new life, we were in a car crammed with possessions and we were barreling once more into the indigo haze, into the thorny, blond bush, somewhere beyond which our next new life was waiting. Dad had a Peter Stuyvesant out in the air, twisting smoke, the twin gray lines of the strip road were tapering crazily into the horizon, and he was saying, categorically: "Two things got me down about Cape Town. One was the weather and the other was people telling me I'd run away from the War. I couldn't *stand* people saying I'd run away from the War."

Which was ironic because it wasn't even his war.

It had become his war only because in 1960 he happened to see a recruitment ad for the Rhodesian Army the same week he received his National Service papers in his home town of Uitenhage, South Africa, and he'd thought to himself: A chance to see another country! What a pleasure! Even though he was only eighteen and it would mean fighting for someone else's cause. And even though his family had been putting down roots in the Eastern Cape ever since their ship, buffeted by ice storms on the Thames in England and ocean winds in the Bay of Biscay, had docked at Algoa Bay with the 1820 Settlers. By the seventies the Rhodesian War had become Dad's war because he'd spilled blood for it and also because he'd married Mom, whose great-grandfather had been an associate of Cecil John Rhodes, who "discovered" Rhodesia. Her ancestry was full of stories about pioneering uncles walking barefoot from Durban to Bulawayo, more than a thousand miles, to save their shoes.

Mom always said that Dad was Rhodesian from the moment he set foot in the country and saw how beautiful it was. Not that South Africa wasn't. In almost every way it was more blessed with visual splendor, more rich in natural resources, and unlike its landlocked northern neighbor, it had the ocean, steaming up to the coast in a smoking white rush. But something about the landscape of Rhodesia spoke to him. He liked its unshowy loveliness. He liked the way of life, and he liked the people, who for the most part didn't think there were many worse crimes than getting above yourself. Above all, he liked the sensation that poured through him as he crossed the Great Green Greasy Limpopo—"this incredible sense of being free." It stayed with him even after he stepped hot and sticky from the train in Bulawayo, aged eighteen, and saw the smart peaked caps of the RLI (Rhodesian Light Infantry) officers, who waited with crocodile smiles and soft, welcoming voices to greet the new recruits. He thought of Rhodesia as the Promised Land, and he'd brought me up to do the same.

Now we were Rhodesian to our souls.

Heat and dust boiled in through our car windows and the leathery smell of cattle and something else—something that forced its way into your nostrils like a dissident spirit and set nervy adrenaline jangling through your veins. Something as old as Africa, like the loamy earth or the sweat of the Africans walking along the roadside, backs as stiff as cats', their heads loaded with sky-scraping stacks of *mielie-meal*, crates of chickens, or economy-size Sunflower oil tins slopping water. They passed in an arc of Viewfinder snapshots.

"How come their heads don't get sore?"

"Their heads are very hard," Mom said. "Shhh, keep your voice down. You'll wake Lisa."

She took off her tortoiseshell sunglasses, pursed her lips in the vanity mirror, and reapplied lipstick in anticipation of the journey's end. I leaned over the wicker carry-cot and smoothed the downy hair of my sister, thinking that, though she'd cried so hard for so long that some days it seemed a miracle she found time to draw breath, she still resembled a Pears' Baby Competition winner. But her skin was thin and clammy. I noticed with alarm that my own arm was as blue-white as hers and snatched it away lest my mother see it and comment. "Are you anemic?" grown-ups were always asking me. "Have you been ill?"

A black sign flashed by: GADZEMA.

If there was a town about, it wasn't apparent.

We flew over a narrow bridge and ramped up the other side. Dad had one eye on his watch, and he drove without troubling the brakes, never once slowing for pedestrians or cyclists. Their only warning was a last-minute toot, at which point they'd jerk into life, see they were about to join the kaleidoscope of twitching butterflies on the grille of the car, and fling themselves sideways, trying desperately to maintain their towering loads.

"*Dad!*"

"Errol, please slow down," Mom entreated. "You're going to kill someone."

"For goodness' sake, you people, I'm not going to hit them. What do you take me for? But why must they walk in the middle of the road?"

He bore down on a bicycle. My fingers dug into the seat, trying to stop the car by sheer willpower.

Mom said: "I don't understand why you're driving like a maniac. If we're five minutes late, it won't be the end of the world."

I didn't have to be in the front seat to know that Dad's blue eyes would be turning Cape-of-Good-Hope-in-a-squall gray, and he said through his teeth: "Any minute now, I'm really going to lose my temper. No ways am I going to be late. *No ways.*"

I twisted around. The cyclist was skidding uncontrolled down the gravel incline, bare toes splayed, scrabbling for a foothold. His back was rigid with indignation. He wobbled to a halt on the edge of the bush and turned his head to glare at us, but by then he was just a speck against the green and gold, and the red dust spun up and erased him.

I faced the wavering strips again, but the atmosphere in the car had changed and I was no longer looking or listening. On my lap were my favorite books, their covers faded and scarred. A dozen times over the past year I'd pressed my palm against their pages and wished that the lives of the characters, the pea-soup fogs on smuggler-crowded moors, the starlit beds of heather and bracken, the wild gallops over mountains and deserts, would flow into my fingertips by osmosis. Now I would no longer have to. Now I had the promise of a horse of my own and life on a farm, all in the middle of a war with terrorists.

I widened my window and leaned out into the charged, leathery air. *Please, God,* I thought, *let me be someone who has adventures.*

2

Before Giant Estate and long before Rainbow's End, we lived in a railway cottage in the no-horse town of Hartley, 120 kilometers from Rhodesia's capital, Salisbury. Mom worked for the David Whitehead fabric factory until two days before I was born, and Dad was a checker on the railways. It was there that he handed Mom an unsealed brown envelope to hold on to during a car journey, and it turned out to contain a live baby cobra.

She'd never really recovered. "What kind of man gives his wife an envelope with a cobra in it? You can't believe what I've had to put up with."

I was a toddler by then, and he'd incensed Mom by housing the cobra, his new pet, in his wooden fishing box in the kitchen. She was convinced it would escape and attack me and was forever opening the lid to check if it was still there. Eventually it almost bit her, and she asked the garden boy to kill it. It had taken Dad weeks to forgive her.

"It was absolutely beautiful," he'd reminisce fondly when reminded of it. "You should have seen the colors."

Then, because we were poor and trying to build a house, we lived with Granny and Grampy, Mom's parents, in Salisbury, where I frayed the nerves of Grampy, who was deaf and not so fond of children, and my uncle James taught me to use a pellet gun and Granny told me how the Owl and the Pussycat went to sea in a beautiful pea green boat and I went to the circus and caught a rare virus and was in intensive care and nearly died.

After nearly a year of Dad working at the Electricity Supply Commission (EEC) by day and the Sunshine Fish & Chip shop till closing, we moved into pink Pussy Willow cottage. There Mom mashed up pumpkin and rice for me and put it in my Beatrix Potter bowl on the windowsill to cool, and at night I climbed up on the kitchen cabinets and ate sugar until I got boils and, when I was cured of those, saw stars and had fainting spells and underwent multiple tests and brain scans until the doctors concluded I was just a "dizzy dame."

Other things that happened at Pussy Willow cottage were (1) I fell into the toilet and was rescued by Samson, our houseboy, which Mom was glad about, but she also told me that it was "not nice for a black man to see your Mary-Ann." (2) I locked the steering wheel on the car after Dad specially told me not to and he chased me round and round the dining table trying to give me a hiding, while Mom shielded me like a small but brave lioness. (3) We went with another family to the Mozambican town of Beira, the seaside resort of choice for white Rhodesians, on one of our first ever holidays. While we were there, Dad and the other husband bought two galvanized-iron baths packed with huge prawns, and Mom and the wife had to peel them for our supper while the men lay on the darkening beach carousing and downing beers. The prawns stabbed Mom's hands with their spiky, gray heads, so that by the time they were on the fire, turning pinky orange, her fingers had, as she kept plaintively reminding us, "swollen up like giant sausages. You can't see between them!"

And though I was morbidly fascinated and, of course, truly sorry for her, I was even more captivated by the sweet, charcoally Beira prawns and the flames shooting up into the black, salty night and the silver shimmer of sea.

We were in and out of our next house, a double-story where we moved when I was six and a half, with hardly enough time to unpack. Shortly after my seventh birthday, we immigrated to South Africa in a way that was presented to me as a happy chance—while on holiday in Cape Town, Dad had popped into the local equivalent of the EEC, Escom, and had been joyfully received and offered a job on the spot. But it felt more like fleeing. On the day of our departure, I was sitting on my parents' bed in our double-story house in Salisbury, watching Dad pack a suitcase, when there was an emergency-loud hammering at the back door.

"Stay here," Dad commanded.

His footsteps faded away on the stairs.

I went to the window, parted the yellow curtains, and looked down. All I could see was the top of a man's head and some shoulders. I was sorry that Mom wasn't with us. She'd been away seemingly forever, first in hospital and then somewhere to recover, and now she was in Cape Town, finding us a house. But I was sorrier still to be leaving the double-story, where I'd made bows and arrows with blunt stone tips in our over-grown backyard after learning about the Bushmen; and danced around the lounge to "The Loco-motion," "D-I-V-O-R-C-E," and "Knock Three Times"; and tossed our fluffy gray cat, Sparky, out of a second-story window to see if he'd land on his feet (he did and somehow survived).

There were shouts from below, and Dad and a stranger in an office shirt suddenly reeled out of the shadows, fists flailing. They fell apart, chests heaving, and shouted some more, and then they came together again and pounded and battered each other and clung to each other in a cruel embrace. My fingers locked on the yellow curtains. Should I run downstairs and try to stop them? Should I hide in a cupboard in case the man beat up Dad and then came after me? Should I act normal if Dad survived and pretend that I hadn't seen anything?

I returned to the bed and sat there in an agony of worry.

When Dad strode back into the room, bruised and carrying some kind of darkness with him, I jumped up and cried: "Why were you fighting, Dad? Why was the man angry?"

The darkness swung on me, and he snapped: "Mind your own business."

Then, as my face crumbled: "It's nothing, see."

Then: "Don't tell Mom, okay."

He smiled and gave me a hug.

The world tilted, wobbled a little, and righted itself again.

Cape Town is where the Indian and Atlantic oceans collide, the last gasp of Africa before the maelstrom of gray-green seas known as the Cape of Good Hope, notorious for wrecking the boats, bones, and good hopes of untold numbers of early explorers. Henry and George Peck, distant relatives of my mother, survived an 1828 shipwreck in False Bay and salvaged enough to open a ginger beer stall. When we arrived there in March 1974, Cape Town was also a place of soaring mountains, breathtaking blue bays, and vineyards graced with Cape Dutch houses, but we lived in the Tygerberg, close to Dad's work but far from the beautiful things. The first time I stepped onto the lawn— or at least the ground where it would be once we planted it—I got a sole full of devil thorns. There was no end to them. It was as if the earth was infested with them.

The house was recently completed and smelled of plaster and paint and varnish and new carpet. It had amber stained-glass windows on either side of the front door and a brass chain to keep out the burglars and murderers—of whom, I was told, there were many. From the lounge window you could see the new-development bareness of our home replicated several dozen times. A flat, straight road stretched so far into the distance it seemed to touch the mauve sketch of mountains. It was a bleakly pretty vista, but it was suburbia again, and more than anything on earth, I wanted a horse. And not just any horse. I wanted a black stallion.

In the absence of black stallions, Mom and Dad bought me a kitten, a seal point Siamese with eyes the color of an alpine lake. He had a fancy pedigree name, but I called him Kim. Kim took the edge off the loneliness, but he couldn't shut out the arguments that had ricocheted around the walls ever since our arrival. For that I used a pillow and buried myself in books. I read every horse and adventure novel I could persuade anyone to buy me, and then I turned back to the beginning and started all over again. At night, I sat at the window hoping to see mysterious lights or people "up to no good," as they always were in books, but nothing ever happened to interrupt the dreary mundanity of our lives.

When winter came, gale-force winds howled around the house, and black widow spiders, known in the Cape as buttons, scuttled through the gutters. Every morning Kim and I would shiver in bed while Mom ran an iron over my school uniform so that it would be warm when I held up my arms for her to slip it over my head. In class I'd found myself on the wrong side of the Afrikaans-English divide. In my limited understanding of the matter, South Africans seemed to spend a lot of time at odds with one another. The Zulus didn't like the Xhosas, and the Xhosas didn't like the Vendas or the Sothos, who didn't like the Afrikaners, who in turn didn't like the English or many, or even *any*, of the Africans, and hardly anyone liked the Cape Coloureds, descendants of Malay and other slaves and shameful Dutch and English unions with not-so-willing Khoi, San, or Xhosa participants, and who were therefore constant, unwanted reminders of a past it would have been easier to forget.

With so many people not getting along, I despaired of finding a friend, but then I met Frederique, a French girl with a pigtail and quarter-moon dimples. Her mother made traditional French apple tarts so flaky and fabulous that Mom, who had a sweet tooth, could never wait to drive me to her house at the weekends, and Freddie and the apple tarts—along with milk tarts sprinkled with cinnamon, deep-fried twists of batter dipped in syrup, known as *koeksisters*, and Snowballs, chocolate and coconut–coated marshmallows from Woollie's (Woolworth's)—became the highlights of my stay in Cape Town. For Mom, those things were just a bonus. She loved every inch of the city and our shiny, clean house.

Dad, meanwhile, was shrinking. In all of the photos from that time, his face is beige, set in discontent, and his hair is flyaway and overlong. In Salisbury, even working two jobs, he'd looked like his namesake, Errol Flynn, tanned and hyperfit from Army exercises. In Cape Town he existed in a permanent state of restlessness, like a zoo animal with obsessive-compulsive disorder. He wore cheap, ill-fitting suits in tan, his hands grew pale and soft, and his unhappiness was obvious.

Toward the end of August 1974, Lisa was born. I'd hoped for a brother right up until Mom walked through the door from the hospital, when I panicked and thought, I want a sister! But even a new sister seemed only a temporary blessing because she cried all the time, as though she were in torment, although the doctors could find nothing wrong with her.

The arguments continued, now interspersed with Lisa's screaming. I cuddled Kim, read by flashlight under the bedclothes, and felt utterly, intensely alone.

On November 4, there was a Babel of sirens and lights outside our school on Gladstone Street, Bellville, and police swarmed all over the road. Next they were in our classroom, asking if we'd seen a Coloured with a limp hanging around the area or entering the house across the road. By morning it was front-page news. Susanna Magdalena Van der Linde, a forty-six-year-old mother of three, had been stabbed to death with scissors. The prime suspect was Marthinus Choegoe, a crippled Coloured man.

The Scissors Murder, as it was known, would become one of the most infamous murder cases in South African history. Three years earlier Van der Linde's forty-seven-year-old husband, Christiaan, had begun a relationship with Marlene Lehnberg, then sixteen, at the orthopedic clinic where they both worked. As the months passed and Christiaan's promises to leave his wife came to nothing, Lehnberg's infatuation turned obsessive. She hired the reluctant, unemployed Choegoe, a patient at the clinic, to kill Mrs. Van der Linde, but on three separate occasions he went to the house and was unable to go through with it.

Undeterred, Lehnberg attempted to persuade an engineering student to do the hit instead. When he balked at murder, she stole his gun. Again she enlisted the help of Choegoe, allegedly promising him sex and a car if he murdered Mrs. Van der Linde. At 9:00 a.m. on November 4, they drove to the house. Lehnberg told police that she stayed in the car, but witnesses supported Choegoe's story that they entered together. Lehnberg struck Mrs. Van der Linde on the jaw with the pistol butt, and Choegoe finished her off with a pair of scissors they found on the sideboard. Lehnberg then squirted Choegoe with green dye from a gas pistol and told him she'd deny everything if he was caught. In fact she was trapped within weeks by a web of her own creation. They were both sentenced to hang, a sentence reduced to jail time on appeal. Christiaan spent the rest of his life in mourning and died a decade on, a broken man.

The grisliness of the crime and its proximity to our classroom had a lasting impact on me. I found it impossible to get the specifics of it out of my head—the green dye, the scissors on the sideboard, and the crippled Coloured man. It was as vivid to me as if I'd actually seen it. Then I heard that an elderly woman in our neighborhood had been murdered by another Coloured who'd somehow managed to breach the chain on her door and throttle her.

After that, Coloureds with scissors stalked my nightmares. They crept down the windy alley beside the house, slipped through my window, and pinned me to the bed. And although I screamed till my lungs almost burst, they were the silent screams of sleep and no one ever came to save me. The circles around my eyes turned purple and then blue-black. Night after night I shook my parents awake and crawled in beside them. When they banned me from doing that, I crept in unannounced and curled up at the foot of their mattress like a stray dog.

On February 11, 1975, fate granted us a dramatic reprieve in the shape of an envelope postmarked "Hartley." Mom had just returned from a visit to Granny and Grampy, where she'd seen Thomas and Sue Beattie, wealthy farmers and racehorse owners with whom Dad had been friends since the Hartley days, when he'd ridden for Thomas on the amateur horse-racing circuit. Over lunch, she'd mentioned that Dad was pining for Rhodesia, felt guilty he wasn't fighting the War, and still had ambitions of one day working on the land. The letter was a job offer. Thomas would pay Dad up to six thousand dollars a year to manage Giant Estate. He'd be responsible for 1,400 acres of maize, 500 acres of cotton, and 3,200 head of cattle.

"Errol, if you do decide to accept, let me know chop-chop," Thomas wrote. "I can take you on almost immediately. . . . Anyway it's up to you now."

To Mom, who loved Cape Town but loved Dad more, it was the most bittersweet of missives. I wanted to pack and leave that very day. Dad was undecided. One minute he was sure that farming and fighting the Rhodesian War was the only life he'd ever wanted; the next, he was equally sure it wasn't. Eventually he made up his mind. A removal van was booked, and the house sale was put in motion.

At the last second Dad got cold feet. "If we stay, I'll buy you a horse," he promised.

But it felt like what it was, an empty bribe. More arguments. One lunchtime he raced home from work with a pair of air tickets and practically ordered Mom and me onto the plane. He would follow by road in our Austin Apache.

"Okay, my friend," he said when he came to tell me the news, "no more long faces. We're going home."

"Back to Rhodesia?"

"Back to Rhodesia."

It felt like a deliverance.

3

It's the morning sunshine I remember, the irrepressibility of it, and how it got everywhere, spilling and staining everything in its path—fabric, walls, and even grass—with its glorious orange; and also the birds layering songs and whistles over one another in a way that was both freely expressed and perfectly organized, like a spontaneous, natural orchestra.

I opened my eyes and blinked away the brightness. Mom was still asleep, hazelnut hair fanned across the pillow. Dad had been gone since first light. I'd heard his smoker's cough in the passage and stumbled out, crumpled with sleep from the kids' room, asking *"Pleeease"* could I ride one of the racehorses, the ones whose fine-boned heads had followed our progress when we pulled into the Beatties' garden oasis the previous afternoon. And he'd laughed, ruffled my hair, and said that when the horse boys came I could ask one of them to put a halter on Trouble-shooter, a glossy, dark bay, and lead me around the yard. So I'd climbed into his still-warm patch with Mom and waited impatiently for the break of day.

So far, farm life had not exactly been what I expected. After our arrival and lots of excited talk about crops and cattle, we'd had lunch at the Beatties' house, where we were staying until our furniture came. Sue was an artist, and the rooms smelled faintly of oil paints. Monet prints hung between framed photographs of Sue and Thomas smiling beside a plethora of winning racehorses. They had three sons: Douglas, aged seven; Hamish, six; and a baby, Gareth, with a crest of red-ginger hair. As soon as we'd eaten, I was dispatched to play with the older boys, which was annoying because I wanted to stay and hear about "The Situation." Over lunch Thomas had told us about a terrorist attack on Shamrock, one of his farms. Sue had heard the screams of the manager's wife on the Agricalert radio. She was reloading weapons for her husband. A police unit had come to their rescue, killing one of the terrorists, whose body was then disposed of down a mine shaft. Afterward they'd found bullets in the wall above the baby's cot.

Thomas himself was like a character out of Dickens, all sideburns and redheaded coloring, with a temper to match but without the carrot topping. Every millimeter of his freckled bulk exuded power—not just muscle, although those were thick enough, but in aura. It was obvious that everyone in the house, apart from Sue, with whom he had a tempestuous but loving relationship, walked on eggshells around him. His sons and servants shrank from him. Even the air seemed to get out of the way for him.

For all that, it was impossible not to be drawn to him. His presence was contagious. He had an infectious belly laugh and a deep-rooted certainty of his position in the home and in the country that seemed a throwback to another age—a time when men like Rhodes bestrode Africa, as Thomas still did, asserting their will. He was entirely self-made. He owned five farms—Giant Estate, Morning Star, Lion's Vlei, Shamrock, and Braemar—a few farm stores, and with his father and brothers, a string of butcheries.

After an afternoon's acquaintance, I was sent away to sleep top-to-toe with Douglas, the closest I'd ever been to a boy by some distance. For ten minutes I lay stiff with shyness, unable to sleep, then Douglas made a tent of the blankets, switched on a flashlight, and whispered: "Do you want to fuck?"

I said: "What's that?"

I thought it might be a card game, like Snap.

"It's when I show you mine and you show me yours."

I thought it over. On the one hand, it seemed too good an opportunity to pass up, but I was also aware that while it was "not nice for a black man to see your Mary-Ann," it was very much frowned upon to show it to white boys. So I declined with reluctance.

"Okay," Douglas acquiesced, "I'll just show you mine."

I propped myself up on one elbow to study it. It looked like a snail when you trod on it by mistake and it flipped over and all you could see was its pale underbelly and its collapsed shell. The only things missing were the feelers.

Heels clicked in the passage. Douglas turned off the flashlight and pulled up his pajamas. Sue said through the door: "My boy, if your father hears you talking, there's going to be trouble."

I had a feeling that trouble in the Beattie household was something worth avoiding, and Douglas clearly agreed. We shut our eyes without another word.

My mother took one look at our new home and burst into tears. Almost nothing had been done to prepare it for our arrival. When we pulled up to the rusting, curlicued gate and surveyed it across a luxuriant field, our initial impression was that it hadn't been lived in for forty years. It was a rambling, old mining house with a pitched corrugated-iron roof, a veranda enclosed with torn fly screens, and a hive of vicious bees in the chimney. The walls were riven with cracks heaped with ant workings, hornets' nests, and white, silky bubbles of spider hatchlings. The bathwater flowed brown. There was an ugly concrete fishpond out the front.

Mom cried for the first two weeks, and Lisa cried with her. She'd prepared herself for the worst—"I know those old farmhouses, I know it's not going to be a picnic"—had even imposed a condition on the move, namely that if Dad could pursue his dream of farming, she could fulfill a lifelong ambition to see the world, but the reality was almost more than she could bear. Dad found it difficult to empathize. He was grateful beyond gratitude to the Beatties for both the house and the job and thankful to be back to fight the War. Neither did she get much sympathy from me. I was so thankful to be back home in Rhodesia and in close proximity to horses, I would have happily slept under a bush.

The house came with a couple of garden boys; a cook-houseboy, Peter, who had a singsong voice and a smile tinged with melancholy; and a nanny called Maud, who, like Peter, was Malawian. Maud immediately became our second mother, and at times she was almost our first. She had high cheekbones and an innate elegance, and the pink-and-white and purple-and-white dresses with matching *doeks* (caps), which Mom had the tailor sew for her, remained spotless throughout the busiest day. There was something very knowing about Maud. My abiding memory is of her watching Lisa and me, hands on her hips, sometimes with amusement, more often with thinly veiled disapproval. And yet, whatever her opinion of us, she was always there, always reliable, always vigilant, always caring.

At the bottom of the driveway was a red-dirt road, which led to the lands in one direction and to the strip road, compound, and farm store in the other. A *vlei* separated us from Chris and Darlene Adcock, who had three children and lived in a mining house even more run-down than ours, and the Beatties' grand house with the racehorses in the paddock.

The farm was three thousand commercial acres of rudely healthy maize, cotton, and wheat, split by the strip road. Feedlot cattle milled behind a screen of auburn dust. The cotton lands were dominated by a rocky, tree- and aloe-covered hill, which we referred to as a kopje but to me was really a small mountain. At its foot was Giant Mine. At the turn of the century, Giant was the second biggest gold mine in a country rich with mineral deposits, including copper, chromite, nickel, lithium, and precious stones, but by the seventies it was largely stripped of its treasures. A stamp mill still pecked optimistically at the ground, but Thomas didn't own it, he merely leased the dumps and hired a couple of miners to work them. The miners had an ill-tempered pet guinea fowl, which Dad maintained was the "cheekiest thing" he'd ever come across. "If you take your eye off it for a second, it attacks you."

Along with the servants, the house had a party line, which meant a black Bakelite rotary-dial phone heavy enough to break your foot if you dropped it. It trilled loudly at all hours of the day or night but we weren't allowed to pick up unless it had our specific ring (three shorts and a long)—although the nosey parkers in the district liked to lift their handsets sneakily and listen in on other people's conversations. I tried it a few times but was always rumbled immediately. "*Ag*, no, can you hang up, please? Haven't you got anything better to do? Is that Frikkie Bredenkamp? Frikkie, is that you?"

Shell-shocked, Mom took to the bed with Lisa and a pile of Lucy Walker books, which were about beautiful young women who find themselves on remote, inhospitable cattle stations in the Australian outback with granite-jawed men who revel in the harsh conditions. Dad, who was not unlike them, was gone from dawn to dusk, six or seven days a week, so I spent my time hanging over the paddock fence behind the Beatties' house feeding titbits to Troubleshooter, while Maud, Peter, and the garden boys swept, scoured, smoked bees from the chimney, and used *bembas*—homemade, hand-beaten, and sharpened scythes—to hack dispiritedly at the waist-high jungle in our yard.

Their activities upset the natural status quo, and we awoke one morning to find a pair of adult *boomslangs* (Afrikaans for tree snake— "boo-um-slung"), the female brown, the male pea green, looped in a bow at the top of the syringa tree in the driveway. The moment Mom saw them, she was adamant they had to go. She had a fear of death in all its manifestations, and venomous tree snakes were just an extension of that. But I'd inherited a fascination with snakes from Dad, who as a teenager had sold puff adders from his uncle Dan's farm to Fitzimmons Snake Park in Durban, so I wanted her to leave them in peace.

"Ha! And what happens when they come down and bite you or Lisa?"

"Why don't we wait until Dad gets home?" I suggested, but Mom was deaf to reason.

She vanished into the house and reappeared with the shotgun, a long-barreled antique that Dad had been given to help him control the wild pig population in the lands. Peter and the garden boys "ah-ah-ahhed!" and shrank back against the wall. Maud and I joined them. There was something in the way that Mom rammed the barrel into the mud while shakily loading the cartridges that suggested someone who not only was unfamiliar with guns but would be well advised to stay that way.

She took uncertain aim. There was a deafening bang, and a large section of the syringa tree detached itself and plummeted to the ground. The snakes writhed uneasily.

Five blasts and several muddy reloadings later, the *boomslangs* exploded out of the sky in an unholy confetti of gristle and bits of bark, twig, and berries. Maud and Peter flew shrieking into the kitchen; the garden boys ran for their lives. I stood transfixed by the fallen snakes, which though decapitated and in pieces, were still writhing and striking in a frenzied denial of death. Then I glanced over at my mother. She was pale as milk, staring down at the barrel of the shotgun, which, packed to capacity with mud, had split in two in protest and peeled back like a banana. "I could have shot my face off," she gasped.

Perhaps it was all too much for her because when she came in to kiss me that night, her voice was cotton wool–full, like she'd been crying. She sat, and the mattress dipped lower. Money permitting, I'd been promised a pine bunk, but until then I was folded into a decrepit farm bed, the springs of which had given up the ghost. It was like sleeping in a hammock.

She said: "Oh, honey, don't you miss our beautiful house in Cape Town?"

I didn't want to hurt her feelings, but I didn't want to lie either, so I said: "It was *lekker*, but I like it here, Mom. Don't you?"

She sighed. "I guess we'll just have to make the best of it, then." After a pause, she said: "You're not too frightened, are you? You're not worried about the War?"

"Nuh-uh."

"Because I don't want you worrying about the terrorists. Dad's got his guns and we're very safe here."

"I know."

"Would you like me to teach you a prayer that Granny used to say to me when I was a little girl and I got scared?"

"But I'm not scared."

"Well, still . . ."

"Okay."

There are four corners of my bed; there are four angels at my head
Matthew, Mark, Luke, and John, bless the bed that I lie on.

"That's not the way Granny says it."

"Oh?" She sounded put out. "What does Granny say?"

Matthew, Mark, Luke, and John, bless the bed that I lie on
If I should die before I wake, I pray the Lord my soul to take.

Mom frowned. "That's not very nice. I think you should leave the last part out. Anyway, just remember that God loves you and I love you."

She bent down to kiss me, and the roses-and-cream scent of Oil of Olay came with her. "Don't let the bedbugs bite."

"I won't."

The door clicked shut behind her, and darkness spilled in like ink. I tensed myself for the bedtime terror of Cape Town, but the bogeymen of my imagination—the Coloureds with the plunging scissors—seemed childish and remote here, and the War was still an unknown quantity. What did it really mean? Even so, I held tight to Kim's Siamese warmth and repeated my prayer like a mantra. And for a long time I lay listening to the stealing quietness of the night and, far away, the stamp of the gold mine, like a heartbeat.

Life began. If the sound track to my former existence had been arguments or an interminable, fridge-ticking silence, now it was the rhythmic blare of African guitars, marimbas, and unison singing from the storekeeper's crackling radio, and the cheerful morning chaos of cows, sheep, hysterical roosters, and rushing tractors. In the evenings, the women returning from the lands on the backs of those same tractors sang call-and-response harmonies as they trundled past our house, the magnolia clouds of sunset flaring up behind them.

Almost the first thing that happened was that Dad brought me an orphaned Hereford calf. To start with, Daisy was nothing but ginger-lashed eyes staring from a mess of angel white curls, all set on top of a gangly chestnut body, but as she grew in stature and confidence, she became a real character. Mom gave me one of Lisa's old bottles and taught me how to sterilize it and warm the milk to the correct temperature, and several times a day I'd feed Daisy and clean under her tail just like a cow would, but using a damp cloth. When she could drain a bottle in a single swallow, I weaned her onto a bucket, first letting her suck a milk-coated hand and then gradually lowering it into the creamy froth.

The adoption of Daisy triggered an influx of pets. We took on a donkey in need of a temporary home and a wiry, black mongrel, Muffy, in need of a permanent one, and Mom found a Siamese companion for Kim—Coquette—at the SPCA. Dad had had his heart set on a Staffordshire bull terrier for years, so he bought himself a couple of puppies, naming the black dog Jock in honor of the book *Jock of the Bushveld*, and the brindle bitch, Jess. Finally the sheep boy, a wizened, toothless man, brought me the first of many abandoned lambs. I called her Snowy and the two that followed Misty and Baringa. I put them into a pen with Daisy and was besotted with all of them.

After two weeks of hand-wringing, Mom decided that if she was going to be a farmer's wife, she would do it with as much style as our meager means would allow. Thomas made the mistake of telling her that the David Whitehead factory owed him free fabric after having leaked effluent onto Lion's Vlei, and for the next few years Mom used the environmental blunder and the emotional license she felt was owed to her in her capacity as a former employee to extract so many reams of free material from the company, they had to plead with her to stop. The sewing machine purred constantly. She ran up curtains, cushion covers, blinds for the veranda, and outfits for me and Lisa. In between, she baked fairy cakes and directed the servants to plant flowers, roast chickens, and do endless piles of laundry.

By midmorning, five days a week, Maud was leaning over a bath foaming with Surf blue powder—"Suffa," she called it—pounding out stubborn stains with the aid of a pine board and a bar of Sunlight ("Sunright"), a greasy green soap reeking of industrial pine. It was sold in long bars and cut down to size. She herself smelled of Lifebuoy, a red carbolic soap, tinged with a cloying perfume, like a cheap pink body lotion bought from OK Bazaars.

When I tried to follow Maud's example and use Lifebuoy myself, for bathing, Mom snatched it away. "Don't be silly, Lifebuoy is disgusting."

"But the *munts* use it to bathe with."

"Yes, well, they're different. Maybe they can't afford Lux."

This lodged in my head as An Accepted Fact about Africans, of which the others were:

If you spoiled them they got cheeky.

They were good at singing and dancing.

The men were useless at weekends, when they spent all their free time in the compound beer hall drinking Chibuku, "the Beer of Good Cheer," a sour-smelling sorghum brew delivered, like fuel, in a big lorry and served in paper buckets.

They had very virtuous babies. "You'll never hear a black baby crying," Dad was always saying as he shook his head at my sister's screams. "Never. Never in a million years."

The older black progeny were hungry for knowledge— were, in fact, so desperate to learn that they were prepared to walk six miles or more to school and, when they got there, apply themselves with dedication—unlike most white children, who would make up any excuse to get out of going to school or doing homework.

In spite of this their parents were, on the whole, not very bright, and those that were tended to be troublemakers.

They were heavy-handed with cleaning products, such as Sunlight dishwashing liquid.

They were all riddled with worms and bilharzia, a disease carried by freshwater snails, which leads to liver damage, bladder tumors, excessive tiredness, and blood in the urine— hence their lack of motivation and tendency to idleness.

But they were, if correctly managed, very good workers.

And so it was that by noon the beds were made and the sheets smelled of sun and Surf, and the floors, which Peter cleaned on his hands and knees, with an old T-shirt and little grunts of effort, assaulted the senses with the paraffin glare of Cobra polish. And no matter how many clothes I tossed onto the floor or threw muddy and grass-stained into the orange hamper, they were back in my cupboard by sundown, ironed and folded as if from the best hotel laundry.

At Giant, the trees and crops seemed greedy for survival, reaching for the blue heavens, the soil a fiery meld of the vermilion blossoms of the

Kaffir boom tree and the skin of the Africans who worked it. Every inch of the earth shivered or wriggled with life. With ants, ant lions, and purple-brown earthworms. With chongololos—ginger-legged black millipedes that rolled into balls if you touched them. With blindworms that slipped through your fingers like polished silver snakes. With seeds that practically germinated while you watched.

Milk no longer came in bottles from the supermarket, pasteurized and bland, but was heaved into the kitchen each day in a moisture-beaded half-gallon drum by the same laughing black men whose practiced hands had greased the teats of the two Friesian cows that constituted the farm dairy. Dispensed into Tupperware jugs, cooking pots, and bowls, it quickly formed a golden skin of cream, out of which Peter churned salty mountains of butter or Mom made lemon meringue pie or which we'd spoon onto tinned Cape gooseberries or stewed guavas. The remaining milk was thick with creamy lumps, and we drank it neat in pint glasses or whisked it into chocolate shakes with Nesquik or malty Milo (both equally good eaten directly from the tin). But no matter how much we drank or how many uses we found for it, there was always more the next day, so we fed it to the dogs, Daisy, and the lambs or gave it to the Africans, who liked it sour with *sadza*, the porridge they made from maize meal.

The only one who didn't appreciate it was Lisa, who, it transpired, was lactose intolerant and unable to digest soya milk or anything else, and who now cried louder than ever.

Elsewhere, everything was cyclical. Medicine, one of our new garden boys, who was not a boy but had pepper 'n' salt hair and a stiff, arthritic walk, never obviously engaged in any activity more strenuous than sitting on his haunches drinking tea from a tin mug or leaning on a *badza* (hoe) staring vacantly into space, and yet under his supervision, or lack thereof, the veggie garden flourished. Within months almost every vegetable we ate, plus bananas, pawpaws, and lemons, came from the garden. The scraps were given to the hens—Rhode Island Reds bought as cheeping, fluffy day-old chicks—or thrown onto the compost heap, which in turn nourished the veggie garden. We built the hens proper houses from brick and great curving sheets of corrugated iron, and they snuggled in their nests, making crooning noises of contentment. In the mornings, their fresh-warm eggs went straight into Peter's frying pan with a sizzle of Sunflower oil. Thanks to the veggie scraps, their yolks were bright orange with an intense flavor, which, combined with crispy bits of smoky Colcom bacon and the caramel zing of fried bananas, exploded into my mouth like sunshine every breakfast.

With meat, it was much the same. Cows and sheep were grazing in the fields one minute and skinned on the circle of grass near the farm workshop the next, their membranes laid out like cobwebs, their juices soaking into the earth. Then they were on the dinner table in the form of T-bones, fillet steaks, lamb chops, or roasts, or packed into bags in the freezer.

The rest of the groceries came from Schofield's supermarket. To get them, Mom and I would leave Lisa with Maud and drive the ten kilometers into Hartley, which was the town Gadzema might have been had it had enough water to sustain the gamblers and gold miners who'd resided there before us. Which, to be frank, was not much. There was one wide main road, known as Queen Street, which did not have enough of a rush hour to merit a traffic light (we called them "robots") and was essentially used as a thoroughfare for people en route to more interesting places. Lining Queen Street were Japanese pickup trucks belonging to farmers and cream Mercedes-Benzes driven by their wives and low Colonial-style buildings in washed-out colors, like some sun-faded postcard from the fifties.

The first thing you saw as you entered the town was Hartley Hospital, which if you were white you wouldn't attend unless you were desperate and probably not even then.

Next came Schofield's, a dimly lit emporium wafting a savory-sweet perfume of cling peaches and *kapenta*, a dried minifish staple of African diets. Schofield's provided gossip and the best breakfast cereals in the world: vanilla wheat flakes called Cerelac and chocolate ProNutro, made from maize. It also stocked Dairibord yogurt with whole chunks of pineapple, strawberry, and *granadilla* (passion fruit), Tastic rice, Marie biscuits, Mazoe orange concentrate, Tanganda tea, Cashel Valley baked beans, Royco tomato soup ("Royco makes you big like a giant!"), Aromat (a Day-Glo yellow, MSG-laden flavor enhancer), and treats like Mitchell's Highlanders shortbread with brown sugar round the rim, melt-in-your-mouth Boudoir "lady's finger" biscuits, and pink-sugar peanuts.

Mom never left the house without doing her makeup, curling her hair, and putting on her best dresses, and she always looked amazing.

She'd walk along Queen Street trailing a cloud of Magie Noire, and men became all smiley around her and constantly tried to help her—not least because she *was* fairly helpless—and she'd return their smiles from under her fringe and become almost as shy as I was, at which time they'd always say the same, unoriginal thing to us: "Are you *sure* you're not sisters?"

Which at that age I thought was funny and really lovely and later came to loathe with a passion.

If you went up one side of the street and then came back down the other, you'd pass Smith's Garage, the Café Capri, Continental Restaurant, Barclays Bank, Town House, Honors fashion store, the Farmer's Co-op, and Universal Autos on the right and, crossing over, Hartley Hotel, Standard Bank, the Post Office, some miscellaneous furniture retailers, a newsagent, and Beatties' Butchery. The butcher's shop had pigs on hooks in the window, wearing yellow jackets of fat and macabre smiles. We went in there to buy prepared meat we couldn't get on the farm, such as spicy coils of *boerewors* sausage, slabs of dried-beef biltong with peppery flecks, steak mince for us, ordinary mince for the cats, dog bones, plump chickens, and polony shaved into pink wafers by a man in a bloody white coat, and tried to make ourselves heard above the screech of the ham slicer.

In our new life, even the bread seemed exotic. There were two bakeries in town, both of them Greek, but Mom always went to Tomazo's in the back streets, where you could smell the bread ovens from half a block away. The back streets had the feel of a foreign country, even though they were only a short hop from the main road. They teemed with black and Indian life, with street-corner tailors and watch menders in lopsided stalls with misspelled signs, with one-man bicycle repairers patching up punctures on the roadside, with cut-price clothes and furniture shops. And of course, there was Bata, shoe store to the nation, where farmers bought their *veldskoens* (fawn-colored, rough suede "veld" shoes) and white kids bought rubber Slip Slop sandals and blacks and whites alike bought *takkies* (white plimsolls), which we all wore till our toes protruded from the sides. Outside the bakery, picannins in ragged clothes that had faded to a universal beige sprawled on the pavement, "cement-mixing" Fanta and Tomazo's buns, which were sweet and as light as air and came in joined-together batches.

Siss, man! I'd think haughtily as I stepped between them. "Cement mixing" was something I imagined only black people did, like eating *kapenta* or frying up flying ants.

And yet I was hardly in a position to judge, because just as soon as I was back in the car, I'd insert a whole, not especially clean paw into the center of one of the hot, boxy loaves Mom had bought and scoop out handfuls of steaming white dough, which I squashed into grubby but delicious dough balls. If Mom had actual plans for the loaves and I was forced, whining, to wait until we reached home, I'd cut them into doorstops and eat the slices warm with Peter's salty butter melting on top and gooey heaps of Cape gooseberry jam.

Regardless of their business in Hartley, the one place everyone stopped at was the stationer's-newsagent-florist–dry cleaner–Doves Funeral franchise owned by my friend Deidre's parents, the Burrowses.

In Dad's world, people were either "terrible" or "super," and which category they fell into had a lot to do with whether they had good manners, in which case they were "lovely ladies" or "absolute gentlemen," or if they'd ever, at any point in their history, displayed the slightest lack of integrity—particularly in sport. Thus Tom Beattie's father, Jimmy, was "an absolute gentleman," because on those starry dawns when Dad drove through to Gatooma for cattle sales, he always insisted that Dad stop by his house for breakfast (a couple of eggs, some *boerewors*, and a steak cooked on a plow disk suspended over hot coals). One of the town merchants, on the other hand, was a "terrible man" because he had a reputation for gambling on anything and cheating at everything. According to Dad, he'd been "flattened" more than once at Hartley Club because he'd lose a game of dice and then say: "I'm just off to the men's." But the members knew his tricks from old. They'd follow him out to the car park and suggest, in low, polite voices dripping with menace: "Let's go back inside."

But Mrs. Burrows occupied the category Dad reserved for people with extremely committed work ethics who could be forgiven almost everything. So although she stood stolidly behind the counter and seemed a stranger to the most basic social pleasantries, he was very fond of her and would always leap to her defense if he heard her criticized.

"Shame," he'd say, "she really works hard, the Poor Lady. She really, really does."

5

All terrorists are black, but not all black people are terrorists.

In the beginning, I identified terrorists mainly by their hair. Ordinary Africans have springy caps of closely cropped hair, but the hair of aspiring terrorists (of whom I've decided there are several on our farm) and those in the news seems to sprout from their heads in electrified clumps, as if it has been teased into position with the special wooden combs used only by black people but without the aid of a mirror. Often it is dusty in appearance, as if the terrorists have been too busy fighting to bother with a bar of Lifebuoy, let alone Palmolive green apple shampoo, and they are seldom without aviator sunglasses and a poorly tuned radio on one shoulder blasting songs of the *Chimurenga*—"The Struggle." *Tsotsis*, who are not terrorists but merely Very Bad Men, such as murderers and thieves, also use the special wooden combs, but they tend to go around with Mungo Jerry Afros, glistening with oily hair relaxer. *Tsotsis* are identifiable by more than just their hair because they smell of Chibuku beer *even on weekdays*, walk with an exaggerated swagger, and accessorize with women who wear red polyester dresses, black bras, and high-heeled shoes in inelegant sizes, which seem supremely ill suited to long walks on farm roads.

At first, the war that we'd come back for was not much in evidence—not in terms of people shooting at us at any rate—although the war machine was. Armored vehicles with names like Hyena and Rhino rumbled through Hartley packed with black, brown, and white soldiers, and passersby, especially me, cheered, waved, and whistled. The Army guys' teeth were white against their dark and sunburned faces, and they smiled through a bristle of guns.

Dad immediately joined the Police Anti-Terrorist Unit (PATU) and went off on call-up for seven days a month wearing immaculate camouflage and dazzling black boots, his hair neatly cut and slicked back. He looked like a handsome soldier out of a book.

In 1962, his second year in the RLI, where he was in the Engineers, Dad was one of only twelve men selected out of a thousand for an exchange program with the British Army. The four months he'd spent with the Gordon Highlanders were among the most wonderful of his life, and he talked of them often. He spent three of the months in Gilgil, Kenya, teaching horse riding to the officers' wives, before setting sail for the coconut groves and translucent waters of Zanzibar. In Zanzibar he danced with the sultan's daughter and was almost eaten alive by ants. The Gordon Highlanders were the last British company to leave the island before the uprising that deposed the sultan, after which they went by ship to the scorching desert heat of Aden. There, Dad recalled, "you had to eat your breakfast before the flies did."

It was a source of constant amazement to Mom and me that Dad, who blew up if the salt was passed to him too slowly at the supper table, was able to cope with the discipline of Army life, but he had a number of qualities that made him a perfect soldier. Among them was a respect for authority bordering on awe. Five hours before crossing any border post, Dad—without doubt the most scrupulously honest person in Rhodesia when it came to any matter that could possibly concern a customs official—would break into a sweat and become paranoid that we might, unwittingly, have committed some customs violation that would see us all jailed. Mom would have to restrain him from throwing our minuscule holiday allowance out of the window just in case we'd brought one dollar more than was legally permitted.

Army officers always favored Dad because he took tremendous pride in his work and bearing while remaining humble. His high school record of achievement describes him as a "young man of very good conduct, honest, reliable and dutiful. He was always courteous and well-behaved and did his best." When given any order, he went directly from A to B without wasting time contemplating C, but not without using his initiative. He'd never forgotten a lesson from his early days in the Army when a captain had caught him and another soldier sitting on the edge of a dam one wintery dawn with a makeshift arrangement of fishing lines and hooks, trying vainly for a bite.

Instead of telling them off for being there, he said: "If you're going to do something, gentlemen, do it properly. How long have you been here?"

"An hour, sir."

"An hour? You've been here for an hour and you don't even know if the fish are any good or if you're ever going to catch them. Aren't those grenades on your belt?"

"Yes, sir."

"Then why don't you use them?"

So they did, and only a few malnourished fish floated to the top, proving that all the patience and skill in the world would have been misdirected.

But the quality the Army liked best in Dad was that he had no discernible fear of death.

Once, when he was a young NCO in the RLI, he was taking a nap after finishing his duties on a Sunday when he became aware of an immense weight on his chest. He opened his eyes to find a cheetah gazing down at him, yellow orbs gleaming. Dad shoved it off and laughed. The cheetah was the RLI mascot, and although it had probably spent its morning disemboweling an antelope, he wasn't alarmed. "They might be fast on their feet, cheetahs, but they're very slow upstairs. No brains."

Another time, he was crossing a dam wall with his PATU "stick" (in this case, one officer and five or six soldiers) when a firefight erupted. They were totally exposed—the original sitting ducks—and there was nothing they could do but stay low, unleash a volley of bullets, and hope.

Afterward his friend Martin asked him: "Weren't you afraid of dying?"

And Dad replied, with complete truthfulness: "I never gave it a thought."

He left the RLI in December 1963, after the breakup of the Federation of Southern Rhodesia (which became Rhodesia), Northern Rhodesia (Zambia), and Nyasaland (Malawi)—in which those countries seceded from Britain—nine months after he married Mom, because, he said, the "Army is not a married person's place, let me tell you." His RLI reference called him a "fine and able NCO. He is intelligent and takes an intense interest in his work. He reacts well to discipline and his bearing and turnout is always very good. He is a very trustworthy person who can be relied upon to do his best at all times."

Dad said: "I think they were writing about the wrong bloke there, but never mind. I think they got me *confused* with someone else."

In our old life, the most exciting thing I ever did was ride my bike around the block wishing it was a Chopper with three gears, but now I had a working farm to explore and an instant set of friends. There were the Beattie boys and the older Adcock kids, Michelle and Bain. On the most searing days of summer, the Adcocks would put a long strip of linoleum and a hose pipe on their lawn, and we'd shoot through the puddles on our bellies.

Mostly, though, I hung out with Douglas. He had his mother's fair coloring and his father's hair-trigger temper, but there was an open likability about him that was very engaging. We pegged cardboard to the spokes of our bicycles to make them sound like motorbikes and charged up and down the dirt roads, performing increasingly insane stunts. We recruited Hamish and played Cowboys and Indians in the long yellow grass around the house, whipping smoking cap guns from faux leather holsters, or used long sticks wrapped in tinfoil as automatic weapons, wore camouflage, and pretended to be soldiers.

In Cape Town, the notion that some terrible injustice had been perpetrated on me because I wasn't a boy had taken root in my head, fueled by the character of George, the tomboy in the Famous Five series, so Douglas became the measuring stick in my efforts to be as good as a boy. I wanted to do everything—ride, run, use a "catty"— as well as or better than he did. "Catties" were catapults made from forked sticks and the inner tubes of car tires. Like the picannins, we carried them everywhere, but unlike them, we never killed birds. Or at least we didn't until Douglas, in a moment of bravado, shot a finch out of a tree near the farm workshop. Right there, he plucked off its downy feathers, built a little fire, and cooked it whole. I was horrified, but Douglas preened over his marksmanship. The nude finch was all bones and no meat, and what flesh there was turned fibrous and was burned and covered in ash by our inept *braai*.

Throughout the day we'd make visits to the shadowy cavern of the farm store armed with empty bottles, for which there was a five-cent reward. Five empties bought a cold Sparletta cherry plum or cream soda. Sometimes we would come away with a handful of pennycools, little plastic packets filled with rainbow-hued ice-lollies, or sweet buns, Chicken Flings, and Corn Curls. When the storekeeper passed them to us, his hands were always rough and his skin was always cool, and his shop had the fragrance of Omo washing powder and *kapenta* and *mielie-meal*.

We'd sit on his shady porch, washing down curly twists of Chicken Flings with cherry plum and watching the tourist cars fly by to Sinoia Caves, where there was a mystical pool with no bottom. The tailor was in permanent residence on the other side of the veranda, eyes half-closed as he waited by his sewing machine for customers, and muscly black youths, shiny with sweat, played drafts with hand-drawn boards and bottle tops.

But nothing was as much fun as bouncing in the cloud-mountains of reaped cotton that was stored in the former Gadzema clubhouse. The clubhouse had fallen into ruin and lost most of its doors and windows, but it still had the original ballroom floor and heaps of atmosphere. If you closed your eyes, you could imagine Gadzema as it was in the days when it was a gold-rush town, awash with illegal gold. When ladies danced and champagne flowed.

In the late 1860s, when Rhodesia still resembled a Thomas Baines painting, with marauding elephants and natives like ebony statues and white-safari-suited Colonials with rifles in the crooks of their arms, Gadzema was so rich in mineral wealth that the land itself was like a living beast with gold instead of blood in its veins. For years Mzilikazi, leader of the Ndebele people, had banned visitors and hunters from his kingdom in the hot, dry south of the country, an area known as Matabeleland, but when he lifted the ban in 1865, Henry Hartley, the son of an 1820 Settler and a white hunter famed for his ability to wipe out staggeringly large numbers of elephants, was one of the first to travel up from South Africa. He found traces of ancient gold in both Matabeleland and Mashonaland, to the north of it, but it wasn't until 1867, by which time he'd joined forces with the German geologist and explorer Karl Mauch, that the scale of the find in and around Gadzema became clear.

"There the extent and beauty of the gold fields are such that I stood as it were transfixed," Mauch said, "and for a few minutes was unable to use the hammer. . . . Thousands of persons might work on this extensive gold field without interfering with one another."

Over the next few decades, fortune hunters, prospectors, and international mining operations like the South African Gold Fields Exploration Company, which employed Baines, poured into the country. Gadzema became a thriving center, but it never lost its Wild West ethos. Between the 1930s and 1950s, when it buzzed with politicians, miners, poker-playing millionaires, daredevil pilots, and chancers of all descriptions, it had two hardware stores, a fabric shop, a club with tennis courts, and a hotel with a back room for all-night gamblers, a twilight zone of cardsharps, roulette players, and blue-gray cigar smoke.

In those days Gadzema had lived up to its name, which was said to mean a "Shining Place." But with no sustainable water supply and the gold dwindling, people had drifted away toward Hartley. Now Gadzema was a ghost town and infamous for only one thing: being the location of the very first murder of the Rhodesian War—that of the Viljoens, a white farmer and his wife, at Nevada Farm, on May 16, 1966, seven months and five days before I was born.

The illegal gold and poker dens might have gone, but the Wild West ethos and a kind of frontier justice were still alive and well in the farming district around Gadzema and Hartley. I learned very quickly that the power we had over animals and Africans in our patch of Africa was absolute. It was not so much that farming families considered themselves above the law, more that they felt it had little relevance to them. The general consensus seemed to be, in a time of war, all bets are off.

"Well, *as you know*, this is supposed to be a conservation area," Dad told me the first time I went out hunting with him and some of the local farmers. Dad had a habit of saying "as you know" about things you couldn't possibly know, such as "Well, as you know, Triatix is the best cattle dip in the world" or "As you know, you can't sow tobacco seed before June first." So he said: "Well, *as you know*, this is supposed to be a conservation area . . . but Thomas doesn't like the game eating his stuff."

I asked: "If it's a conservation area, why are we going hunting for kudus?"

"Well, as you know, everyone around here sort of like does their own thing."

In Gadzema, hunting and drinking, fishing and drinking, going to friends' houses for *braais* and drinking, playing rugby and drinking, and going to Hartley Club and drinking were the main social activities. Along with doing deals on the black market or flirting with death or disaster. Jeremy Smith, the pilot who sprayed the crops at Giant, was never happier than when he was darting under power lines in his yellow biplane, flying so fast and so low that afterward he'd have to untangle cotton flowers from his wheels.

The hunting nights felt forbidden, which to begin with, was their appeal. I'd go bouncing into the blackness on the back of a pickup truck or Land Rover with Dad and three or four other farmers. Someone would hold up a silver spotlight with a length of lethal cable, patched together with insulation tape, hanging off it, and the mosquitoes would whine and pitter-patter against the hot bulb as the platinum beam cast a pearly-jade band across the cotton or wheat. I'd try my hardest to be the first to see the red eyes of the kudus, duikers, or bushpigs. I'd stand against the cab, with the bar of the truck bucking under my hands and the hairy, rugby player thighs of the farmers and a rifle or two on either side of me. They'd all have Lion beers or Castle lagers in their hands and be in khaki shorts (except for Dad, who only ever wore long pants) and knee-length socks held up by garters. They'd be wearing Bata *veldskoens* ("fellies") on their feet, and they'd all be the same shape—solid with T-bone steaks and beer, their bellies like women's in the advanced stages of pregnancy. In time, Dad would take on their silhouette, but he would never be like them, any more than Mom could ever be like their wives. With his tattoos, mahogany skin, and film-star eyes, Dad was something apart from them. Not better or worse, only different.

In his own mind, though, he was something lesser, a manager rather than an owner, a "dogsbody." In any social grouping he'd always take on the menial role, if only because his work ethic and frenetic energy wouldn't allow him to sit still. And so on hunting nights it would be Dad who drove the truck or guided the spotlight, Dad who went to the side of the fallen kudu to check that it had been shot cleanly with no suffering, and Dad who helped the Africans who'd accompanied us to load it onto the vehicle.

The other men threw out comments into the mosquito-cursed darkness, mainly to do with the adequacy or inadequacy of the blacks, who came in only two categories: good or bad.

"*Ja*, he's a good *munt*," one might say approvingly. "The best in my bloody compound. Isn't that right, Fanwell?"

"Yes, *bas*?"

"You're number one in my compound. Not that that's saying much."

Or, if the kudu was not secured properly and fell off the truck or some other confirmation of idiocy occurred: "*Got*, he's a useless *kaffir*, that one." And to the worker: "*Upi lo skop gawena*? Why don't you use your brains, you bloody useless . . . ?"

No one in our house ever said the word *kaffir* (except in regard to the Kaffir boom tree), which felt wrong and dangerous and ugly. Mainly we referred to Africans as Africans or "boys" or "girls" or *munts*, which had an ever-so-slightly disrespectful feel about it but was there in the Fanagalo phrase book in black and white, *muntu*, as meaning nothing more sinister than a person or a human being. In which case, we were *muntus*, too. Terrorists were "terrs" or "gooks" or "floppies," a reference to their floppiness after being shot.

In the end, I went hunting only two or three times. Initially I blocked my ears to the epithets and my nose to the beery gusts, and when the deadweight of a kudu crashed onto the bed of the truck, I stroked its curved neck and spiral horns and enjoyed the illicit thrill of touching a precious, wild creature I could never have touched even ten minutes previously, when its heart still beat and it still had freedom and the wind off the cotton land in its lungs. But when I went out on another night, an ache came into my chest when the almond-eyed kudus fell, and this time when I stroked them I felt no illicit thrill, only the ghastly, cold stiffness creeping across their silken fur. In death, their innocent eyes were sightless and blank, and the magic that had made them so special was gone.

I never went hunting again.

6

From the moment the alarm woke him at four-thirty, Dad was like a racehorse out of the stalls. Unless he was asleep or fishing, in which case he tended to be semianesthetized by beer or in that still place he was able to access when hunting, he took life at a gallop. It was rare to see him walking. Instead he negotiated the house and farm in a half-run, as though at any second he might break into a full sprint. If he found time for a tea break, he'd come tearing into the yard in his truck, rush through the kitchen issuing polite but urgent orders to the cook—"Coffee and a sandwich please, Peter, quickly, see"—fling himself down in the lounge, take a hurried gulp of boiling black coffee—"Ooo, oww"—a few quick drags on a Peter Stuyvesant, and devour a slab of Tomazo's bread spread with butter and Oxo or Gouda sprinkled with salt, in three bites. Only then would he pause long enough to take us in.

"Lovely cheese," he'd say seriously, "*lovely* cheese. Have you had some?"

Then he'd be off again, the soles of his *veldskoens* squealing like racing tires on the concrete floor of the passage, his FN automatic rifle, which went everywhere with him, in his hand.

Peter would watch him from the kitchen window as he dashed out to his truck with Jock flying after him, a glimmer of amusement in his dark eyes. "Eeeh, but the *bas* has strong regs [legs]," he'd marvel. "He all-a-time running very fass, like guinea fowl."

The downside of this roadrunner routine was that Dad tended to be highly impulsive and impetuous in some regards, and utterly intransigent in others—traits compounded by the fact that in his first year of working for Thomas he had a total of five Sundays off.

It was on one of those Sundays that he decided to buy me a horse.

Ever since our move to Giant, the thoroughbreds in the fields behind the Beatties' house and in particular Troubleshooter, a former champion two-year-old racehorse, whom I visited regularly with treats, had been constant reminders of how desperately I wanted a horse.

"If I had a horse, I'd be up at five in the morning grooming it and mucking out the stable," I told anyone who would listen.

And Dad would nod in support. "She would. I know she would."

Finally, he managed to secure a day off. Mom made a special trip into town to buy the *Herald*, and Dad asked Thomas if he could borrow the cattle truck at the weekend. All week I poured over the classifieds, trying to decide whether to go for a show jumper, an Arab, or a thoroughbred colt that would grow into a black stallion, but Dad would consider only Charm, a two-hundred-dollar fourteen-year-old bay mare, 14'2" hands high.

Charm resided at a stable yard in Salisbury, so on Sunday we climbed into the cattle truck and embarked on the hour-long drive, stopping only to collect lunch supplies from the store. At first glance, Charm fell some way short of my vision. She had short, stumpy legs, a swayback, was blind in one eye, and looked like she was a frequent visitor to the trough. But I was so overjoyed at the prospect of getting a horse, I decided to reserve judgment until the test ride. It was possible that Charm had hidden qualities. She could be a fearless jumper, a turn-on-a-hair gymkhana horse. Her advanced years were something of a worry, but experience counts for a lot in the dressage ring. I helped her owners—the kinds of jolly horsey people my mother was convinced I'd come to resemble purely by association, all unkempt hair, florid, confident faces, and saggy bottoms in ill-fitting jodhpurs—saddle her up. They led her to a flat, scrubby paddock, in the center of which was a large anthill, a termite-sculpted mini-mountain, topped by a tree. I mounted and rode away.

Although a little sluggish, Charm seemed willing enough. I trotted her in figures of eight and then coaxed her into a canter, imagining how good we must look to her owners. Boy, can that girl ride, they'd have been thinking. Who knew that Charm could perform like that?

My reverie was interrupted by the consciousness that we were going uphill. For reasons unknown, Charm had decided to take a short-cut over the ant heap. I looked up to see a tree branch rushing at my throat. It was too late to duck and way too late to take evasive action. To avoid being impaled or decapitated, I had no choice but to collapse backward onto Charm's hindquarters. Charm took this as a signal to spring forward into a panicked gallop. This sudden lunge, combined with the downslope of the ant heap, was too much for me to recover from. I rolled off her back like a sausage off a grill and hit the ground face-first, ingesting a tablespoon or two of dirt and a little manure along the way. I was winded and in pain—albeit mainly from embarrassment. Out of the corner of my eye, I could see Dad and the owners hurtling toward me with flailing arms, like ungainly contestants in a sack race. Charm was grazing nearby.

Dad was the first to reach me. "Dozy Arab," he said tenderly, sitting me up and giving me a comforting squeeze. "Didn't you see the tree?"

The owners fussed over me and apologized profusely for Charm's errant behavior and the existence of the tree, but it was plain they agreed with Dad. The looks on their faces said: What an imbecile. Since the rules of horsemanship dictate that one has to remount immediately after a fall, I had no choice but to climb gingerly back into the saddle and put Charm through her paces once again. This time I managed to stay onboard. However, my pride and my dream of a black stallion were in tatters. The combination of the cattle truck, which couldn't easily be borrowed again, and the need to save face made me fairly certain that we would be driving out the yard with a fat, stubby-legged pony on the back.

"Do you want her, do you?" encouraged Dad, beaming over my shoulder at the owners. "Super little horse. She'll give you lots of happy years."

I nodded miserably.

He ruffled my hair affectionately. "Dozy Arab," he said.

The moment Charm arrived at Giant Estate, she announced her retirement. That is to say, she would agree to be ridden only after she had worn herself out running in circles around the paddock in an effort to avoid being ridden. Out on the ride, no amount of kicking or cajoling could induce her to proceed at anything other than a pace that suited her. Occasionally, on the homestretch, the thought of the food trough would move her to an enthusiastic canter, but more often than not the most she could manage was a walk or a leisurely trot.

In spite of these foibles, I was absolutely devoted to her. Horses were my all-consuming passion, and if Charm didn't fit my vision, I would alter my vision to fit Charm. In my mind's eye, Charm and I became Army scouts, scrambling up kopjes draped with tiger spider webs the size of volleyball nets, ever alert for danger. How Charm would really respond if we gate-crashed a party of terrorists—an ever-present possibility—I shuddered to imagine, but I spent many enjoyable days planning our escape.

My dream, though, was to become a gold medal–winning cross-country event rider, and to that end I forced poor, blind Charm to leap logs or hurtle down the steep kopje, or I crouched low over her neck as she cantered grudgingly along the cotton fields, envied only by Douglas, who was a little afraid of horses and was beaten if he was bucked off Clear Moon, his spoiled, purebred, dapple-gray Welsh mountain pony. When he fell off in our garden, Thomas swiped him so hard he flew clean over a bed of cabbages.

Apart from riding and hanging out with Douglas in my new tree house—a miniature mud hut with a thatched roof built high in a syringa tree in the backyard—I still read every minute that I wasn't sleeping, at school, or feeding Daisy and my small herd of lambs. I read so much it was almost like a sickness. Unfortunately when I read, I couldn't hear, and when I was thinking about what I'd read I couldn't hear either, which seemed to drive the people around me into a frenzy. They called me dozy, half-asleep; yelled at me to wake up, to stop daydreaming, to look alive. Dad told me if I didn't close my mouth I'd get flies in it. Sometimes I'd emerge from the ecstatic transports of some pony story to find myself in the midst of a telling-off by my mother. She'd be standing in front of me with her mouth moving, obviously highly exasperated, and I'd have no way of knowing how long she'd been there and have great difficulty taking in what she was saying.

But on the whole my parents encouraged my reading. For years we didn't have a television, and even when we got one there was never anything to watch apart from the news, weather, and occasional British comedy *(Rising Damp)* or American show *(The Beverly Hillbillies* or *Little House on the Prairie)*, so most evenings we just talked and read and fell asleep by nine. I only ever read *Snakes of Africa* and horse and Enid Blyton books; Mom read Lucy Walker, *Europe on $10 a Day*, and fat novels about exotic locales, like *The Far Pavilions* and *Sayonara;* and Dad read Harold Robbins, which I was banned from ever opening, and also Oliver Strange Westerns, about a gunfighter called Sudden. Sudden rode a big, black horse he worshiped, named Nigger, and did his best to avoid violence but was constantly being called upon to rescue hapless ranchers from cattle rustlers, evil developers, and other gunfighters with a less strict moral code.

My sister just sat around bemused with Gareth, her ginger-haired playmate. A year after her birth, she had a head of pretty blond curls, but she was allergic to most foods and was still quite seriously ill. Peter diagnosed her condition as a side effect of spring. "When the new leaves come, Missy, all-a the babies, they get sick," he told my mother.

Mom divided her time between obsessing that Lisa was dying of malnutrition and, under pressure from Peter and Maud, running a clinic for farmworkers. She stocked up on economy-size bottles of cough mixture, diarrhea medicine, horse liniment, Phillips' milk of magnesia, bandages, Disprin, gentian violet, and Mercurochrome from the Farmer's Co-op, and treated a steady stream of patients at the kitchen door (our front door). The line grew daily until it was out the gate and down the road. At that point Thomas, who had been unaware of Mom's Mother Teresa ministrations, drove by the house and saw it. He had a fit. He screamed so loudly that all of the patients, even the lame, ran for their lives.

"I'm not having this," he shouted at Mom. "I can't stand it. They're always looking for new ways to get sick."

Mom was upset because running the clinic had made her feel that she was helping in some way, and I was annoyed because I used any encounter with the farmworkers to improve my Chilapalapa. Chilapalapa, otherwise known as Fanagalo, was a simplistic form of Ngoni (Zulu, Xhosa, Ndebele, and related languages), amalgamated with snippets of English, Dutch, and Afrikaans. It had evolved out of a need on mines and farms to create a common language that could be quickly learned by an ever-changing migrant labor force, one that could be composed of numerous tribes. It had been spoken throughout Southern Africa since the turn of the century. I'd picked it up from Dad, from Medicine, and from Granny's Fanagalo phrase book, which made me laugh with its unlikely scenarios and dire warnings:

> Look out for the teeth of the crocodile: they are very dirty and if you get scratched the place will become septic.—*Basopo mazinyo ga lo-ngwenyana: yena maningi doti; futi, noko yena limaza wena, lo-ndawo yena bolile.*

> Perhaps it is a lion. No, I see now, the grass is on fire.— *Mhlaumbe yena kona lo-ngonyama. Hayi, mina bona manje . . . lo tshani yena baswa.*

> I think there is perhaps another white man underneath the motor car. There! See his hand.—*Mina kabanga mhlaumbe yena kona lomunye pantsi ko lo motokali. Nanku! Bona la sandla gayena.*

> If you don't open your window at night the carbon monoxide from your coal brazier will kill you.—*Noko wena hayikona vula lo festele ebusuku loskelem smoko ga lo tshisa malahle zo bulala wena.*

> Don't eat underdone pork.—*Loskati wena yidla lo-nayma ga lo-ngulube, pega yena stelek kuqala.*

Once I'd mastered basics of pronunciation, such as *l* being *r* and *r* sometimes being *l* and *o* sounding like *or*, so that *lo*, meaning "the," became *raw*, it was incredibly easy to learn. Some words were literally English words said with an African accent. *Bicycle*, for instance, was written as *baisikil* in the phrase book. I loved being able to understand Dad's communications with the cattle boys, or discuss my carrot and lettuce seedlings with Medicine, who'd made me a special vegetable bed of my own, or listen to a Wrex Tarr record—which was full of humorous Chilapalapa story-songs like "The One-Legged Chicken Cocky Robin" or "Jamesi Bondi"—and laugh in all the right places.

Of course, if Maud or the garden boys wanted to discuss anything privately, they just lapsed into Ndebele or Shona. Then I didn't understand a thing.

Toward the end of the year, I entered Charm in a friendly family cross-country event held on a farm in nearby Selous. Competition made Charm lift her game, but her stubby legs, unseeing eye, and large stomach meant that we careered clumsily around the cross-country course, missing most of the logs and water jumps, and the next day she was simply not of a mind to participate in the silliness of the gymkhana. By then, neither was I. Midway through the cross-country we'd been overtaken by Rowan Lewis, a boy of my age whose family were renowned horsemen. He was with a friend, and he was riding Tempest, a rangy bay with the taut, highly defined muscles of a prize polo-crosse horse.

"I didn't realize they allowed donkeys to do the cross-country," he said, grinning down at Charm. He turned to his friend. "Did you? Or is that a zebra?"

Still, at least I had a horse, and we had a new addition to our growing menagerie, a baby warthog so exquisitely ugly we christened her Beauty. She was the most lovable creature I'd ever known. The smallest thing sent her into spasms of ecstasy, especially having her back scratched. She spent most of the day racing after the dogs with her spindly tail vertically upright or lying on her side in the sun. I'd put my face against her hot stomach and run my fingers through her wire-stiff mane. In the evenings, she hoovered up *sadza* and milk or cream-laden bonemeal with an expression of unadulterated bliss, and then she'd climb into one of the hessian-padded tractor tires we kept under the carport for the dogs and sink into a coma, her beauty-queen eyelashes curling up from her cheeks.

On my ninth birthday, I woke to a slice of orange sunshine and the crinkle of presents. Mom liked to put our gifts on the ends of our beds so that they were the first things we saw, and heard, when we opened our eyes, but this time there was also a bridle hanging from a hook on my dressing table, its snaffle bit gleaming with a watery shine, and folded over the back of a chair, a maroon *numnah* to put under Charm's old saddle. It felt like the happiest day of my life so far. Mom came in and cuddled me and sat with me while I unwrapped my other presents—mainly books—and wallowed in the pretty paper and became intoxicated with the new-leather smell of the bridle.

Later she baked me a chocolate birthday cake with Hundreds & Thousands and waxy red candles on top, and I licked the bowl while its vanilla-cocoa aroma filtered around the house. When it was ready, we carried it through to the dining table. I blew out the candles and wished to be a famous rider when I grew up. Then I relocated to the sofa, where I had my new books fanned out around me like lives waiting to be lived. Lisa was on the sofa beside me, Dad was smiling up at Mom, and I was in the middle of them all with a mouthful of warm chocolate sponge, secure in the force field of their love.

7

In the early days, when the Beatties and the Adcocks were our best friends in the way of rural towns, where families flung together by circumstance form friendships as obsessive as teenage crushes and live in one another's pockets for six months or even six years and then, by tacit agreement or because some boundary—sexual or social—has been overstepped, never speak again, we were forever at their houses for meals or beers, and a couple of times we went out to Shamrock with the Beatties and bruised every sticking-out part of us shooting down a natural waterslide hewn among the gray boulders of the Umfuli.

We roared out there one Sunday after a week of heavy rains. The sky was a glary white, as if the storms had leached all color from it, and as we drove a cacophony of insects swelled up in chorus to greet us. Douglas, Hamish, and I stood on the back of Dad's truck for the duration of the journey, watching the road through streaming eyes, and we shrieked with joy whenever he slammed full-pelt into dusky pink puddles. Mom and Lisa rode in the cab with Dad; Sue and Gareth went ahead in a second truck with Thomas.

Bumping down the marshy track to the river, Thomas's truck got stuck in the mud. He leapt out and began cursing and shouting as though the vehicle were a deficient worker, but Dad soothed him by volunteering to run to the farmhouse at Shamrock, several miles distant, to fetch a tractor and chain. While this was going on, we could hear the rain-swollen river crashing behind the trees, but the sight of it halted us in awe. This section of the Umfuli was usually streamlike and picturesque. Now it was a speeding, caramel blur.

"There's not going to be too much swimming today," Sue told the boys.

"Ah, Mom," whined Hamish, but one glower from his father shut him up.

We kids piled onto the trucks and unloaded the gear. We stacked the FN rifles beside the deck chairs close to the surging waters and dispensed the beers, Cokes, Fantas, and mixer bottles of Schweppes tonic water and lemonade into a tub of crushed ice. The hot sun winked through the leaves, which partially shaded the clearing. Lisa and Gareth played in the shade, their blond and red-ginger heads leaning close together. Mom and Sue opened up a foldout table and laid out Tupperware containers of cucumbers in vinegar, sliced beef tomatoes with onion, coleslaw, and potato salad. Flies came buzzing around.

"If you kill one fly, a thousand come to its funeral," Mom remarked.

"A bit like the gooks," someone said, and we all laughed.

The *braai* was an oil drum cut in half lengthways, with cut-down pipes soldered to its underneath as legs. Every farming family had one. While Thomas poured drinks and cracked jokes and reclined in a deck chair with a beer in a confident, landownerish way, Dad, the willing helper, built the fire with blocks of dry wood and readied himself to run for the tractor and trailer. Douglas asked if he could go along.

"It's quite a long way, my boy, but *ja*, you can come if you want to."

"I'll come, Dad, please can I come?" I cried, jigging up and down with keenness.

"Why don't you stay behind, my friend?" counseled Dad, a little impatiently. "You won't be able to keep up."

"I will. I will be able keep up."

Douglas laughed scornfully. Dad shrugged, and the two of them broke into a brisk jog. Barely a mile down the road I was attacked by a fierce stitch and had to limp back to the others, humiliated. Mom tried to console me, but there was no way she could appreciate the true ignominy of it, of not being as good as a boy—not even slightly.

In no time at all, the runners returned with the tractor. The smoke from the *braai* had created a blue pall in the clearing, and the aroma of char-grilled steak and fat leaking from the *boerewors* set my stomach rumbling, but I skulked in the shadows as Dad and Douglas, the Men of the Hour, supervised the rescuing of the truck. After that, Dad jumped into the rushing river to cool off. He was laughing, holding on to some reeds, talking to someone on the bank, when it came into my head to do something brave. Something *crazy.*

Unnoticed, I slipped in upstream. The water was warm and it hissed in my ears and I could feel the unrelenting force of it kneading my abdomen as I clung to a fallen tree.

"Catch me, Dad!" I shouted, and I let go.

And in the instant before I shot forward, I saw shock grip his face and realized too late that I'd made a terrible mistake. That if the river steered me away from him by even a couple of millimeters, I'd be drowned or gone forever—sucked into the green realm of crocodiles. But there was nothing I could do. Inconsequential as a leaf, I bowled along on the torrent, so fast and far out it seemed impossible he could reach me, let alone catch me. Then all of a sudden, his frantic fingers were clamping my wrist. There was a war among the current, his muscles, and the tearing reeds, and then somehow he had won and he was propelling me up the riverbank and clambering after me, half-yelling at me, half-hugging me, his breath coming in gasps. "My friend, are you out your mind? What if I hadn't managed to catch you? *Hey?* You could have . . . You would have . . . Nnn-nnh."

Through a screen of tears I saw him shake his head violently, like a dog, to dispel the thought. Then, mindful of the Beatties and of Mom, who was dealing with the lunch and was oblivious to our little drama, he forced a smile back onto his face and teased: "There were nearly some very well-fed crocodiles in the Umfuli this evening, that's for sure."

The possibility of death; the freedom of life. It was all over in a second.

It was now that the notion of being a hero began to burn away at me. All around me people regularly performed astonishing acts of courage or audacious daring. I heard about them on the news, from Mom, who read the paper, and at the troopie canteen in Hartley. They were in my books, in the lyrics of John Edmond's *Troopie Songs* and in those of "The Ballad of the Green Berets." Dad seemed to do them in his spare time.

As a consequence of all these heroics, I was continually on the look-out for situations that might result in me too saving the day, at least in some small sense. One morning I was trotting round the edge of the cotton lands when I spotted a wild cat perched on the upper branches of a skeleton tree. I pulled Charm to an emergency halt. I couldn't iden-tify the species of cat, but from where I sat, craning my neck, it ap-peared to be enormous. Not leopard-size, but not domestic cat–size either.

In no time at all I'd convinced myself that the cat was a threat to man and livestock—something to be stopped at all costs. I slapped Charm's neck hard with the reins and set off for home like a Pony Express rider, only slower. And even as we galloped I knew that there was no point to what I was doing, but I did it anyway because I wanted the drama of it and, deep down, the attention and maybe the praise. I forgot all my resolutions regarding hunting and allowed myself to be carried along on a tide of adrenaline and power.

Dad was away on call-up, so I forced Charm on to the Beatties' house, where, between gasps, I communicated the life-and-death urgency of the situation to Thomas. We swerved from the yard in a skid of gravel, sending dogs scattering. I put my hand on the barrel of his rifle to stop it from sliding along the seat of his truck, and all the way to the lands I kept looking at it and being torn between wanting the cat to be there, so I wouldn't be in trouble for wasting Thomas's time, and want-ing it to be gone to a place of greater safety, so I wouldn't have to deal with whatever came next.

The wild cat was exactly where I'd last seen it, outlined against the sky, regal as a sun god. It was perfectly still.

Thomas shaded his eyes with a freckled hand. "It's only a civet cat!" he exclaimed. "They don't generally cause problems. Why the bloody hell do you want me to kill it?"

And yet even as he spoke, he was cocking the rifle and taking a hunting stance. He paused and stared down at me. Magnified by his milk-bottle glasses, his blue irises stared right into my soul. Into my black heart.

"I don't . . . I just . . . I-Isn't it dangerous?" I stammered, but he'd already turned away and was concentrating on bringing the cat into his sights.

I wanted to beg him to stop, to remind him that I was only a child and probably a stupid one at that, but nothing in my life had equipped me to halt a man of Thomas's forceful charisma in a course of action I had initiated, and so I stood cold as a winter morning at his side, accessory to a senseless murder.

He fired. The civet cat fell to earth in slow motion and hit the dirt with a thud.

Thomas snatched her up by the hind legs and swung her onto the back of the truck. Her amazing pelt, with its pooled spots of black on platinum, was soaked in blood. Before our eyes, her spirit seemed to flee from her.

A sickness far beyond nausea, born out of the most hideous shame, seized my throat and left me wordless.

"Isn't she beautiful?" Thomas said. "Next time you see an animal like that, leave it alone, hey. She wasn't harming anyone."

I never forgave myself for that. When soon afterward I saved one of the Beatties' racehorses from colic after recognizing the symptoms and knowing the cure from a book I'd read, I didn't feel like a hero, I felt like I was working off a debt. Nobody treated me like a hero either. On any farm, but especially on an African farm, life and death continually conspire to become intimately acquainted, and everyone does their bit to keep them apart.

8

In January 1976, aged nine, I packed a black tin trunk with the required number of forest green knickers and went uncomplainingly off to board at Hartley School. That was what most white farm kids did, partly because the distances and frequent petrol rationing meant that day schooling was rarely viable, partly because it offered the freedom of a childless existence to parents already let off the hook by maids and other servants, and partly because, at the height of the War, the schools were deemed to be safer than the farms.

That was true in the main, but Hartley Primary was presided over by Don Clark. Mr. Clark had a spiky military haircut, through the prongs of which his scalp provided an accurate barometer of his moods. Mostly it just showed scarlet. I learned very quickly that while girls at Hartley School were punished with rulers over the knuckles or made to write lines or sent to Mr. Clark for a dressing-down, boys were regularly subjected to the rule of the rod. Kevin Lunt was so frightened of him that he used to eat his tie from nerves. By the end of every term, all that would be left was a stump.

Less than an hour after entering the red soil and hospital green environs of Hartley Primary the previous April, I, too, had been reduced to a gibbering wreck by Mr. Clark. Things had gone wrong almost immediately when Miss Power, the Standard One teacher, introduced me to the rest of the class.

"Nutsa?" she said. "Is that how you say your last name?"

"No, it's—"

"Coetzee?" she said, adding an Afrikaans twist.

I tried to correct her, but that one word was the bane of my existence, and all that came out was a strained whisper.

She cupped a hand over her ear. "Kininter?"

"Yes," I said, just to shut her up. "Yes, yes, yes."

I sank into my seat, bitter and humiliated. Under my breath I cursed Grandfather Frederick, who'd abandoned my dad and left us with an unpronounceable Dutch name. At intervals, Miss Power broke into my depression with incomprehensible questions about long division. Eventually she lost patience and threw me out into the corridor. That's where Mr. Clark discovered me. Forty-five minutes after enrolling, I was receiving a bowel-loosening lecture on the very severe consequences of laziness and inattention at Hartley Primary in front of my new classmates, while Miss Power nodded approvingly. I never got to grips with long division, and I left school no wiser.

Our Standard Two teacher was Ursula North, a blond bombshell who dressed exclusively in primary colors. Like Miss Power, she seemed to take an instant dislike to me, but whereas Miss Power had a nice side and was essentially harmless, Miss North would become so beside herself with frustration at what she saw as my daydreaming and overall dimness that she'd twist my ear until I squeaked with pain and thought it would break off, or hiss a grim warning so forcefully into my ear cavity that my eardrum tickled.

Halfway through the year, my friend Michelle Swanepoel, a pale, emaciated girl, committed some small crime that was considered serious enough for her to be sent to Mr. Clark's office. Such was the terror Mr. Clark inspired that Michelle decided not to go. She hid in the toilets for ten minutes and returned with some story about how he'd told her not to do it again. Miss North was suspicious. It was unlike Mr. Clark to be so forgiving. She went over to his office to find out if Michelle was telling the truth.

Moments later, Mr. Clark burst into the classroom with a roar so terrible that I felt like a rhinoceros had just collided with my heart. His scalp was an apocalyptic purple, and his spikes quivered madly. "MICHELLE SWANEPOEL!" he screamed.

Michelle went gray with fright. She raised a tiny, thin hand. Her memory is of being frozen with fear.

Mr. Clark swooped on her like a buzzard, lifted her from her seat by the collar of her school dress, and hurled her against a vacant desk. Then he grabbed her again and threw her in a different direction. She crashed into the freckled frame of one of the boys and slid down to the ground, her face a ghastly blue white. He seized her by the shoulders, stood her up again, and gave her a final, violent shove. She landed with a smothered yelp and lay on the ground whimpering softly.

"Don't you *ever*, EVER, lie to your teacher again!" spat Mr. Clark, and then he marched shaking from the room. Even Miss North looked unnerved.

The following day Michelle's father, "Swannie," confronted Mr. Clark in his office, informing him that if he ever again laid a hand on his daughter, he'd murder him, in such convincing terms that the secretary ran from the room crying, "Swannie is killing Mr. Clark!'

The girls' hostel was run with draconian efficiency by our matron Mrs. Du Plessis, and supervised by Mrs. Clark, who had a gruff but kindly manner. She had a great sense of humor, and I liked her enormously, although Michelle, who had wet herself in front of half the hostel because Mrs. Clark refused to let her go to the toilet during prep, didn't have quite the same regard for her. In winter Mrs. Du Plessis and Mrs. Clark roused us at six and forced us to stumble around the misty golf course on cross-country runs, pursued by mosquitoes the size of dragonflies, our ankles gritty with dirt and dew. In summer we swam laps every morning in the chilly blue pool, floundering among the frogs and gelatinous clumps of frog spawn, teeth chattering. Both activities were followed by communal showers in a bathroom reeking of Dettol. We used the same red Lifebuoy soap that my mother disdained at home, lathering it over our bulging white tummies. Afterward we stood combed, dressed, and at attention for an inspection of our beds, which had to be Army-perfect with hospital corners.

The worst day of the week was Friday, when we had malaria pills and fish and chips for lunch. The fish smelled like tripe, and its nauseating aroma circulated around the school for hours before it actually reached the dining table. Coupled with the malaria pills, which dissolved like bitter poison on your tongue no matter how quickly you tried to swallow them, it made for the vilest meal on earth. Breakfast was usually French toast and syrup, or scrambled eggs you needed a steak knife to penetrate, or Maltabella, a chocolaty *mielie-meal* porridge.

Dinner was meat loaf or liver and onions followed by banana custard or Zambezi mud—a weak cocoa blancmange—or a semolina pudding we called frogs' eggs.

Within its prison structure, boarding school came with a strangely exhilarating freedom. There were no parents to prevent you from eating ten slices of white bread spread with butter and sugar at dinnertime; no one to tell you not to remove acacia thorns from the soles of your feet with a shared sewing needle and no antiseptic (I awoke one morning to find an angry red line stretching from a fresh puncture on my right foot to the top of my thigh and had to be rushed to Dr. Bouwer with blood poisoning), and no one to point out that there was no sense in running away from home if you were rarely there and were perfectly happy when you were. Running away was something I discussed regularly with my friend Lisa Trumble, who was a day scholar and the daughter of my mother's closest friend, Carol, using a tourist map illustrating the attractions of Rhodesia.

"We'll go by boat to South Africa or maybe take a raft," I told Lisa, tracing the blue lines of various rivers past a watercolor of Zimbabwe Ruins. "The hard part's going to be getting across the border. We'll probably have to sneak across at night. Then all we have to do is follow the Limpopo to the sea." I hadn't got as far as studying a map of South Africa and was unaware that the Limpopo actually met the ocean in Mozambique.

Lisa clapped her hands together gleefully. "What will we do when we get there?" she wanted to know.

An unwelcome picture of myself and Lisa homeless, filthy, and hungry on the beach while our devastated mothers had nervous breakdowns back home surfaced in my mind. "Lots of things," I answered vaguely.

My best friend was Jilly Kirkman, who, like me, was horse-mad. She was tiny, wiry, and intense, and the nicest person I'd ever met. After net ball, tennis, hockey, or athletics practice in the afternoons and the orange quarters that followed, we'd pretend to be horses and cavort around the fir-lined sports fields, whipping ourselves with twigs.

At break time a bell-ringing prefect would hurry the length of a sun-speckled tunnel of red poinsettias, and we'd burst from our classrooms and crowd, squealing around the ice-cream boy, who rode a bicycle with a blue-and-white cooler on the front, at the school gates.

We were after Bengal Juices and Pink Panthers—plastic packets of chocolate or strawberry milk. We'd shake them vigorously, pierce a tiny hole in one corner, and squirt the bubbles into our mouths. On hot days they were pure delight. We'd drink them down, gobble our peanut butter sandwiches, and rush off to the sports fields, where we convened every break to play marbs (marbles) in the camphorous shade of the firs.

Here, as everywhere, the golden kids held sway. They were sports stars, like the Walters girls, Carol and Lee, and three of my classmates, Juliet Keevil, Bruce Campbell, and Mark Cremer. Almost everyone liked Mark, a handsome farm boy whose eyes shone with merriment. He teased me and everyone else mercilessly, in a gentle, funny way devoid of any malice, but not even he could compete with Juliet and Bruce for popularity.

Juliet came from one of those homes where the parents are completely devoted to each other and all of the siblings are good and true and brave and everyone is actively involved in the school and community, and she brimmed with a confidence that was unnerving. Her white smile was on permanent display because she was talented at sport as well as intelligent and very pretty, so her life was a round of trophies and praise and prizes and gold stars.

Juliet was close to Bruce Campbell, who had corn-colored hair and clear, olive skin and was the image of a young Robert Redford. He, too, was good at everything. All the girls had a crush on him, and all the boys wanted to be him, but most of this adulation went over his head because he was down-to-earth, deeply decent, and only really interested in nature. His best friend was another Bruce, Bruce Forrester, who sat beside me in class. Both Bruces shared a love of wildlife, falcons, and ecology, and the two of them were inseparable. But Bruce Forrester was shy and a bit reserved and often homesick, and so he, like Jilly and I, hung around mostly on the fringes of the marble-playing group.

Even here, the War interceded. In class we had drills to prepare us for grenade attacks, flinging ourselves under our desks, where, we were told, we'd be safe from upward-blasting shrapnel, and there were posters warning us to stay away from a variety of Frisbee- and cookie-cutter-shaped bombs. We talked about terrs all the time and how they cut off some victims' lips and ears and made them cook them and eat them. Everyone knew someone or lived close to someone who'd died or been attacked. We did a brisk trade in Rhodesia stickers, which we put on our little brown suitcases. They said things like RHODESIA IS SUPER and SAVE WATER, BATHE WITH A FRIEND, but they also carried more sinister messages, such as LOOSE TALK COSTS LIVES and STICKS & STONES CAN BREAK YOUR BONES BUT WORDS KILL. Those were the ones I liked best because they implied that, in the deadly business of war, we must be as important as Secret Agents if the carelessly spoken words that fell from our lips on the playground as we rolled our marbs and guzzled our Bengal Juice could lead to the loss of life.

When she wasn't twisting my ear or spitting into it, Miss North spun wonderfully romantic yarns about the history of Southern Africa. We heard about Cecil John Rhodes, who during the Matabele Rebellion of 1896 rode unarmed into the Matopo Hills to negotiate with the rebel chiefs and bring about a lasting peace; about David Livingstone's discovery in 1855 of Victoria Falls, which the Africans called *Mosi-oa-Tunya*, "the Smoke That Thunders"; and about the famous greeting of H. M. Stanley, who was sent in search of him: "Dr. Livingstone, I presume." We learned that Mzilikazi, the first king of the Ndebele nation, was forced from his Transvaal kingdom by the Boers and Zulus, and that his son Lobengula, who succeeded him, was generous in granting hunting and mining concessions and allowed the Pioneer Column, the first white settlers, into the land that would become Rhodesia. We learned, too, about the geography of our country, which had an abundance of natural marvels like Victoria Falls, one of the Seven Wonders of the World, and buffalo-lined Lake Kariba, the second biggest manmade lake in the world, and Zimbabwe Ruins, once believed to be King Solomon's Palace.

In summer, Mr. Truman the groundskeeper seemed perpetually to be mowing the sports fields, and the scent of cut grass would float around the classroom as we drew pictures of circles of wagons spewing flames and Zulu warriors with shields and rivers running with blood. That was when Miss North was talking about the Boer pioneers, the Voortrekkers, who in 1835 undertook the Great Trek, a mass migration to escape the rule of the British-controlled Cape Colony. They negotiated areas of settlement with Dingane, king of the Zulus, who later double-crossed them, sending ten thousand impis to attack four hundred of them in the Battle of Blood River, a battle from which the Voortrekkers emerged victorious.

I listened to all this and felt a part of it. My paternal great-grandmother Daisy Sarah-Ann Edwards was a cousin of Dick King, who famously rode 1,000 kilometers in ten days to raise the alarm about a British colony held under siege by the Dutch Settlers at the Old Fort in Durban. He also walked 120 miles to warn the Voortrekkers of imminent peril from the Zulus.

Dad's mother, Ivy Stella, was the maternal great-granddaughter of James Edwards, the 1820 Settler who'd sailed out from Deptford, London, on the *Aurora*, and the paternal great-granddaughter of Johann Heinrich Albert Croft, a missionary responsible for translating the English dictionary into Xhosa. Family lore had it that, after Piet Retief, leader of the Voortrekkers, was murdered, James Edwards retired and lived on Retief's farm.

The 1820 Settlers were a group of four thousand emigrants who traveled to the Cape Colony in ships from a Britain in the grips of a savage winter. More than ninety thousand applicants had responded to the Colonial Office's offer of free passage and one hundred acres per man for those prepared to pay a ten-pound deposit and make a new life in wild Africa, a scheme supported by pamphlets boasting of the Cape's exotic but useful flora and fauna—Aloes! Elephant's teeth! Wild Pigs! Quaggas! This state-sponsored emigration was thought by some historians to have an economic basis—unemployment, poverty, and social dissent were rife in Britain. But according to *The Story of the British Settlers of 1820 in South Africa* (by H. E. Hockly), it had only one real purpose and that was to create a settlement which established a "sturdy and reliable human buffer between the warlike Kaffir tribes on the eastern, and the European Colony on the western, perimeter of the area to be occupied and developed by that buffer."

On my mother's side my ancestors were mainly English and Irish. My great-great-grandfather Hugh William Donnan was from Belfast and was an architect and master builder who, I was told, had been an associate of Rhodes during the creation of Fernwood, a Cape Town estate that later became a parliamentary retreat. He and my great-great-grandmother lived in Fernwood Manor on the estate. Charles Leonard O'Brien Dutton, Granny's father, served with British forces in the Boer War and later became government secretary of the Bechuanaland Protectorate (now Botswana).

In geography, Miss North and other teachers taught us about African culture and customs such as *lobola*, a marriage dowry usually paid in cattle. There were numerous tribes in Rhodesia, but the main ones were the Mashona and the Matabele, traditional enemies who'd long ago declared an uneasy truce. The whites—predominantly of British or European (German and Dutch) descent—were in the minority by many millions (in 1969 Rhodesia had a population of 229,000 whites, 14,000 Asians and Coloureds, and 4.8 million blacks), but we ran the country, which we were confident was better for everyone, particularly since our prime minister, Ian Smith, had more or less said that the blacks wouldn't be ready to govern themselves for a "thousand years."

On the rare occasions I ever watched the news, Ian Smith always seemed to be on it. He had a noble face that was somehow trustworthy and resolute, and he was always in a suit and tie, with never a hair out of place. Everyone I knew idolized him. He'd come on the TV and talk about our war against the Communist guerrillas who were trying to take our country away from us, and about the British, who'd been cross with us ever since we told them we didn't want to be ruled by them anymore. Years ago they'd persuaded the United Nations to impose sanctions against us to punish us for our rebelliousness, since when we hadn't lost a minute's sleep because we were self-sufficient in everything we needed, including beer, and our friends the South Africans made sure that we had oil.

Even petrol rationing wasn't exactly a hardship because people brought along portable *braais* and cooler bags full of Castles and Lions and meat to Smith's Garage in Hartley, and we'd sit in the sunshine eating T-bone steaks and telling war stories under a blue sky of freedom, and just generally laughing and sharing and being proud of our resilience.

Ian Smith had been responsible for the Unilateral Declaration of Independence (UDI) on November 11, 1965, a date engraved on our hearts. That was the day we'd announced to Britain and the rest of the world that we were going to do things our way in the future, whether they liked it or not. Ian Smith's address to the nation had passed into legend, and no matter how often I heard it, it never failed to move me.

> I believe that we are a courageous people and history has
> cast us in a heroic role. To us has been given the privilege
> of being the first Western nation in the last two decades

to have the determination and fortitude to say "so far and no further." . . . The decision we have taken today is a refusal by Rhodesians to sell their birth-right, and even if we were to surrender, does anyone believe that Rhodesia would be the last target of the Communists and the Afro-Asian block? We have struck a blow for the preservation of justice, civilisation, and Christianity, and in the spirit of this belief have this day assumed our sovereign independence.

We were a *courageous people*, and history had cast us in a *heroic* role.

I used a Magic Marker to write the name of my country decoratively on my school books, beside the pictures of horses and hearts containing pop stars' initials. Charm, Donny Osmond, and Rhodesia, my first loves.

9

One Monday morning I was lying in bed hoping that the Umfuli River had flooded in the night, meaning we wouldn't be able to cross the bridge into Hartley and I'd have a day or two off school, only to find that something even better had happened: my school uniforms had been stolen in the night. It was Mom who finally figured out that we'd been burgled. After everyone but me had run around earnestly searching for the uniforms, she noticed that her watch was missing. Then she spotted dirty marks and fragments of glass in the dining room. But what really upset her was finding that the toothpaste and toothbrushes were gone.

In a week or two the burglar was captured. For reasons that were unclear at the time and have grown no less inscrutable over the years, he was brought to our house in a ball and chain to reenact the crime, flanked by two police constables, one black, one white. He had the mulatto skin and small frame of a Bushman. We gathered on the veranda and stared at him accusingly. The remains of our possessions, bedraggled and smoky, were wrapped in a pink blanket—*our* pink blanket—at his feet. Our anger matched his.

"Okay, so show the *bas* what you did, how you got into the house," ordered the white constable. He was standing between my parents with his arms folded. The black constable, who was translating, kept a loose hold on the burglar's bicep.

The burglar made a pantomime of gathering his thoughts. He knew that from here on in his life was going to be hell, and he was determined, in the midst of his misery, to have the last laugh. He began by describing how he'd spent the first part of the evening sitting under the canopy of the camel's foot tree in the front garden, watching and waiting. When the last light went out, he broke a pane in the dining room window. He took what he could carry from the lounge, and the school uniforms and some linen from the clotheshorse in the passage. Then he came into my room. After rummaging through my cupboard for clothes, he swiped the pink blanket from my bed—just removed it with a careful flick.

Dad made a strangled noise that sounded like "Yussis!" His face was corpse white with patches of mortician's red. He was a study in suppressed rage.

The burglar's voice rang with defiance. Every sideways flick of his bloodshot brown eyes seemed to say: "Do you know how easy this was for me? Do you know how easy it would have been to do something much worse?"

He continued with the theater, narrowing his eyes to demonstrate peering through the crack of my bedroom door. He'd heard my sister's cry and seen my mother go through to the kitchen, and had taken the opportunity to dart into the bathroom, where he'd pocketed the watch and all the toothbrushes and toothpaste. Before making his escape, he'd waited for Mom to return to her room. She was wearing, he said with a smirk, a "*picannin* dress," a small dress.

If there was a lascivious note in his tone, I was too young to pick up on it, but what was obvious was that his implication—that the sight of Mom in her short, transparent white nightdress, illuminated by the flickering passage light, had aroused dark thoughts in him— was calculated to offend and that, by pointing it out to my father, while in the protective custody of the police, he was exacting his final revenge.

"You bloody black bastard," cried Dad, and he launched himself at the burglar, getting in two Army-hard punches in the time it took the constables to react.

"No, Errol!" shouted the white one, and there was a tangle of limbs and the *thwock* of bone on flesh as they struggled to contain him. The burglar straightened, panting. Sweat drizzled down his forehead in soapy ribbons. When the constables tugged him away, the look in his eyes was no longer tempered by misery. Now there was only hatred.

Dad accompanied the trio out to the yard. "Man, that felt good" was his parting remark. *"Man, oh man!"* He laughed cruelly. Mom glared at him as he passed. The feral odor of the prisoner and the stink of smoky clothes lingered in the humid air.

"I don't know why your father can't control his ugly temper," Mom said furiously. Her anger rose to join the toxic stew on the veranda. "Still, it gives me chills to think of that awful man taking the blanket off your bed. While you were sleeping."

I said nothing. It terrified me that my instincts hadn't woken me up. That in the first real test of my ability to sense and survive danger, I'd failed abysmally.

Mom and I sorted through the pitiful contents of the pink blanket. They were soiled in a way that washing could never fix.

We threw them away.

In the school holidays I'd go around the farm with Dad and Jock, his shadow. At work, Dad's eyes were permanently narrowed against the sun, idleness, and the rising smoke of his Peter Stuyvesant cigarettes (I kept hoping that he'd switch to Lexington, which had the best advert: "After Action, Satisfaction"). I'd try my hand at reaping cotton or eat the sweet, new ears of wheat or follow him through the maze of maize, dwarfed by green stalks, their tassels wriggling high above us in the azure expanse of sky.

The cattle dip was one of my favorite places on the farm. The dip was long lines of protesting cows dragging their cloven hooves until columns of fine dust coated my teeth and put gritty stars in my eyes. It was the thud of heavy bodies, the clicking of hooves, the moos of protest, and the calls and whistles of the cattle boys—"Dip, dip, dip, *deeepa!*" At rhythmic intervals, it was the belly flop of cows succumbing to the low-roofed tank of poison, followed by the chemical assault of Cooper's dip on my nostrils. And afterward, as I walked among the wet cattle, which shuddered and moaned and shook the foul droplets from their backs in the recovery area, it was warm, gloopy mud and dung oozing between my toes.

Through it all Dad would be chain-smoking or filling in numbers on the back of a cigarette packet, his arms resting tensely on the rails of the corral, forever poised for bad news—a missing cow, a lame calf, or the tiniest sign of ill treatment. The cattle boys twisted the cows' tails and gave them a little shove if they hesitated too long on the edge of the dip, but if they dared to use a stick or if it came to Dad's attention that, through negligence, an illness, fracture, or wound had gone unnoticed and untreated, causing one of his precious cows—his "beautiful girls," he called them—to suffer, he'd go berserk.

The cattle boys moved at the same pace as the cattle, as if their body language had just automatically come to mirror their charges' over the years. Their overalls were always open to the waist or rolled down over their sinewy stomachs and tied around their hips, and their toes, gnarled and cracked from years of walking, poked through the sides of their gum boots. The significance of cattle as symbols of wealth and success in African culture meant that the cattle boys commanded a great deal of respect among their peers, as well as from Dad, but they and Dad were continually engaged in a game of one-upmanship.

He knew their little weaknesses, and they knew his. He'd do things like offer them a lift on the back of his truck but neglect to mention that they'd be sharing the space with a huge python he was transporting in a sack. At some point the sack would move and they'd be bailing out in all directions, while Dad doubled over the steering wheel with helpless laughter. The cattle boys didn't really need to play practical jokes. They just contented themselves with enjoying Dad's misfortunes, which generally had to do with his stomach, which rebelled against many of the daily occurrences of farm life. Lancing an abscess or inadvertently standing in chicken manure, for instance, would be enough to make him violently ill. Even the thought of something that made him queasy made him queasy. He went through a period when he was sick every morning into Mom's cannas, so strung out was he on nerves in case he did a less-than-perfect job for Thomas.

Because he was on the front line of any treatment of animals, Dad was regularly mauled, kicked, and brutalized by the creatures he loved, and it was these incidents that the cattle boys lived for. One time he was examining an Ngoni bull with the wide, curving horns of an ox when it swung its head and gored him in the abdomen. Incredibly, it missed any vital organs.

"Hell, the *munts* laughed," a grinning Dad told us when he came home. Bizarrely, he seemed to relish these interactions. "They thought this was an absolute scream."

He wouldn't hear of going to hospital to have the goring wound examined but simply packed the puncture with animal wound powder and carried on as usual.

• • •

Wherever Dad went, Jock followed. Any time Dad's truck could be seen streaking among the cotton, wheat, and cattle, Jock would be at the window, dark ears flapping in the wind and a grin on his broad Staffordshire face. Just as there are people on earth who are born with a unique inner light, so there are animals, and Jock was one of them. Before he was a year old, he had all of the qualities of his namesake. Dad valued courage in animals and humans more highly than any other characteristic, apart, perhaps, from good manners, and Jock had bravery and good manners in spades. He wore his black coat like a sable cloak over proud shoulders and squat, elastic muscles, and even as a puppy he was never given to fooling around but was serious and bodyguardlike, watching Dad's every move.

When Jock was about nine months old, Dad stopped his truck on the edge of a cotton land at Morning Star to study an immense, blue-bottomed male baboon. It was sitting on its haunches and raking leaves toward it in a sort of protective wall. In a flash, Jock had dived out the window. The baboon simply scooped him up with a massive paw and ripped off his hind leg with curving ocher incisors. All that connected Jock's leg to his body were a few tendons and arteries. Dad rushed the dog to Tinks Rabie, the vet, and Tinks gave Dad his word that Jock would be as good as new when he'd sewn him up. And he was.

I wasn't at the dip on the day Jock began barking the urgent, staccato bark that in Africa means only one thing. Dad was at the crush, weighing cattle, but he was running before he'd even fully registered the sound, vaulting over the fence into the cattle camp, yelling for Jock to stop, to come back, to save himself before it was too late.

Jock was fifty yards into the savanna, his tail pointing skyward in a fierce curve. Above him, draped the length of the three large shrubs, was a black mamba.

In Gadzema people always said that you could tell black mambas because their heads are shaped like the coffins most of their victims end in, but to me they were identifiable purely by their aura of evil. They're not actually black but a grayish green or beige, with small, sinister eyes, and it's their eyes that set up a childhood conviction in me that one of them was the original snake in the Garden of Eden. Riding Charm, I'd sometimes think about the theory that an angry black mamba could outdistance a running horse, and the one thing I knew for certain was that if it was Charm doing the running, that wouldn't take very long.

Before Dad could make a move to grab Jock, the mamba had dropped from the bushes and was streaking toward an anthill with the Staffy baying after it. When Jock sank his teeth into its side, the snake came over in a monstrous arc—hellish black mouth stretched wide— and bit him four or five times in quick succession. Then it poured into a hole like molten lead. In the insanity of the moment, Dad grabbed its tail and tried to drag it from its burrow, but its grip was unbreakable. The cold, gray scales slipped easily from his grasp.

It took Jock seventeen minutes to die. By then Dad was on the outskirts of Hartley, racing manically to the vet for help he already knew could be of no earthly use.

I was on my bunk bed reading when I heard his truck door slam, heard the back door go, heard Peter exclaim: "Ah, ah! *Yena file?*"

I thought, Someone or something's dead! and strained my ears for Dad's response, but all I caught was the sympathy in Peter's singsong voice: "Eeeh, *bas*, sorry, sorry, sorry. Tch! Sorry, sorry, sorry."

I cast aside my book and flew into the passage. The body of Jock hung limply in my father's arms. His dark eyes were glazed, his tongue lolled blackly, and foam dripped from his mouth, splashing on the polished floor.

A little scream burst from me. Mom was startled from the lounge. One hand flew to her mouth and the other grabbed the fingers of Lisa, who stared up at Jock with a bewildered curiosity. When he spoke, Dad's words were torn from his chest, as if dredged from a place of fathomless agony. "Black mamba . . . dip . . . seventeen minutes . . ."

It was the only time I ever saw him cry.

He wrapped Jock in a blanket and carried him out into the garden, and somehow we knew not to follow him. I climbed onto my bunk and stayed there till my face was stiff with salty tears. Dad's shadow passed under the tree outside my bedroom, alone apart from his burden. I saw him set it down. And through the open window I could hear his great, gasping sobs and the sharp sound of the spade committing his beautiful black dog to the red earth.

10

For me it was the first lesson in how Africa gives and snatches away. For Dad it was one lesson too many. He would have other dogs, and he would care for them and get pleasure out of them, but he would never love any of them the way he loved Jock.

Then Beauty was ripped to pieces after following the milk boys to the Beatties' house. Sue telephoned Mom and said in the matter-of-fact way of farmers' wives: "I thought you should know that our dogs are busy killing your warthog."

Devastated, I redoubled my efforts to protect the lambs in my charge, cuddling them to me during feedings, when their warm, furry mouths tried to drink from anything they could reach—my hair or even my chin—their waxy hooves digging into my thighs. Every lambing I received a flurry of new orphans until eventually I got three in one day and Dad put a stop to it. But the deaths of Jock and Beauty had proved to me that love wasn't enough. You needed God on your side, or luck, and you needed knowledge.

I decided that, like my friend Jilly, I'd be a vet when I grew up, but unlike her, I'd start the training right away.

I found a wooden trunk in the spare room, cleaned it up, and raided the first aid kit for basic supplies. I pestered Dad for any remnants of farm antiseptics and antibiotics he could pass my way, and if the new vet, Eric Staples, was summoned to Giant, I'd hang over his shoulder and on to his every syllable and pounce on any syringes and needles as soon as he discarded them. I also learned what I could from Dad, who

did all of the farm's nonemergency animal treatment, helping him
to deliver a couple of breeched calves. I'd started reading James Her-
riot's *It Shouldn't Happen to a Vet*, and I proudly soaped up my forearm
and plunged it into the hot, snug cervixes of the cows just like James
did, feeling for the miracle of life: the wet calves and their tiny, soft
hooves.

My mother, meanwhile, was preparing to become a lemon millionaire. When Mom was a child, Granny had suffered from prolonged
periods of clinical depression, and for years Mom had spent months at
a stretch with Grampy's friends the Mowbrays, who lived in a palatial
spread on the outskirts of Salisbury. They had multiple servants and a
polished silver dinner service and an emerald lawn so verdant that it
gave off the cool, green scent of abundance. It was those visits, Mom
once admitted, that had fostered in her a taste for the finer things in life,
even though her own parents were dirt-poor and we weren't doing
much better.

As a result, my mother was always trying to think up get-rich-quick
schemes. Legend had it that in 1874 Thomas Hartley had shot an elephant and found a piece of white quartz beneath it, a strong indicator
of the presence of gold, so when Medicine found a piece of rose quartz
in the garden, Mom was sure we were sitting on a gold mine. When that
didn't pan out, as it were, she turned her attention to the lemon tree,
which she'd pruned and nurtured over the past year and which had
rewarded her by producing so many lemons that from a distance the
tree itself resembled a giant lemon. Having convinced herself that it was
her passport to riches, Mom spent a busy few weeks tracking down special citrus-holding pockets and organizing a sales outlet, and then she
and Medicine filled sixty pockets with fruit.

Sadly, the whole enterprise was a triumph only of enthusiasm.

"It's truly amazing how the cost of the pockets was almost exactly
what we made from the lemons," Dad said sardonically. "I just can't get
over it, myself."

Overnight Lisa recovered from all ailments and allergies, stopped crying, and became a lively, curious toddler with sparkly brown eyes.
This brought its own set of problems because Maud was busy with
laundry and other chores in the mornings and Mom had a limited
attention span. She'd be chatting away on the phone, glance vaguely

out of the window, and spot Lisa and Gareth playing with a night adder.

My parents took little or no notice of where I was or what I was doing. I almost always went riding on my own, often through thick bush in remote cattle camps, where any number of fates could have befallen me, but it wasn't those that concerned my mother; it was details like whether or not I was wearing a sweater on a cold day. In this she and Dad were opposites. She was overprotective. He yelled at me if I showed any sign of wimpishness.

She said: "Wear your hard hat. Please ride carefully. Don't go too fast."

He said: "What's the matter with you? Can't you go any faster? Have you forgotten how to ride? Stop sniveling."

Very occasionally a switch would trip in Mom's mind and something that, on another day, would have produced dire predictions of death or mutilation would seem quite fine to her. For example, when I was a teenager and our car broke down in the Lion & Cheetah Park while we were taking her Indian travel friend Pat on a tour, she had no hesitation in ordering me to get out and push, even though there was a pride of nine lions thirty feet away.

Unwisely, I did just that.

Maud was the only one who really kept an eye on me. She had an almost telepathic way of materializing whenever Douglas and I were about to do something mischievous or forbidden and saying, in a way that caused chronic guilt: "WHAT ARE YOU DOING? *Basopa*, watch out, or the *bas* is going to beat you!"

Where Dad's attitude came in handy was when I wanted to do something that Mom considered dangerous, like ride the racehorses, which I'd been inspired to do after listening to Dad's stories of his amateur racing days. He'd met Thomas when he offered to stand in for a jockey who'd lost his nerve moments before he was due to race, and had ridden so well that from then on Thomas would have no one else on his horses. Dad won scores of races for Thomas and became firm friends with him in the process. But his proudest moment came when the old man Jimmy Beattie said to him: "Errol, I want you to ride in *my* colors today."

"Hell, I rode that day," Dad would recall emotionally. "I think I won four races that day. I'll never forget that day."

It's because I wanted to win four races like my father that I ended up on Butcher Boy, a trophy-collecting racehorse, wrestling with all my puny strength at the reins as he bolted for the main road. That's the reason I made the decision to jump rather than become strawberry jam under the wheels of a tourist car, and that's why I found myself sitting dazed under a tree on a sun-baked *vlei*, watching blood fill my left gum boot and begin to trickle over the side.

Cautiously I pulled up the leg of my jeans. A cavern of split flesh and white bone greeted me. I pushed my jeans down. It hadn't happened.

A plume of dust indicated that help was on its way. I stayed where I was until Dad bundled me up with an "Oh, hell's teeth, lovey" and whisked me back to the house. With Mom alternately panicking that I was about to lose a leg, showering me with kisses, and hurling recriminations at Dad, they transferred me into the back of the car on a heap of blankets. Then they argued all the way into town over which one of them was to blame, pausing only when I gave the occasional moan for effect. Dr. Bouwer was not at his surgery, so we drove miles down the Black Adder Road to find him, and he interrupted his tennis game to follow us back into Hartley and patch me up with three neat layers of stitches.

At home, Mom made up a bed for me on the couch and put my crutches in easy reach. She was in her element nursing Lis or me, and she came over repeatedly to stroke my hair and berate Dad for irresponsibly encouraging me to engage in hazardous pursuits, something that was doing untold damage to her health: "It's a wonder my hair is not snow white."

A couple of days later they hosted a party, and I lay in bed with my mummified leg up on a pillow and a glass of nonalcoholic punch, some chips, and a blended cream cheese and tomato and Worcestershire sauce dip on my bedside table. I felt a bit sorry for myself, but I was also quite relieved to have been spared the festivities outside. After a recent beer-fueled visit by a group of neighboring farmers, Mom had told me she didn't want me sitting on their laps anymore.

"Why not?"

"Because it's not nice, that's why."

"Why isn't it nice?"

"Because men can be a bit funny sometimes, that's all."

"Why are they a bit funny?"

"Don't ask stupid questions. Why don't you just listen to your mother *for once*."

On my first day back at school, Miss North, a tottering dynamo in a navy blue suit, red platform heels, and scarlet enamel earrings, made me crawl around the parquet classroom floor on a measuring exercise until my bandages were covered in dirt and blood and plasma seeped through. When I hopped over to show her the damage, she eyed the stained gauze with a grimace and snapped: "Oh, for God's sake, go to sick bay."

Sick bay was two spotless hospital beds in its own special building. There, well-meaning Sister Honey Metcalf smothered the torn stitches with a sticky blue ointment. For two days I lay in the starched perfection of the sheets in that time vacuum peculiar to illness, where the sounds of the world arrive at your ear filtered through a dense, dislocating silence, and the hours pass in seconds or even in years. My only visitor was a smiling black maid who arrived bearing trays of scrambled egg, meat loaf, and Zambezi mud.

"He-llo, *Masikati* . . . Good ufter-noon," she called out in greeting the first time I saw her, and her voice was like music in the sterile chamber of the sick bay.

"Hello. Good ufter-noon," I answered, unable to resist mimicking her careful accent. *"Maswera sei."*

"Taswera kana maswerawo—yes, it was a good day," she replied and laughed. "You speak Shona?"

"No," I said, feeling a bit of a fraud. "Only Chilapalapa."

The morning, afternoon, and evening greetings were the only Shona I knew.

She pointed to my bandaged leg and said: "It's brokken?"

I explained about Butcher Boy and how heartless Miss North had made me crawl around the floor until my stitches split open.

"Aa-ah!" She jumped back as if she, too, had been dealt a blow by Miss North. "That's terri-bill! Shem," she murmured with compassion. "Shem, shem, shem."

It was impossible not to smile, not to feel comforted, not to be cocooned by her caring.

By the fourth day a severe infection had set in, and I had to be rushed off to Dr. Bouwer. He cleaned the wound and prescribed further antibiotics, but nothing could be done about the torn stitches. The resulting scar turned keloid and spread across my shin as I grew, so that I spent the first three-quarters of my adolescence standing with my legs in knots trying to hide it and the last quarter flaunting it as a battle scar.

It was while I was at home, recuperating for the second time, that I found the *Encyclopaedia Rhodesia*. I'd borrowed it from the school library months before and forgotten to return it. Instantly I panicked. I had visions of being sent to Mr. Clark, who would scream at me, fine me, and possibly throw me at a desk. It occurred to me that the solution would be to get rid of it altogether. If there was no book, I reasoned, there would be no late date to get into trouble over.

I hopped outside to the wood-burning boiler, a brick kiln that heated water for the house, and put the book on the step while I stirred up the pulsing orange embers. It felt sacrilegious to put the entire encyclopedia into the fire at once, so I decided to start with the title page and one or two others that didn't seem to matter.

"*Hayikona, hayikona. Yinindaba?* What are you doing?"

I jumped guiltily.

Maud was standing behind me with her hands on her hips. "You want to put the book in the fire? Why? What for?"

"Because," I said rudely.

"What is 'because'? Give it to me." She held out her hand. When my parents weren't around, some of the niceties of Maud's language went out of the window.

"Do you want it?" I said doubtfully.

"*Nxa!*" She turned her head away and laughed derisorily, as if the question was too ridiculous to merit a reply.

"Okay," I said, relieved not to have a burned, unreturned library book on my conscience, "you can have it."

I forgot about it until the next day, when Thomas came to the house. I heard him ranting in the lounge and stayed well away. After the civet cat incident, I'd done my best to avoid him. The voices of my parents rose and fell. Then I heard my name being called. My parents only ever used my name when I was in trouble, so I walked through on leaden feet.

The first thing I saw was the encyclopedia.

That was when it came home to me that even small sins are found out eventually. In Cape Town I'd nicked a boy's eraser because it smelled of bubble gum and had a special brush to sweep away the rubber crumbs, and because I was sure we were too poor to afford one like it, and later I'd attempted to shave his name from it with a kitchen knife. But the ink he'd used had soaked deep into the rubber, and although I sliced and sliced, his name showed through like a brand. In the end, I had all of the guilt with nothing to show for it.

Mom said in a dread-filled half whisper: "Something terrible has happened. We think . . . we think Maud has stolen your school encyclopedia."

She explained how, the previous evening, Thomas had stopped and searched Maud on her way back to the compound and had found the book in her bicycle basket. He'd questioned her at length about it. When she kept insisting I'd given it to her, he'd accused her of lying. He was convinced that she'd stolen it, and he wanted to hear me confirm it.

I listened with growing disbelief. Even at that age and in that time I found it chilling that Thomas would intercept Maud on the deserted compound road late at night, would search her basket and interrogate her. Thomas, with his thick white chest and redheaded temper, knew Maud, *had* known her for years, and should have trusted her; should have respected her more than to go rummaging through her belongings and humiliating her.

Ashamed, I mumbled to a square on the olive green carpet: "I *gave* it to her."

"Say that again," Dad ordered in his quiet voice, which was a lot more frightening than his yell.

I raised my eyes and met the hostile laser of Dad's and Thomas's. I said: "She didn't steal it. I gave it to her."

There was a shocked silence, and then they all turned on me and wanted to know how I could have done such a heinous thing, not only stealing school property but giving it away to the nanny, and didn't I realize how much trouble I'd caused—the police had nearly been called—and that I was to return the book immediately and apologize and pay the fine.

"You think you're big stuff, do you?" Dad demanded. "You think you can do what you like?"

Mom was mostly thankful that Maud was innocent.

Maud was livid with me. "Why you want to make trouble for me?" she scolded. "*Bas* Beattie, that one is too much cheeky."

"I'm sorry, Maudie, I'm so, so sorry," I said, and I was. Very.

But she wasn't to be placated. *"Wena mampara, wena,"* she said scornfully.

I was a useless person, and not one in a position to disagree.

11

To me, the War began in earnest the day that Miss North told us one of our classmates had shot himself in the night. His father was away on Army call-up, and he'd been trying to be the man of the house. A loaded rifle lay on the rug beside his bed. He'd got out of bed and stepped on it.

All of us were shocked, and some children were crying, but none of us could really take it in. How could a boy who'd sat just a few feet away from us, fearing Mr. Clark, struggling with his homework, looking longingly out at the sunshine, have been erased overnight like an unwanted picture? Soon he was just one of many. After years of trying to contain the guerrilla threat within the country, the Rhodesian government launched cross-border raids in June 1976. By the end of the year, the list of innocent and not-so-innocent victims of the new killing fields of Rhodesia was already a couple of thousand names long.

For the first time there was a feeling that we were a Nation at War. A troopie canteen opened up next to Smith's Garage in Hartley, and I'd go in there with Mom and stand in a corner with my legs twisted in such a way as to hide my scar, watching the Afrikaner women, the best cooks in the district, serve bush-weary soldiers with *babotie* (an eggy mince curry), roast pork with crackling and applesauce, fruit salad from white bowls, syrupy *koeksisters*, or icing-sugar-dusted sponges packed with cream and strawberries.

The troopies had their own language, and snippets of conversation about close shaves with "flatdogs" (crocodiles) on the Zambezi, or *don-*

nering (killing) gooks out in the *shateen* (the wilderness) at Gona-Re-Zhou (a name meaning "refuge for elephants"), would drift over to me as I hovered awkwardly. They'd say: "My God, those floppies took a pounding. We *really* gave them a hiding."

At Giant, squads of soldiers stopped by to drink *shumbas* (Lion beers) in our living room, and at two or three Lisa would stand in the middle of them and charm and entertain them with long, involved stories about airplane crashes, acted out for extra effect. As someone routinely paralyzed by shyness, I found it incredible that she and I were actually related.

The person most cheered by the escalation of the War was Dad. He was descended from a long line of soldiers, and the Army was in his blood. His grandfather on his mother's side, Johannes Croft, a gentle German, had been a POW in Britain during the First World War, once so hungry he'd eaten his boots to survive, and Dad's parents had met in the military. Ivy Stella, my grandmother, was working as a clerk in the mail room of the WAF in Pretoria when she met Frederick Antonie, a Dutch soldier, and he was the love of her life. When they married, she felt her world became "more beautiful."

Toward the end of the Second World War, Frederick—whose own father was, Dad said, "one of the hugest [only Dad pronounced it in the Afrikaans way, "yugest"], fattest men you've ever seen in your life," so "yuge" that he had to hire a special picannin to tie his shoelaces and wash his massive feet in a plastic bowl—was posted to Italy. The day Granny Ivy gave birth to Dad's brother, Neal, she received a telegram to say that Frederick was missing in action. Dad was only eighteen months old. There are two versions of what happened next. One is that Frederick returned to South Africa a changed man and took to chasing Ivy around the house with knives. The other is that he never returned to Stutterheim, where Ivy and the children were waiting for him, but went directly to Port Elizabeth, where he was later discovered to be living with a woman pregnant with his baby.

Either way, Ivy's world was blown to bits. She was a slight, attractive woman, all cheekbones and blue eyes, and she had already experienced more than her share of heartbreak. Her stepgrandmother, a former governess to the German kaiser's children, so it was said, had tried to murder Ivy's father by lacing a blancmange with arsenic. When she heard that she'd mistakenly killed her favorite grandson, Ivy's beloved younger brother and best friend, Bertie, instead, she dropped dead of a heart attack. The loss of Bertie haunted Ivy all her life.

After the vanishing of Frederick, Ivy remarried twice. For as long as I could remember, she'd occupied a knife edge between living and dying, so that all of our relationships with her were conducted with heightened intensity, with extreme love, because you never knew if she was going to be around the next time you saw her. In reality, her tiny, frail frame was pure steel. Her sense of humor never failed her. She was the axis around which the whole family (the South African branch of it, at any rate) revolved.

As soon as he heard the news reports of the first external raids, Dad became determined to join the Selous Scouts, a mixed-race, SAS-style Special Forces unit, which specialized in infiltrating guerrilla ranks. Their survival and tracking skills were some of the most advanced in the world, and Dad put himself through a grueling training regime at Giant to prepare for the notorious selection course. No matter how exhausting his day on the farm, he'd sprint up the high kopje with brick-filled rucksacks or shin up ropes in the garden.

Mid-1976, Dad joined the other would-be Selous Scouts recruits at Nkomo Barracks in Salisbury, where they were searched for fishing hooks, and a hornbill was sent along their lines to hunt out any food. Twenty-five kilometers short of the training camp at Wafa Wafa, near Kariba, the recruits were dropped off, paired up, and told to run the remainder of the way with a sandbag and rifles. Many never reached Wafa Wafa, and those who did found that there was no food and no barracks, only a few mud huts. No meals were provided for the first five days. To further torture the men, on the third day, a baboon carcass was hung in the square to rot in the sweltering Kariba heat.

"If you wanted to be a hero, you went and cut yourself a piece of baboon meat," Dad told us afterward. "Of course, the people who did that were horribly sick."

Luckily for his weak stomach, he didn't last until the fifth day, when the baboon would be cooked and fed to the starving men, maggots and all. On the fourth day, Dad was watching the crestfallen failures load their gear into the truck that would take them away when the driver called over: "Any of you guys interested in joining the Grey's Scouts?"

The Grey's Scouts were an elite, mounted infantry unit named after a volunteer force raised during the 1896 Matabele Rebellion. Unbeknownst to Dad, they'd been in the midst of re-forming.

"*Get me on that truck,*" Dad cried, almost knocking the driver over as he hauled himself onboard. "Here I am running up hills and climbing ropes when I could be on a horse! Hell, why must I run when I can ride?"

Back in Salisbury, he sprinted all the way from the Selous Scouts' barracks to the new home of the Grey's Scouts, arriving there dripping with sweat, still filthy from the previous few days.

"Sir," he panted, "I'd like to apply for the Grey's Scouts selection course."

"Well," drawled the recruiting officer, "if you're that keen . . ."

The Grey's Scouts call-up schedule was twenty-eight days on, twenty-eight days off. When Dad joined them, they were still training horses and recruiting farriers, and he helped in the building of the new Grey's Scouts barracks at Nkomo, chopping down mopani trees as bone jarring as concrete.

The night before his first exercise, I sat at his feet in the spare room while he stripped and cleaned his FN and sorted through his ration packs, creating a mini "rat" pack for me. This became our ritual. Dad would take the rehydrated mashed potato, rice, curry powder, peanuts, and tins of Lucky Strike sardines, beef stew, and chopped ham ("chopped fetus," the troopies called it), which he traded with the African soldiers for their delicious Nyemo beans. Once he had everything he needed, I loaded the spare packets of sticky coffee and tubes of jam, butter, and condensed milk into my old school satchel. As soon as he was gone, I planned to put on my own Army uniform and gum boots, pop a few caps in my revolver, patrol the perimeter fence on foot, and have a well-earned rat pack meal (usually flask coffee and condensed milk on bread) in my tree house.

Now I sifted bullets through my fingers and asked: "Don't you get scared, Dad?"

"No *ways*. If you're fit and well trained, nothing's going to happen to you."

Twenty-eight days later he was back, blasting through the door in full camouflage, rifle in hand, and the smell of him—an unforgettable brew of horse sweat, man sweat, saddle leather, crushed pine needles, and damp earth—evoked the Grey's Scout life like nothing else. I was in a rapture of envy. His eyes were tired, but they blazed like aquamarines against his sunburned skin, and his face was alight with the adventure of it all. He scooped up Lisa with one tattooed arm and squeezed me hard with the other. Over black coffee, he told us how, after being transported with their horses to northern Inyanga, close to the Mozambique border, they'd ridden 400 kilometers in two weeks. "The horses just lived on apples."

From high mountain passes they'd been able to see and be seen for miles, and everywhere they went there was evidence of the "bush telegraph"—villagers beating drums or sending up threads of smoke to warn the terrorists of their approach—going before them.

"Because of that we had numerous contacts but few kills," Dad reported matter-of-factly.

Then a horrific accident. A horse had overbalanced while being led along on a treacherous path and plunged screaming to the bottom of the mountain. The whole stick was rattled. They stripped the poor creature of its tack and cut off a front hoof, which was individually branded and had to be carried back to base for identification purposes.

Years before, we'd been camping in Inyanga with Sheila, who was Scottish and then a colleague of my mother's, and her Spanish husband, Joseph, a chef whom I remember chiefly for the sublime hot chocolate donuts he made in their café. Sheila's parents had a house in the mountains, and we pitched a tent in their garden. On our first night there, my mother left the campfire to rummage in the dark tent and put her hand on a furry caterpillar. Within seconds, her hand was a swollen fireball of agony. The gas lamp was brought, and Sheila's mum began the laborious task of finding each and every hair and removing them with tweezers. To distract themselves from the tedium and the pain, Sheila and my mother laughed about silly things like their office diet of samosas from the Bengal Tiger and banana fritters with cinnamon sugar and lemon from Flanagan's, which they'd ordered every day until the chef at Flanagan's demanded to know if they were pregnant.

The night took on a mountain chill. The hours slipped away. After a while I was glad to snuggle into my sleeping bag just beyond the circle of hissing white light, and to lie there with my feet resting on an African hot-water bottle (a brick heated in the coals and wrapped in hessian), smiling up at the sparkle of stars, until they and the bending silhouettes of the women blurred and vanished into oblivion.

Despite the caterpillar drama, I remembered Inyanga as a place of fairy glens, gossamer mists, and vivid greenery—"like Scotland," Sheila said. The air had the cold, clean bite of the trout-packed mountain streams, and in the mornings and early evenings the Chimanimani Mountains melted into the distance in smoky folds of violet and blue. Years on I could picture, as easily as if I'd ridden alongside him, my father, rifle in hand, kicking his horse up vertical slopes of pine, or descending into valleys where gaboon vipers hid among the ferns in fat, autumnal coils. Given such a setting, even the bloodied hoof, carried like the dog tag of a fallen hero, sounded romantic, and I wished again that I could be a boy, or even a man, on a strong horse with an oiled gun, defending my country.

12

Ever since Dad had gone fishing with his friends—most of whom Mom detested because they drank too much and encouraged him to do the same—and brought home a vundu, a great maroon-bellied, prehistoric catfish, bigger than I was and many times heavier, I'd pestered him to take me fishing, and not only fishing but camping. But he was always away on call-up or too busy on the farm. Finally he agreed to take me late on a Saturday. He knew, he said, of a special place on the river at Shamrock, a place I'd never been to before, and he was certain the fishing would be good there. We didn't have a tent, but we had groundsheets, blankets, and an Army sleeping bag, and we'd sleep under the stars near the water.

To get there, we'd have to take the Lowood Road.

The Lowood Road was a gravel route that wound through some of the remote farms in the region before looping back to the Sinoia Road, a diversion nicknamed Sunset Boulevard. Until very recently, Mom and I had risked it just because it was worth it to visit Sybil Norman, a gifted wildlife artist. Sybil worked with oils on anything from dinner plates to calabashes, and her cheetahs, kingfishers, and other animals were so exquisitely rendered they almost lived. She and her husband, Brian, owned a wheat farm opposite Braemar on the edge of the Tribal Trust Lands (areas of land held in trust for African tribes, which in 1973 amounted to 21 million acres, a quarter of the country), a hotbed of terrorist activity.

After a tour of Sybil's studio, we'd sit out on the terrace watching hoopoe birds nod across the lawn like brown-crested pharaohs. A servant would deliver a coffee-and-walnut sponge or scones dripping with jam and cream to a table draped with a starched white cloth, while Sybil poured tea from a magnificent silver urn. The garden dropped away steeply to the irrigated lands. As the afternoon wore on, shadows deepened the blue-green hue of the wheat, and the sprays created pockets of mist. Puffs of smoke from the compound fires floated above the violet backdrop of the distant kopjes. It was a scene of surpassing tranquillity and gave the illusion that all was right with the world. That we hadn't just massacred twelve hundred terrorists at a training camp in Mozambique. That we weren't in the middle of a war.

But by January 1977, when Dad and I set out on the long-awaited fishing trip—both tense and agitated after a standoff at the house regarding the weather—traveling the Lowood Road had become a bit like running the gauntlet. In parts, the blur of trees was interwoven as suffocatingly as any jungle, and the proximity of rocky kopjes—home to leopards, *dassies* (rock rabbits), and Bushman paintings—made them likely locations for an ambush.

It was on this road that Dad had seen a leopard bathing in the red glow of dawn. It was sunning itself on an anthill as he crested a rise, and its arrogant beauty was so arresting and the sight of it so rare, leopards being both nocturnal and intensely shy, that he pulled over to stare at it. In a flash Muffy, echoing Jock, was out the window. The leopard bounded up snarling and took off into the bush, the fuzzy black scrap hurtling after it. Dad was already mourning her as leopard bait when she returned unscathed, crooked tail wagging.

That incident, coupled with another at Lion's Vlei, where Muffy backed a Sable bull into a circle of rocks and held it there in defiance of its great, curving horns, convinced Dad that, while she could never replace Jock, she had every bit as much heart as he'd done. But like Jock's, her big heart would be her undoing. She was eventually killed by a much larger dog.

Somewhere beyond Morning Star, the air became oppressive. Even the birdsong ceased. With every passing mile the safe warmth of our ramshackle farmhouse seemed to dissipate. It was as if, without knowing it, we'd crossed some outer margin of civilization into a lawless frontier of paralyzing loneliness.

I was thinking about Muffy and about the bullets in the wall above the baby's cot at Shamrock when, from a long way away, Dad said: "D'you know how to look for land mines, do you?"

"What?" I stalled. I tried to rewind and make sense of the question. I had no idea how long he'd been speaking. Outside the window, balancing rocks cast mutant shadows over the road.

"Don't say 'What?' Why don't you *listen* to me when I talk?" He sucked in his breath in sudden fury and released it in a pressure-cooker hiss. "I saaaid, Do you know how to look for land mines?"

Twin rods of panic stabbed me in the gut—panic at upsetting him so early in the trip, and at being at his mercy so far from the protection of my mother. I shook my head quickly, and tears pricked the backs of my eyes.

"Well, the main thing is, you look for new diggings or disturbed earth. Anything that looks sort of like unnatural, like it's not supposed to be there."

"Are the land mines big?" I imagined them like trip wires, snaking under the road.

"You know, not really. The gooks even hide them under pieces of cow dung."

"Then how do they know if your wheel is going to go over them?"

"It's sort of like the law of averages. Sooner or later, somebody is going to set one off."

"But if they're that small, how are we meant to see them?"

His mouth twitched. *"Ag,* if it's done professionally, you've got no chance really."

For the remainder of the way I strained my eyes for imperfections on the road. It turned out there were many. A spill of grain from a tractor, choppy crosscurrents of multicolored soil, faded piles of antelope droppings, scattered foliage. Despite the likelihood of land mines, or perhaps because of it, and because we could be ambushed at any time, Dad rarely went slower than 100 kilometers per hour. And so I rode alongside him with my heart in my mouth, watching cowpats slide under the wheels, just waiting to be blown to smithereens.

At Shamrock, we turned off before we reached the main farm, rattled over a cattle grid, and bounced along a wooded track. Through the bush came the iron smell of rain. Dad squinted out at the sky. The sunset was equal parts pink and thunder gray.

"I don't like the look of *this*," he said. "I don't like this look of this at all."

We parked on the edge of a rocky river crossing, alongside a tangle of bulrushes. Red-beaked waxbills spooked away in a straggled whir of wings. We unloaded our fishing gear and planned our spots, but I could tell by the look on Dad's face that the trip was already a write-off and that he was giving himself hell for not obeying his weather instincts back at the house and probably imagining he'd been talked into it. I began to worry that I'd get the blame. A threatening breeze ruffled the silken flow of water. Dad cast an injured glance at the blackness above and strode into the bush to gather firewood.

A little while later, I was kneeling by the coals in a dizzy paradise of *boerewors* spice and smoke when there was a great, mineral-laden *whooosh* and the rain came over the river in a waterfall wall. "Holy Moses!" yelled Dad. And then we were on our feet laughing and gasping at the cold sting of it, and Dad was wincing as he herded the spitting *boerewors* into a container with his fingers while shielding himself from the onslaught.

We flung ourselves into the truck and slammed the doors, but already our hair was plastered to our faces and goose bumps rose like chicken flesh on our skin. The rain clattered hard against the roof and ran in broad, silver ripples down the windshield, opaque as mercury. It pressured the river into singing like music played at the wrong speed. Our world was reduced to a dully echoing cave. Hemmed into the cab with my father, I was struck dumb with shyness. It was rare to get him as a captive audience. Usually, he couldn't sit still. Usually, he paced or fretted or cursed himself for not anticipating the ringing of the phone or the wants, needs, or desires of every person in the room or at the dinner table. And he growled at us for not anticipating his. But now he was temporarily confined. And, as was his wont when confronted with disaster, unexpectedly cheerful.

"What a shambles." He chuckled, unscrewing the lid of the flask and sloshing a steaming stream of condensed milk coffee into it. "Sorry about the fishing, my friend, but this is beautiful rain for the cotton and cattle. B-eau-tiful rain."

He practically cheered, he was so joyful.

We salvaged what *boerewors* we could and ate the burned bits with doughy doorstops of Tomazo's bread, cold roast chicken, tomatoes, and a liberal dusting of salt.

"Tell me some stories, Dad," I pleaded. So he smoked and told me of another rainy night back when he was a boy in Uitenhage, when the man whose luckless job it was to remove the barrel of shit and piss twice weekly from the family outhouse slipped while negotiating the steep path to the back gate in a downpour and nearly drowned himself in its contents.

I always laughed at that story but not nearly as much as I did at Dad's face, which still paled at the memory of the lingering stench. What I loved most, though, were the pictures he painted of a magical winter he and Neal had spent on his grandfather Croft's Gubu farm, the year that he turned five years old. Of his father playing "You Are My Sunshine" on his guitar while snowflakes drifted past the window. Of him and Neal building a snowman beneath an oak tree bowed under slabs of glistening white. Of two Africans riding up to the farmhouse on Basuto ponies to see his grandfather, their cloaks brilliant splashes of color against the snow.

He was only a small boy, and his parents were already three years divorced, and he could have had no way of knowing then that he'd only ever see his father twice when he was a child, or that those moments would stay freeze-framed in his memory as perfect hours just as this would stay freeze-framed in mine.

When I grew light-headed with tiredness, I said: "G'night, Dad."

"Good night, my friend. Sleep well, see."

I locked the truck door and packed a pillow against it. My clothes were still damp, and I shivered against the unyielding plastic seat, swaddled in a thin rug, dozing fitfully. I tried not to think about the terrorists, who might stumble across us while laying their land mines, and took comfort in the fact that the frogs and crickets, said to fall silent at the first sign of danger, instead sang on valiantly into the slowing rain. And all through the night I was aware of Dad wide awake and the cold barrel of the FN between us, and the whiff of sulfur and blast of rainy air that accompanied the lighting of each new cigarette, and the tension in him, which at home caused my stomach to knot into nervous balls or just plain terrified me, but here, in this wild place, was a soldier's tension and was appropriate and made me feel safe.

13

Perhaps it started then—a kind of low-grade fear that's so subtle and constant that in no time at all it passes for normal, as natural a part of the physiological fallout of war as strains and pains are in the life of a career athlete. It was there when I rode Charm alone through the tiger-spider-web-draped wilderness on the high kopje, where sometimes only a single bird sang, like a harbinger of doom. It was there when Dad left to go into the Army and there when he came back. It was there at school and at Hartley Club, a tennis, rugby, golf, and squash club that was the social center of the district, where the beer aggression gave me an afraid feeling when I walked in. And it was there when Mom was rushed into a Salisbury hospital for an emergency operation on a cyst and lay there, yellow-white and fragile, with the purple eyelids of a newly hatched bird, as if life could ebb from her at any moment.

"You mustn't worry about me," she said over and over in a small, barely alive voice that made me worry a thousand times more.

I'd made her a cake, a green one with watery chocolate icing and a big dip in the middle. Michelle Adcock hadn't baked before either, so earlier that day we'd experimented together. Michelle's first attempt was an unqualified success, but I was a slow learner and had to have three goes, during which the Adcocks' kitchen became an elaborate spin painting of flour, cocoa, green food dye, and egg. Despite copious quantities of baking powder, each of my cakes was more of a flop than the last. Michelle made the mistake of gloating in Dad's hearing, and he barked at her in my defense and made her cry.

Now I set my best cake on the hospital locker. Mom was disappointed in it, I could tell. "Didn't you use baking powder?" she murmured and gave me a weak smile. Then, seeing my face, she squeezed my hand and said: "Thanks, honey. I'll eat some later." And I knew that she wouldn't.

Her purple eyelids slid shut again, and she sank back into the pillow. Dad shuffled his feet and fumbled for his cigarettes. His mother's many ailments had made him impatient around illness. To hide my hurt, I opened the locker to put away the clean nightie and underwear we'd brought for Mom. The sweetly comforting fragrance of marshmallows and Johnson's baby powder floated out into the ether- and surgical-spirit-clogged air. But it was not sweetly comforting enough. We kissed Mom good-bye and left.

And on the way home I cried, because the failure of the cake felt like some failure of love.

It was when Mom came out of hospital that I found out about the lost babies, the ones before me and Lis. She was brushing her hair in the mirror when she told me about them, and in my imagination they came and stood between us like wraiths.

The oldest of the babies, the first, had been five months old when she "went to meet the angels," and I'd almost, almost had a big sister named Launa. But Mom explained that after I was born a butcher-doctor in Gatooma had done something bad to her tummy, and that was why she'd been told she would never have another child and why she had to keep going into hospital for operations. She touched her belly. Until a few days ago, there'd been a line of spiky stitches across it that made it look as if someone had tried to saw her in half.

"Lisa was a miracle baby," Mom explained.

I digested this information in silence. I would have liked to have been a miracle baby, too. "Launa," I said at last, "that's a funny name." My eyes fell on the orange clothes hamper. "Like 'laundry basket.'"

Some well of pain, deeply buried, surfaced briefly in an attacking rage, and Mom hit me so hard with the hairbrush that a red wheal sprang up on my arm. I cowered away, and still she kept shouting at me and hitting me. But that wasn't what scared me. I understood that she was wounded and was mortified to have been the cause of it. And I understood now why she was so protective of us. No, what scared me was that for a split second I'd glimpsed something behind her eyes— some interior life I wasn't privy to, which afterward would always leave me wondering if our lives were exactly as they seemed.

Before I could think about it further, Peter lost his mind.

Which, I have to say, didn't surprise me in the least.

In our first year at Giant we'd been visited by Mom's younger brother, James, whom I adored, and his live-in lover, Maggs, who was a hippie artist from England, a rare bird in our area (the hippie part, that is). She'd immediately earned my allegiance by bringing me a box of books: one on astronomy, a Dr. Seuss, *Struwwelpeter*, a novel about cats and mice written by a thirteen-year-old, and best of all, an encyclopedia of horses with a black stallion on the cover.

The thirteen-year-old's novel inspired me to write a book of my own, and I filled a tiny notebook with a drama about a sheep who looked a lot like Snowy and a snake in a woodpile. Mom took me over to the Dons' farm, close to Morning Star, because Lou Don was the nearest person we knew with a typewriter and I'd heard that publishers only liked manuscripts that were typed. Unfortunately I'd also heard they only liked typing that was mistake-free, and that was the thing that defeated me.

James had a Dean Martin haircut and a Zeus-like torso from years of competitive sport. He'd spent eight years at university rather than the expected four because he was having too much fun to leave. "My problem was, I got so far without doing any work, and then when I had to work, I didn't know how," he told us.

Everything about James was languorous and sleepily contented, like a cat that had spent too long in the sun. He'd escaped being drafted into the Army, not intentionally but through some clerical error, and although he felt guilty, his conscience didn't prick him enough to make him enlist voluntarily. That detail, combined with his general slothfulness, was too much for my father, who had a workaholic's intolerance for the slack and a soldier's contempt for the draft dodger. Added to which, he'd never forgiven Grampy for telling him he should be more like James and drink milk rather than beer.

"If *that*," he'd fumed, "is what happens when you drink milk, *well* . . ."

The morning they left, we gathered outside the kitchen in the sunshine while the garden boys packed their Renault with bags of fresh vegetables and eggs. Mom had her pale hand on Dad's sun-scorched arm, and she was nodding as he said, "Only a pleasure, only a pleasure," in response to James's thanks, not altogether sincerely, and Peter was smiling broadly from the kitchen step. That's when it happened. That's when Maggs, flush with good food and good cheer, flung her arms around the cook and kissed him.

Time stopped. The earth swam away and took me with it, and I felt like I was watching from above, from a cloud, and seeing Maggs's joy and James's awkward squirm and my parents speechless and me looking from one to the other, sensing that some terrible taboo had been violated. And in the middle of it Peter, standing stricken.

I was always convinced that it was the kiss that sent Peter over the edge. That the shame of being kissed by a white woman had sent him into a downward spiral from which he'd never really recovered. Call it the foreshortening of memory, call it what you like, but he was never the same again. He continued to work for us for a year and a half, but his singsong voice rung out less and less often from the kitchen. Early in 1977 his wife committed suicide, and his melancholy smile vanished altogether. Her family blamed Peter for her death, and they paid a witch doctor to put a curse on him. That's when he really started to unravel.

Behind his back the garden boys decided he was crazy. I'd stand with them in the veggie garden, digging in my own patch, and if Peter emerged muttering from the house to chuck a bucket on the compost heap, they'd tap their skulls and go: "*Yena penga, lo cook.* He's mad, that one."

"*Hayikona*," I'd say, half defensively, half agog that Peter, in between his increasingly eccentric butter churning, was becoming slowly demented.

"Sure, *picannin missis,*" Medicine insisted. *"Yena penga stelek."*

We were eating breakfast when we heard shouting in the garden. Mom and I rushed outside to find Peter, who hadn't turned up for work, wavering like a drunkard under the syringa tree. His cook's shirt was wrinkled, and all the buttons were undone. A leather pouch dangled from his neck. Sweat pooled like white water on his dark chest.

"What's happening, Peter? What's going on?" Mom demanded in a voice that was supposed to convey authority and disapproval but came out more as an alarmed shriek.

He babbled incoherently at her.

"What's wrong with you? Are you drunk?" She turned to the garden boys. "Medicine, what's he saying? Has he been drinking?"

None of us noticed that Peter was holding a broken milk bottle behind his back until he was in midlunge. The garden boys, the targets of his wrath, leapt out of range of the spears of glass, but Peter just went stiff. He cocked his head as if he were listening to the commands of a distant voice. Suddenly he gave a primal yell and, without so much as a glance in our direction, sprinted away. The last time we saw him he was clearing the garden and paddock fences in a series of effortless bounds.

"He was like a show jumper," my mother told people afterward.

14

But back then we were all more resilient. Mom turned thirty-one in February 1977 and began gathering brochures and flight schedules for the dream holiday she'd promised herself since childhood. The original plan was for the whole family to go, but Dad's conscience wouldn't allow him to take a vacation from the farm or the War, and I took my lead from him.

"Why would I want to leave my horse?" I asked an uncomprehending Mom.

My idea of a holiday was Beira and the charcoally prawns, or the train journeys of my early childhood, where the compartments smelled of leather and varnished wood and sooty railways and if you flushed the toilet you could see the tracks whipping by underneath and on the way to the dining car the carriages wrenched alarmingly at their moorings as if they planned to fly apart just as you stepped between them. After a while, the skimming scenery would become South African and we could buy beaded Zulu bracelets or Smarties candies or dried fruit from station vendors. When dusk loomed outside the windows, uniformed attendants as spruce as Army lieutenants would transform our compartment with folded-down beds made with starched white sheets and cozy, soft blankets. The sleeps on the rocking top bunk, soothed by the rhythmic *clickety-click* of the tracks, were unforgettable.

Mom had liked the trains once, but now her dreams were of Europe in the spring, specifically Greece, Switzerland, Austria, England, Scotland, France, Spain, and the Canary Islands, all of which she visited on that first trip. In the end she went alone. Lisa was sent to stay with Granny for six weeks, and I was mainly at boarding school or at home and nervy with Dad. A couple of times I went to stay with Granny and Grampy in their Salisbury flat, which had African violets on every surface and lots of cat pictures. Grampy had his own room, so I slept in the bed beside Granny's, and in the mornings she brought me coffee in a china cup, a saucer of Marie biscuits, and a glass jar of condensed milk on a tray.

Grampy spent an inordinate number of hours pressing sharp-smelling tobacco into his pipe and reading. He liked cats, not children. In his room was a wooden plaque that read, WHEN YOU'RE DOWN IN THE MOUTH, THINK OF JONAH, HE CAME OUT ALRIGHT. But Granny was warm, smiling, and wonderful. She'd take me with her to the Anglican Cathedral of St. Mary and All Saints, which was smoky with frankincense and myrrh, and had a charismatic, snow-haired dean with a beatific face and flowing robes, and a powerful spiritual atmosphere that made me feel I really was in God's house.

Granny had grown up in Mafikeng, which at that time was the capital of Bechuanaland, where her father was government secretary of the protectorate. As a girl she'd raced bareback across the landscape on barely broken ponies with no bridles. In the early twenties, when she and her teenage sister, Ruth, were galloping alongside the white train carrying David, Prince of Wales, her horse ran into a barbed-wire fence and somersaulted. The prince, who was waving to them from the window of the dining saloon car, stopped the train and gave orders for the girls to be rescued.

Granny had a family tree tracing her lineage through her father, Charles Leonard O'Brien Dutton, back to A.D. 742, the birth date of Charlemagne, king of the Franks, who was crowned Holy Roman emperor by Pope Leo III on Christmas Day 800. Our ancestors had amazing names like Pepin, *roi de'Italie,* on one side and Hrolf, the Ganger, on the other. A note attached to the family tree said that Ghisela, a descendant of Pepin, had been offered to Hrolf by her father to keep the peace but that he accepted her only after satisfying himself she was of suitable height. Hrolf was followed by William Longsword, Richard the Fearless, Richard the Good, Robert the Magnificent, also known as Robert the Devil, and on down to William the Conqueror in 1066.

The William the Conquerer connection was a little unclear. Some members of the family said that we were directly related to him, some said it was through a cousin, and some said our ancestor had been his navigator.

One of our relatives, William Smith O'Brien, the brother of my great-great-great-grandmother, was an MP who campaigned for the repeal of the British-Irish Act of Union and became an Irish revolutionary. He was the leader of the militant Irish Confederation, which was outlawed in 1848. In July of that year his supporters attacked a police detachment in County Tipperary in an abortive revolt known as the Battle of Widow McCormack's Cabbage Patch. Afterward he escaped on the chief constable's horse. He was captured, found guilty of high treason, and sentenced to be hanged. So many people petitioned on his behalf that the sentence was commuted to transportation for life, and he was sent to Tasmania for five years. He was granted a full pardon in 1856, and returned to Ireland but not to politics.

My favorite ancestor story, though, was that of another great-uncle, Jack, a merchant seaman who'd inadvertently boarded a gun-running ship. His final letter reads:

> Dear Frank,
>   I don't know how to begin, but don't be in alarm. I hope
> 'tis all for the best. I shipped in the steamboat—beginning
> at Kingston for Lemon Bay in Costa Rica, with passengers.
> She has turned out to be a notorious blockade runner,
> which has already landed different cargoes of arms and am-
> munition. Instead of going there she came to Cuba, and was
> captured by the Spanish man-of-war *Foonedo* [?] on Friday
> night last. We and the ship were brought here. Several have
> been shot. Yesterday we were tried by court martial and this
> morning sentenced to death at 3:30 p.m. Don't fret; pray for
> me (which I must do for myself when I've finished writing).
>   Your loving brother,
>   Jack

Granny was highly critical of my mother for leaving her husband and children to go traveling, but Mom would not stand for being made to feel guilty. "I've put my family first for fourteen years," she told Granny. "Fourteen *years*. Now I'm going to think about *me* for a change."

The fourteen years part wasn't strictly true, because I was only ten, but since I was fully supportive of her going because it was her special dream and it raised the possibility of an exciting overseas present, and because Dad didn't mind in the least and Lisa was too young to care and it was our opinions that really mattered, Mom flew away on May 19.

After Peter went AWOL, Maud had revealed herself to be a superb cook, and so it was she who took care of Dad and me, feeding us "cottagey pie" and chickens thickly dusted with paprika and flour and slow-roasted with lumps of dripping. They were lip-smackingly good, as were the crispy roast potatoes that accompanied them. The next day we always had chicken soup. She also made a tomato and "onn-yonn" gravy, which was delicious with everything, especially *sadza* and *boerewors*.

With Mom in Europe, I seized the opportunity to try out my python-handling skills. Once I had a horse, my goal had been to get a python or, better yet, a file snake, a shimmering, coral-colored creature of mythical docility, although the Africans believed that the sight of it foretold an imminent death in the family. Dad promised to find me one. The file snake proved elusive, but true to his word, Dad brought me two pythons. The first I called Charlie, but his sheer size—around eighteen feet long and as thick as a truck tire—meant that he had to be confined to a large wooden trunk and released after a fortnight on com-passionate grounds. He and I were acquainted only through a crack in the lid. When I put my face close to it, an air of rain-soaked leaves and mice drifted up.

Next came Samantha, who at seven feet was more manageable. Maud was extremely disapproving. She, like most Africans, hated snakes, and all of them believed that the harming of pythons would bring drought to the area—a superstition held just as strongly by the white farmers. To date, the nearest I'd been to a python was at the Snake Park during our school camp at Resthaven, an eco-lodge where we'd been taken by our lovely Standard Four teacher, Mr. Mitchley. Mr. Mitchley wore learned little glasses and was a nature buff and a passionate advo-cate of conservation. He indoctrinated us with bush etiquette in the form of classroom signs like TAKE NOTHING BUT PHOTOGRAPHS, LEAVE NOTHING BUT FOOTPRINTS and saw to it that we learned the art of ecology through a variety of wonderful school projects. At Resthaven, we stud-ied Bushman cave paintings and were shown the correct way to hold a python and how to skin a goat. These were by far and away the most valuable lessons I learned at junior school and among the very few with any practical application.

At home Dad helped me take Samantha out of her box, and I sat on the couch with her head in my right hand and her slender tail in my left. That way, I'd been told, it would be easy to unwind her if she got a little rambunctious and went into constrictor mode.

There was a knock at the back door, and Dad went to answer it. He was gone a long time, dealing, I guess, with some farm crisis, and I felt very grown-up sitting there all alone in the silent lounge with a cool, weighty python on my bare legs. She was, I thought, quite beautiful. Her sculptured head was much more mammalian than those of other snakes and her camouflage colors were almost iridescent. Even her eyes seemed warmer. While I was admiring her, she flipped a couple of coils over my left forearm. I didn't take much notice because I was bonding with her and feeling something approaching love for her, but then she began to squeeze. Instantly I was rendered helpless. With my unwinding hand incapacitated, I had no chance of freeing myself. More coils quickly followed. During the wrapping process, a kind of expertly exe-cuted Chinese bangle, my fingers turned a bloodless yellow and were drawn ever nearer to her jaws.

I debated what to do. Should I present myself at the back door—a thin white child trussed, like *The Jungle Book*'s Mowgli, by a large, exu-berant snake—and risk giving the visitor cardiac arrest, or should I just hope that Dad returned before it was too late?

I was on the point of being devoured when Dad hurried back into the room.

"Hell, lovey, are you *trying* to get bitten?" he cried, seizing Saman-tha's tail and unwrapping her forcibly. Somehow she ended up loose on the carpet. Enraged, she began to pursue him round the room, throwing herself at him in full-body strikes while he yelled and dodged and tried to fend her off with a cushion.

I ran into the passage, slammed the door, and left them to it. The first rule of snake safety is: Don't be a hero.

Traveling changed my mother as dramatically as farming and the Grey's Scouts had changed Dad. It confirmed to her that the world was so much more than the confines of our mismatched farmhouse and the suffocating ennui of Hartley, the club, and the endless drinking. After that, the house filled up with brochures on Canada featuring leaves you couldn't imagine seeing in nature, snapshots of Kashmiri children in valleys of wildflowers, leprosy mission charity appeals, and copies of *Time* magazine. In Europe, she'd been befriended by some Americans, who'd influenced her pronunciation—vitamins were now "vidamins" and tuna was "toona"—and presented her with a subscription to *Texas Highways*. Every quarter for the next five years we pored over photographs of vast, impossibly ordered landscapes, Morgan stud farms, and inviting roads of shining black asphalt.

But it was *Time* I liked the best, not for the articles but for the double-page spreads of Marlboro-advertising cowboys on quarter horses, rounding up mustangs, fording rapids, or standing moodily etched against wintry, cedar-lined ridges. I plastered them on my walls with Sticki-Stuff and imagined I was one of them. Combined with *Texas Highways* and snatches of *Happy Days*, *The Beverly Hillbillies*, and *Hawaii Five-0*, they gave me an impression of an America peopled with range riders, eccentrics, and cool, leather-clad heroes, where even the scenery seemed laundered.

The manner of Mom's return set up a pattern. We'd wait for her on the windy top deck of the airport in Salisbury, eating steak sandwiches slathered in tomato sauce and breathing in aviation fumes, and when the passengers disembarked from the plane, Mom would be the one in the sari, the sarong, or the silk kimono; the one with all the baskets. She'd be wearing an amazing hat, and she'd be tanned or at least flushed from her travels, and beaming like she was lit from within in a way that she never, *ever* was on the farm. Dad was always on edge, regarding her half with awe and half with resentful suspicion about who she'd met and what she might have done without him, so we rarely reached home without a fight. And before she'd even unpacked her suitcase, she'd produce a brochure or let something slip in conversation and I'd know she was already planning her next trip.

The success of her travels made Mom hungry for life beyond the borders of Giant Estate, especially since Dad was away for six months of the year on call-up. She took over from Chris Adcock as Thomas's bookkeeper, running his Hartley office, a "filthy, dusty" hole-in-the-wall beside the Burrowses' newsagent. While spring cleaning, she uncovered a falling-apart box labeled DANGEROUS at the back of a filing cabinet. It was packed with dynamite. Old dynamite. Dynamite sweating crystally puddles of nitroglycerin. Mom was out of the office so fast she left skid marks. Thomas insisted it was safe, but she refused to go back until it was gone. So Dad, who wasn't bothered by such things, slung the box onto the back of his truck and bumped away over the farm roads to find a place to dump it.

He'd taken Samantha off to the wild as well after she'd almost (unbeknownst to my mother) consumed Coquette, Mom's special Siamese cat.

Once in Hartley, Mom entertained herself by becoming a campaign volunteer for "P.K." van der Byl, minister of foreign affairs for Ian Smith's Rhodesian Front, in the 1977 election. Mom loved politics—not for the dreary details but for the personalities, and apart from the prime minister himself there was no larger personality than Pieter Kenyon Fleming-Voltelyn van der Byl. A hawk-faced Afrikaner aristocrat from the Cape, he styled himself a gentleman farmer and had a reputation as a lavish host. His pithy quotes and rallying calls to troops and country made him hugely popular. He'd say things like "If the battle should wax fiercer, there can be no question of surrender. We shall contest every river, every crossroads, every village, every town, and every kopje."

He was also a well-known womanizer who would marry a Liechtenstein princess, and once, when Mom was working in his office, she looked up to find him leaning against a doorframe running an eye over her. "*My*, but you're lovely," he breathed fruitily.

Mom's sudden emergence from her chrysalis was not to everyone's liking. It created a tense undercurrent with some of the local wives, who thought that Mom was after their husbands or that they were after her, and it sharpened the knives in Hartley. I'd go with her to the troopie canteen, and as she walked in, a pretty, vivacious innocent, some of the women would shrink away like sea creatures that close up to protect themselves, like Venus flytraps, their mouths pinched tight like dogs' bums.

But the gossip swirled around her and left her untouched, and glances that even I, a dreamy kid, picked up on went over her head. She was too busy planning ahead for cherry blossom time in Japan or how to save the lepers.

15

Slowly, but with a steady, crackling intensity, like a bushfire surging out of control, the world beyond our perimeter fence began to take on a more sinister shape. Even Lisa sensed it. One dinnertime she burst out: "Mom, when you die, how will I find my way to the children's home?"

Then Dad's cattle were held up by a mob in Hartley. The herd was being driven from Giant to another of Thomas's farms, Lion's Vlei. After watching the cattle cross the Umfuli River Bridge on the outskirts of town, Dad went ahead to wait for them at the stockyards. When they didn't arrive, he jumped in his truck and went to look for them. He found the herd close to the Location, a black township near the railway siding consisting largely of corrugated iron shanties, ugly brick houses, and twirling refuse. A pong of rotting orange peel and human waste always hung over it like a cloud. A militant crowd, many armed with sticks, had surrounded the cattle in protest at them passing too close to the malnourished maize plants that grew among the rubbish, and the steers were milling around anxiously, emitting high-pitched moos of panic. The cattle boys stood sheepishly to one side.

Dad drove into the middle of the mob and leaned out of the window. "Are you going to let my cattle go, are you?" he asked in a polite tone of warning.

"No," one of the ringleaders replied, and the crowd advanced on him threateningly.

Casually, so as not to alarm them, Dad reached into the truck's dusty cubbyhole, took out his revolver, and fired two shots into the air. Within seconds, the area was deserted. The herd and Dad, his ears ringing, proceeded to the stockyards as normal.

Around the same time, Snowy was kidnapped.

Most of my lambs and calves had to return to the herd as soon as they were old enough to fend for themselves, but Snowy, my sheep, and Daisy, my Hereford calf, as our first, honorary orphans, had been allowed to stay on. Daisy even let me sit on her bony back, and I'd swing my bare legs against her sun-warmed, ginger flanks. Then Snowy was snatched from us in broad daylight. That was upsetting enough, but her reappearance, two weeks later, was worse. Medicine took me to see Snowy lying stiff on her side behind a garden storeroom. Her stomach was distended, her wool matted, and her gray tongue curled from her mouth. She'd been killed elsewhere and delivered to us like a message.

Like a sign of some kind.

Like revenge.

Then Maud came to Mom with a story about an elderly goatherd being killed by two white farmers. The Africans were in an uproar over it. According to the rumors, on different days both men had found the goats scattered and the goat "boy" sleeping, and both had beaten him to teach him a lesson. Days later he was dead.

Mom wanted to go to the police, but Dad refused to let her do anything on the basis of compound gossip. He yelled: "Think about what you're saying. These people have families. They have *children*. Their lives will be completely destroyed, and for what? How do we even know if it's true? Maybe he just died of old age."

I thought: What about the goat boy's family? Doesn't anybody care about them?

But because I thought that grown-ups knew best and because the burglar experience had taught me that justice in the rural districts worked in mysterious ways, I let it go, hoping, like Mom, that it was nothing more than the talk of men who'd sat up too late in front of their fires and *kayas* (houses, usually mud huts), smoking *umbanje* (marijuana) and drinking Chibuku, and that if there was any truth in what was said, somebody else would come forward. The goat boy's family, for instance.

But nobody ever did.

On January 10, 1978, I walked into the classroom for the start of Standard Five to find that instead of the usual joyous end-of-holiday babel, children were just standing about in lost, whispering groups. One or two had tear tracks, like pink gashes, on their faces. Bruce Campbell was crying openly, his golden head bowed.

"What's wrong, Bruce?" Juliet was asking him worriedly. "What's the matter?"

Uncharacteristically, he growled at her and shook her off. Mr. Clark came in and was white and somber and nervous, and that was when I knew that something horrific had happened. Something there would be no stepping back from. Something that would change us.

Bruce Forrester, the boy I sat next to in class, was dead—murdered, along with his father, friend, and grandmother, in a terrorist attack on Rainbow's End farm. In a voice unfamiliar in its gentleness and compassion, Mr. Clark explained that it had happened the previous evening. The previous evening, Bruce had still been alive. My eyes went to the empty chair in the classroom and my chest emptied in response, like the sea going into retreat.

The quiet boy with nature in his eyes had been due to start school with us this morning.

Due to have a future and a life.

At home, my parents were stunned by the news. Both of them knew the Forresters and liked them enormously, and both had special memories of Bruce's father, Ben. Dad had spent an exhilarating day with Ben and a group of game rangers, trying to trap wildebeests in temporary enclosures known as *bomas*, back in the days when Ben was stocking the game park at Rainbow's End.

He was, Dad said, a "first-class bloke. *First class*. An absolute gentleman."

Mom had met Ben once, but she'd never forgotten him. He'd come into Thomas's office, and she'd caught herself staring at him, actually staring, because his face was so beautiful. Almost angelic, she'd thought at the time. He had the biggest, greenest, most innocent eyes she'd ever seen. He was tall and lean and tanned, and he held a bush hat in his broad, brown hands. "It wasn't that he was good looking in a Hollywood way," Mom said, "it was more in an innocent sort of way. There was something very gentle about him. He was like a shy boy who's grown up to just love animals and nature."

Up until now the War, even as it edged nearer to us, had always been at one step's remove. At school we talked about it, we were afraid of it, it occupied most of our waking thoughts, but it was unreal and surreal, as though we were starring in our own movie. The stickers on our suitcases, the grenade drills, the waves to the sunburned troopies and dashes to school with parents armed with revolvers and automatic weapons—they had all seemed like a big, crazy adventure. Even when two boys in our school shot themselves dead with their own guns, it was still a game, because when all was said and done, those were just accidents. Then Bruce had been killed, and his picture and those of his father, grandmother, and friend were in *The Herald* in grainy black and white, and it wasn't a game anymore.

It wasn't a game at all.

Rainbow's End
1978–1980

Jenny the giraffe

1

When I think of my life, it is as a life divided: before Rainbow's End and after it. We arrived there when I was eleven years old—shy, gawky, and horse obsessed, with long, pale legs of an anemic colt. We left when I was almost seventeen, by which time Rhodesia had become Zimbabwe. The years at Rainbow's End had changed me irrevocably. When I walked away, I went believing, as the African author and aviator Beryl Markham once did, that "if you must leave a place that you have lived in and loved and where all your yesterdays are buried deep, leave it in any way except a slow way, leave it the fastest way you can."

I left Rainbow's End as fast as I could because there is no other way to leave a place that has come to embody all of your childish dreams and many of your nightmares. Or a country where most of your truths have been shown to be lies.

That, though, came much later. In the beginning there was just a falling-down house in a tangle of bush on the banks of a slow-flowing river. It was late July, a time of mint-fresh mornings and infinite winter skies. In recent weeks Dad had become concerned that he might erupt like Kilimanjaro if he spent another hour in the employ of Tom Beattie (they were too similar was the main problem), so he'd approached Richard Etheridge, the farmer who'd called the security forces on the night of the Rainbow's End attack, for advice about finding another manager's position. Richard and his wife, Catherine, owned Stockdale, a lushly bountiful citrus estate that bordered Rainbow's End on the

Umfuli. Not only were the Etheridges the most connected people in Gadzema but they were also two of the kindest, and Dad was still smoothing his hair, twisting his hat in his hands, and apologizing for existing when Richard said: "I'm going to arrange for you to meet a very good friend of mine . . ."

The friend was Roy Lilford, Camilla Forrester's brother. The job was managing Rainbow's End, which had stood empty since January 10.

"How soon do I start?" Dad said.

I remember our first journey there in a series of filmic images, made no less vivid by time:

A black plow disk with the white-painted farm name partially obscured by dust and a restless wand of hot pink bougainvillea: RAIN-BOW'S E-N-D.

A tall game fence stretching away to infinity. We follow its commanding line, gravel popping beneath the wheels.

Tobacco barns, rising ten tiers into the sky.

A slate gray road and, at the end of it, a stand of sighing silver gum trees, their chestnut bark peeled back like open wounds.

Then, finally, the house itself, as forlorn and unloved as a tombstone in a forgotten cemetery.

We climbed out of the car and stood in a huddle staring at it. At the damp-stained walls and rotting thatched roof and the dark trees crowding in on it. It had taken a lot of persuasion and a fair amount of raging for Dad to get my mother to venture even this far. "But why *that* house?" she kept saying with a shudder. "Surely there's somewhere else we could go? Couldn't you find a different job or work things out with Thomas? Why must we live in a house where four people have been murdered? It's creepy."

But once Dad had set his internal compass, all decisions were final. He'd accepted the job. Not for all the lovely mansions on earth would he go back on his word.

"Isn't it beautiful?" he enthused now, as though, if he only said it loudly enough, with enough conviction, it would become reality. "Have you ever seen a more incredible setting in your life—with the river and game park? *Ag,* you know, the house is probably a bit run-down, but Roy says he'll fix it up and make it nice for us. He's promised me. *Promised.*"

Then he was striding away across the scrappy yellow yard, and we were trailing after him, not knowing what to think or how to feel, and an African in overalls was running to let us in.

"It's so gloomy," Mom said, and she shuddered again.

We stepped across the threshold into a small hallway. Cold rose from the concrete floors in a chilly wave, bringing with it a shut-up farmhouse smell of thatch, old floor polish, and *sadza.* Ahead of us was an empty lounge. There were signs of recent sweeping but little else. The windows were cloudy; cobwebs spanned the ceiling; geckos scuttled across the grit-covered shelves. Apart from two bullet holes on the wall, there was no evidence of the bloodbath that had been, but it was hard not to imagine it. My eyes wandered involuntarily to the space where the sofa would have stood, and into my mind came a picture of one of the boys crawling behind it to try to escape the hail of bullets and then, after the men had gone, coming to terms with the killing silence, the crimson tide.

We opened doors and windows as we went, and squares of white sunlight crept in and warmed the floors and rooms. Every footstep set up a chain of echoes. Like a lot of Rhodesian homesteads, the house had been constructed cheaply and simply, without architect or design, and was long and sprawling, with random additions and extensions. We learned later that it had been built using an unbaked brick known as Kimberley made right there on the farm, and bonded using Rainbow's End ant-heap clay (unburned) rather than cement.

In essence, the house was an L shape, with the hallway dividing the two wings. The short part of the L was the master bathroom and bedroom, where Sheila Forrester, lying ill with cancer, had been shot through the window by the departing terrorists. The second part consisted of an unadorned lounge and dining room, followed by a breakfast area and a kitchen with a stainless steel sink, enamel-painted units, and a corrugated-iron roof. There was also a walk-in pantry and a laundry room with smoke-blackened walls. A woodstove caked with sooty grease and greasy ash was housed beside the back door.

From the dining room, a passage led to a cavernous bathroom reeking of mildew. It had a rust-stained tub, a shower that coughed and spat purified river water, and a line of ants heading for the basin. Next door were the bedrooms, in one of which Camilla had sat reading Julie *The Snow Goose* on that summer's afternoon just six months earlier, with no idea of what was to come. The rooms were separated by an archway and would be shared by Lisa and me. Aside from a few random items, such as a lamp and a twist of cable, they were bare.

All through this strange, painful tour, I kept waiting to be assaulted by the ghosts of Rainbow's End's past. It was only when I saw a circle of bullet-shattered glass in the window of what would be my bedroom and, beyond it, a glimpse of green river and the game park as flaxen as a Rift Valley plain, that it hit me there was no sense of evil in the house. No feeling that malevolent spirits lingered. If anything, it was the opposite. There was something good about the place, something peaceful.

"There's nothing bad here, is there, Mom?" I asked, looking to her for confirmation. And as we stood almost humbly in that room which had seen so much and yet now, with the sun slanting across the concrete floor and the stillness broken only by the healing crooning of doves, was almost monastic, she had to agree.

Years on, when she gently mentioned that contradiction to Camilla, Camilla's response was that it was because there'd been so much love in the house. If there were ghosts at Rainbow's End, they were happy ones.

And so it was done. Over the next month, we made several reconnaissance trips from Giant as the moldy gray thatch was ripped from the sawdust-spewing beams and replaced with creosote-treated gum poles and honey-colored grass. African women sat in gossipy circles under the trees preparing it, their legs stretched out in front of them, mugs of tea near at hand, and it was they who brought laughter to the house for the first time in half a year. They combed the special grass, cut it, and knotted it into tightly packed bundles, and then we climbed up homemade ladders to watch the thatching boys, all highly skilled and much in demand, work their magic. Elsewhere, three stables were pegged out with string and then erected and thatched by farm builders in a matter of a week, and a paddock of gum poles was put up around them. In the front corner of the garden, near the water hole, a veggie patch was marked out with bamboo stakes, and lettuce, carrot, pea, and zucchini seedlings planted. The raggle-taggle orchard was pruned. Every wall, stable, and outbuilding was whitewashed and the trees that cast the coldest shadows over the house felled.

On Friday, September 1, 1978, with the security fence so newly put up that tendrils of wire and shavings of metal were still scattered in the grass, we took the slate gray road past the tobacco barns to our new home. Our belongings had gone before us, traveling, ingloriously, on a tractor and trailer, and Charm and two ex–Grey's Scout horses, Persian Lady and Cassandra, who was in foal to Troubleshooter (a foal I'd already laid claim to), were following on a cattle truck. Medicine and Maud were coming, too, and Maud would live alone or with her children if they were visiting in the freshly whitewashed servants' quarters—"the cottage," as my mother called it—beneath the eucalyptus spread of gums.

I was bubbling with excitement, overflowing with it. And when I saw the house, all golden-roofed and with glowing white walls, and the lawn greening beautifully from a month of water and care, I overflowed some more. It was utterly transformed.

I took my sister's hand, and we opened the game park gate and ran down to the edge of the Umfuli.

"Watch out for crocodiles," my mother shouted after us. "And don't go near the water, you'll get bilharzia."

We paid no attention to her but did keep a wary eye out for the ostriches, Cheeky and Beaky. We'd been warned that Cheeky in particular had a history of attacking people who ventured into the game park on foot (striking them with his immense prehistoric toes), although since we couldn't tell them apart, both were lethal propositions. But as far as we knew, none of the other wildlife presented a problem. On our first tour of the game park, we'd encountered the giraffe, an ethereal, otherworldly creature, and the wonder of having a giraffe at the bottom of the garden had enchanted me ever since. But it wasn't only the giraffe. It was the place. It was the winter grass pricking the bottoms of my feet and the swirl of the Umfuli around my ankles and, when Lis and I stood on the overgrown boat dock, with the banks of the river rising high above us and the roots of the trees poking through like veins, it was the musical clamor of nature.

We followed the curve of the river around to the cage where the Forresters had kept fish eagles. It was about thirty feet high and almost as wide and stood in a grove of yellowwood trees, through which the water and a mysterious, jungle-covered island, rising from the river in impenetrable walls of green, were visible. The perches that had once supported the majestic eagles had long since toppled or fallen askew, and the habitat of reeds and vegetation was mostly dead. Yet the spirit of the birds still seemed strong here. An air of loneliness more tangible and eerie than anything I'd felt in the house emanated from the cage.

"Come, Lis," I said quickly, "let's go back now."

Inside the house a coat of light, bright white had given the rooms an airy, welcoming feel, and many of the doorways had been turned into archways. Everywhere Mom's love of color showed. The kitchen was lime green with matching gingham curtains; the master bedroom had an Oriental theme, with peacocks, roses, and Japanese prints. A gray mare defended a chestnut colt above the living room fireplace. The cavernous bathroom was pawpaw colored—or at least the door, wooden bath mat, and sundry bits were. The taps still spat brown borehole water, but the shower had been cleaned, and it worked after a fashion.

So did the woodstove, which Dad assured us would produce the best food we'd ever eaten in our lives. "The *roasts*! Man, oh man!"

To assemble the delights he claimed could be prepared on it, we'd employed a cook so ancient he was known simply as Madala: old man. To help Medicine, we had also taken on Gatsi, a clean-cut Mozambican with a constant, bubbling laugh, and a horse boy called Luka, who was young, muscle-bound, and taciturn, and unnerved me by having hair that fitted my eight-year-old self's idea of terrorist-styling to a T.

Alone in my room, I put up my Olivia Newton-John pictures and the Marlboro men with their rapids-fording quarter horses, and tidied my vet box, which was in disarray after its journey on the tractor and trailer. My clothes and books had arrived in a decrepit khaki suitcase, and now I emptied them out onto my half of the pine bunk bed. The bottom half was in Lisa's room next door. Over in the corner was my white dressing table. The only piece of furniture still remaining from the time of the Forresters was a wooden cupboard, which had been given to us for storage. I went over to it and put my hand on the door.

That's when I saw it: a maroon punctuation mark of dried blood. A kind of comma, like a life interrupted. I ran to the bathroom, soaked a handful of tissues, and tried to erase it, choking back tears. Reconstituted, it came alive again, became *blood* again. And it threw me back to the classroom, to the seat beside Bruce, and his sea blue eyes and the light dusting of freckles on his limbs in his school uniform were so clear to me I could almost touch him, and I could still picture him grinning over his shoulder at handsome, olive-skinned Bruce Campbell and the two of them talking about falcons or poring over their conservation projects. But the thing that bothered me most was that I had known him all that time, three long years, and I couldn't remember a single word he said, just the *sense* of him.

It made me hate the tricks of memory. Hate the war that had torn the breath from him and left me here, undeserving, as if destiny had called me to walk a mile in his shoes. Hate the guilt that made me want to flee from the room and never come back.

But outside the birds were singing as if a more magnificent day had never dawned, the sky was billowing through the fresh, young leaves of the msasa like cobalt silk, and the familiar sounds of farming were riding in on the clean breeze. I exhaled. Blood was only blood. It was not a ghost. I scrubbed it off hard and flushed the tissue down the toilet, where it sank in a red and white swirl. Then I returned to my room, took an armful of clothes, and slid them onto the wooden shelves. It was a cupboard. Just a cupboard.

At sunset, we sat out on the front lawn on our hard metal garden chairs and watched the game animals gather at the water hole. Laughing doves were CUK-*coo-coo*ing on the branches above our heads, and behind us in their new paddock the horses were snatching at the virgin grass and snorting uneasily at the warning coughs of the impalas.

The whole population of the game park seemed to have turned out for our arrival. Small groups of impalas were nosing their way out of the thicket of trees that ringed the brown dam, white bunny tails swinging, and the wildebeest was standing with his front hooves in the mud and his hindquarters up on the bank. Everything about him was comical. His expression was bemused, his neck was a wrinkly stump, and his girth cut away sharply to neat gray hips, giving him the appearance of a wildebeest weight lifter. Even his mane resembled a mullet. His head was turned in our direction, and he was shaking his horns theatrically. The ostriches patrolled the fence line, their heads bobbing up and down like periscopes. Only the giraffe was missing. Finally, she, too, appeared, moving past the house with a graceful swagger. We'd already decided to call her Jenny, not Gracey, as she was presently known.

Dad smoked and sipped a Castle lager, white foam clinging to his upper lip; Mom celebrated with a glass of Nederburg rosé; and Lisa and I swigged Cokes from greeny bottles, which we clinked with our parents' glasses: "Cheers."

I rocked in my chair and let the fox terrier puppies chew my toes. Despite my father's sincere protests, they'd been pressed upon him by his new boss, Roy, who bred the dogs with love but without regard for the shallowness of the gene pool. When you went to his house, they were up against the security fence in a snarling, yammering pack. But Patches and Pebbles were still cute and innocent in the way of most babies. Lisa slid down to the grass with them, and they tumbled over her legs and bared ridged pink palates, and their little teeth clicked and snagged. I felt a sudden rush of happiness. We were all together and no one was fighting.

And at some point I became aware that I was seeing, really noticing, Africa in a way I'd never done before. The way the bush turned a deep, dense black long before the sky ever did, and the silhouettes of the acacias became gilt-edged or shot through with scarlet, as though at any moment they might spark off the fiery ball behind them and spontaneously combust. The way the guinea fowl became unconvincingly airborne as they rose crying to roost in the trees and the bright tunes of the day birds surrendered to the more melancholy sounds of the night creatures. And how the aromatic smell of the vegetation turned cool and sweet at dusk, as if the sugars in the grasses were on the march; and how, right now, it was mingling pleasantly with the smoke from the woodstove and the caramelized juices of the imminent lamb roast and the creosote on the still-wet gum poles of the paddock fencing.

The sun melted into the river. As night drew in, a profound peace stole out of the bush and engulfed us.

Dad's cigarette glowed in the dark. "This is the life," he said.

"Isn't this heaven?" Mom agreed dreamily. She prodded me. "Just think, you'll be able to tell all your friends you've got a pet giraffe."

But that wasn't what I was thinking. I was thinking how deliciously remote Rainbow's End was. As if no one existed but us. That already it felt like our home, like *our* farm, and that the future stretched like an unending road ahead of us, electric with promise.

Then I remembered the blood on the cupboard.

Later I lay in bed with the windows wide open and listened to the noisy percussion of the frogs down at the water hole and the rasping song of crickets and the urgent beating of drums and whooping of women in the far-off compound, which was half African lullaby, half infinitely threatening, like some war dance of savages. On that first night at Rainbow's End, I fell into sleep feeling fear and elation simultaneously.

2

If ever a paradise was invented for a child it was Rainbow's End. The garden alone was a feast of exotic fruit. Of white and purple prickly pears, which we picked using gloves of newspaper to save our fingers from the thorns ("If you use your hends, you will cry," Madala counseled. "Even after two days, you will cry") and ate cold from the fridge by the nectar-laden handful. Of citrus, mangoes, granadillas, and mulberry trees black with fruit. The flexible white boughs of one of the trees had interwoven to form a perfect cradle, and I spent countless afternoons in the shelter of its rough leaves, reading and gorging on mulberries, until my face and pages were splattered with violet and my stomach ached.

Outside the security fence, the unkempt orchard supplied guavas, pawpaws, pomegranates, and peaches, though these last were undernourished and bitter with worms. There was a second vegetable garden beyond it, where we grew bigger produce like potatoes, pumpkins, spinach, and corn. Here, as at Giant, the scraps went to the hens. Their accommodation in the orchard was less grand than they'd been used to, but their run was much larger, and the hens took advantage of it with sand baths so ecstatic they created mini–dust storms. Their body-confidence made me smile. The rooster was too pompous and arrogant to be entirely likable, but the strutting cheerfulness of the fat red hens was that of chubby, big-bottomed African women who not only rejoice in the build nature has given them but celebrate it with impromptu bouts of tribal dancing.

But these things were only the start. The farm itself was a thousand acres of tobacco, maize, and cotton, with herds of red-backed cattle cutting through the savanna. There were miles of sandy roads to gallop along and dams to swim the horses in. Surrounding the house on three sides was the game reserve, one hundred wild acres of thorny bush, sun-bleached *vleis*, deep gullies, great twisted trees, and abandoned mine workings. A roughly plowed road wound through it. In spring it was a vision of wildflowers.

The game gathered at the water holes at sunrise and sunset, and spread out around the reserve during the day. The fifty or so impalas split into smaller herds and browsed between the msasa and mopani trees or out in the open on the *vlei*; the wildebeest spent most of his time near the dam on the south-west border of the reserve; and Jenny the giraffe, who was tame enough to approach but not to touch, hovered anywhere she thought there might be company, most often by the game gate in front of the house, at the water hole with the ostriches, or under the outstretched arms of the mountain acacias on the Umfuli's edge.

The river was a mesmerizingly beautiful and endlessly changing playground. In the dry season, a sandy beach appeared among the reeds, and Lis and I carried our lunch down there or skipped along the weir wall. In the rainy season, the force of water thundering over the weir created turbulent Jacuzzis among the rocks below it, and I paddled in them alone or sometimes with Lisa or a friend and waded, suicidally, along the wall. When the river was at its height, the weir was always slick with algae, but the adrenaline rush of testing my strength against the power of the clear, gushing water never lost its thrill.

For the first time in our lives we found ourselves in direct communion with nature. Crocodiles sunned themselves on the sandbank near the weir, mouths wide open to allow the egrets to pick clean their fearsome teeth; masked weaverbirds squabbled noisily in the gum trees; and impalas bounced around the water hole: trampolinists testing new springs.

Vervet monkeys vaulted over the security fence like furry gray gymnasts and tormented my mother by sitting in her strawberry patch—paws full of fruit and juice dribbling down their chests, their brown eyes sparkling with "Who, *me*?" cheek—until Gatsi or Mom ran shrieking at them with sticks. Usually the youngsters rode on their mothers' backs as surely as rodeo cowboys, but there was a day when the troop scattered so fast that they left behind a baby. We put it in Lisa's old wicker cot, and for three weeks it lay curled beneath a flannelette blanket and was just exactly like a human baby in every respect. It even cried like a baby, only more softly. It had a wizened pink and gray face and liquid brown eyes of the most divine innocence, and it clung to Lisa's Paddington Bear as if its life depended on it. When I lifted it from the cot to feed it, it would lie against my chest as helplessly as a newborn, and I could feel the heat of its skin and its tiny rib cage through my shirt.

For the most part nature is intolerant of human intervention, especially when it comes to its young, but the baby monkey proved the rarest of exceptions. When the troop returned nearly a month later, Gatsi carried it outside the game gate and set it on a tree stump. As soon as he'd retreated out of sight, its mother came for it. She sniffed at it, checked over her shoulder for pursuers, then tossed it onto her back and loped away.

Not all of our new creatures were quite so endearing. Much to Mom's distress, snakes of every species spilled from every hole and crevice. Boomslangs lay in wait on dining room chairs or dangled from the roof beams. Adders meandered lazily through the veranda shadows. Huge pythons tucked into our chickens and eggs, and then, unable to squeeze back through the chicken wire, dozed off where they lay with hen-shaped lumps in their middles until Dad was called and, with his bare hands and often in complete darkness, lifted them gently into a sack and carried them to the other end of the farm. Like his soldiering, his dealings with snakes and unruly animals had an insane bravery to them.

In the first culling of impalas, we made biltong, cutting the meat into thin strips, rubbing it with salt, sugar, bicarbonate of soda, coriander, and coarse black pepper, then marinating it overnight in a roasting pan with Holbrook's Worcestershire sauce and brown vinegar. The following day, we soaked up the excess moisture with kitchen towels and used opened-out paper clips to hang the meat on a wire line strung along the hot, breezy veranda outside my parents' room. Five or six days later it was cured enough for Dad, who liked his biltong wet and soft and greasy, sliced thinly with his Swiss Army knife, and eaten in front of the television. I preferred mine powder dry, salty spicy, and snapped into fragments, carried in my pocket on long game walks and eaten in the sunshine with a cold Coke.

Mom wouldn't touch the stuff. To her, raw meat, cured or not,

equaled toxoplasmosis, a parasite-borne disease that, in the worst-case
scenario, leads to fever, headaches, seizures, nausea, and eye and brain
damage—though, fortunately, not death.

Snakes and biltong aside, she was already hopelessly in love with
Rainbow's End. Mom liked to paint a picture in her head of how life
should be and then set about re-creating it, and the thatched-roof cot-
tageyness of the house with the giraffe out the front and the river flowing by was the perfect palette. Giant had not exactly worked out.
Rainbow's End was going to be the fulfillment of her fantasy that Lis
and I grow up in an Enid Blyton idyll of niceness.

But I'm jumping ahead, because on our first weekend at Rainbow's End
something happened to change everything. It was a Sunday, and we
were trying out the new television. It wasn't actually new—probably
hadn't been new for close to a decade—but it was a television nonethe-
less, with big plastic knobs and a veneer of fake wood. Like the cupboard, it had come with the house. The new TV offered up a powdery
collection of gray and white shadows, frequently interrupted by Apolo-
gies for the Breakdown in Transmission, which was to do with RBC-TV
and couldn't be helped, and an incessant, infuriating rolling, which
could, but only after a prolonged battle with the rusty aerial out in the
garden.

While Mom stood in the lounge directing operations, Lisa and I
were intermediaries at the lounge door and out on the front lawn.

"Backwards or forwards?" Dad called.

"Backwards," I told Lisa, and the pole shrieked in response.

"Try forwards," Mom said.

"Forwards," I instructed Lisa.

"Stop! *Stop!* No, now he's gone too far."

"Too far," I told Lisa. "Forwards or backwards?" I asked Mom.

From his post at the aerial, Dad yelled: "For crying in a bucket, you
people."

"Tell him to keep his hair on," said Mom.

I leaned out the door. "It's fine," I told Lisa.

"It's fine," she relayed to Dad.

He strode in from the garden, flung himself in his chair, and took a long swallow of Castle. A look of beer-relief passed over his face. The smell of hops and Lion matches wafted in my direction. "What's on the box?" he asked, raising his voice above the din from the kitchen, where Madala's supper preparations were in progress. Maud padded through in Bata *takkies* and stopped by the dining room table. She clasped her hands in front of her apron. "Good night, *bas*."

"Night, Maud." A muscle of dislike twitched in Dad's jaw. He turned around but not really.

"Night, madam."

"Good night, Maudie, thank you," my mother said vaguely. She was buried in *Look & Listen*, the television guide. The fact that there was only one channel heightened rather than lessened the anticipation. "News's coming on," she told my father. "Let's watch the news."

Over their heads, I caught Maud's eye and grinned. She was trying not to laugh. Every evening we went through the same routine and every evening we both tried not to laugh. She gave me a funny little wave. I waved back surreptitiously. Lisa giggled.

The bell tinkled, and we took our places at the dining room table. Madala's hand trembled slightly as he lifted the lid on each pot, releasing a bubble of steam. "Gem squashi," he intoned, "mash potatoesi, lemb chopsi, beansi, grevvy."

"*Ja*, Madala, thank you," said Dad, stabbing a chop with more force than was absolutely necessary.

"Thanks, Cookie." Mom smiled.

"Thank you, Madala," I added, putting a spoon into the buttery hollow of gem squash and scooping out the stringy yellow flesh. If they were young enough, I ate them whole, seeds, skin, and all, and they dissolved on my tongue like squash heaven.

It was coming up to six, and the news was about to start. In under an hour the total-eclipse blackness of a farm night far from city lights would set in, but already the curtains were drawn in a bid to prevent us from being shot by terrorists targeting our illuminated silhouettes. If we were staying with friends or dining at the house of a family who didn't observe the dusk curtain curfew, Lis and I went into a panic. *Why* weren't the curtains closed? Didn't they care about the terrs? Weren't they afraid of being *shot*?

I worried about it even when we went on holiday to South Africa, where there were no terrs. And when we'd been on our first and only overseas trip (to Spain, Switzerland, and Greece) earlier that year, the lack of terrs and curfews had plagued me like a phantom limb.

Dad snapped: "Sit up straight and eat properly, Lisa." Chewing sounds sent him into a frenzy.

Mom gave Lisa a supportive squeeze under the table. "Shhh, the news is coming on."

The headline item was the story of a Viscount airliner, the *Hunyani*, which had gone missing from radar screens five minutes after taking off from Kariba airport at 5:05 p.m. Fifty-two passengers were onboard. Shortly before it vanished, the pilot was heard to call out: "Mayday, Rhodesia 825, help me. We've lost both starboard engines. We're going in."

"God," gasped Mom, "those poor, poor people."

"Shame," Dad said with feeling. "That's too terrible."

What we didn't know then, would not know until Mom went into Hartley to get *The Herald* on Monday, and then, because of the shock of it, every day of the week after that, was that while eighteen of the fifty-two passengers survived the crash-landing of the *Hunyani* in the Urungwe Tribal Trust Land near the Zambian border, ten had died in a hail of bullets shortly after staggering dazed from the wreckage, gunned down by terrorists posing as rescuers. Moments before they opened fire on the group, one of the men shouted: "You have taken our land." Anyone still breathing was hacked to death with bayonets.

In all, eight of the eighteen plane crash survivors lived to tell the tale, three by managing to escape during the chaos of the massacre, and the remaining five because they were away seeking help from local tribespeople at the time—help that was not forthcoming. Most Africans were too scared, or too hostile, to offer assistance.

It was hard to swallow the emotion of it. It welled up in your chest and hurt like a broken heart. In a country at war, death—even everyday death—is never just a rite of passage but is connected to you, and each loss of life chips away a piece of you.

When I returned from boarding school after a three-day week, it was to find that RBC-TV had broadcast a BBC interview with Joshua Nkomo, in which the ZIPRA leader chuckled gleefully as he explained that it was his forces which had brought down the *Hunyani*. "The Rhodesians have been ferrying military personnel and equipment in Viscounts, and we had no reason to believe that this was anything different" was his justification for it. Mom couldn't get over the fact that in newspaper photographs he was wearing a diamond-encrusted Rolex. At the weekend, *The Herald* confirmed what a lot of people already suspected: the Viscount had been downed by a heat-seeking SAM-7 missile.

On Sunday, September 9, there were emotional scenes outside the Anglican Cathedral of St. Mary and All Saints in Salisbury—the church where I'd been christened, where I'd sat so often in the pews with Granny, brain foggy with the incense-thickened air. Two thousand mourners gathered beneath the tear-streaked figure of Christ, in the rainbow glow of the stained glass. Hundreds more thronged on the steps outside. Most were silent, but some were too grief-stricken or vengeful to contain themselves. It had come to light that Ian Smith had been in secret talks with Nkomo. One placard read: P.M. SMITH—GIVE NKOMO A MESSAGE WHEN NEXT YOU MEET HIM SECRETLY: "GO TO HELL YOU MURDERING BASTARD."

At Rainbow's End, we turned up the volume on the radio as the Dean, the Very Reverend John da Costa, began to speak. He said that, although he was of the belief that clergymen should stay out of politics, there were times when it was necessary to speak out "in direct and forthright terms, like trumpets with unmistakable notes." This was one such time.

> Nobody who holds sacred the dignity of human life can
> be anything but sickened at the events attending the crash
> of the Viscount *Hunyani*. Survivors have the greatest call
> on the sympathy and assistance of every other human
> being. The horror of the crash was bad enough, but that
> this should have been compounded by the murder of the
> most savage and treacherous sort leaves us stunned with
> disbelief and brings revulsion in the minds of anyone
> deserving the name "human."
>   This bestiality, worse than anything in recent history,
> stinks in the nostrils of Heaven. But are we deafened by
> the voice of protest from nations which call themselves
> "civilised"? We are not. Like men in the story of the Good
> Samaritan, they "pass by, on the other side."
>   One listens for condemnation by Dr. David Owen,
> himself a medical doctor, trained to help all in need.

One listens, and the silence is deafening.

One listens for loud condemnation by the President
of the United States, himself a man from the Bible-Baptist
belt, and once again the silence is deafening.

One listens for condemnation by the Pope, by the
Archbishop of Canterbury, by all who love the name
of God.

Again, the silence is deafening.

So impassioned were his words that they seemed to travel down the
airwaves and resonate around the room as we listened. He said he did
not believe in white supremacy or black supremacy, but that no man
was better than another until he had proved himself to be so, and
that those who governed or who sought to govern must prove themselves worthy of the trust that would be placed in them.

He said that the ghastliness of the ill-fated flight from Kariba would
be burned upon our memories for years to come, but in asking who was
to blame he spared no one. His was a lament for the failings of the
church, society, politicians, and the United Nations; for the television
networks and filmmakers promoting violence as entertainment; for the
men who pulled the triggers, who in all probability, had attended
church schools; for those people who called themselves believers, many
of whom screamed loudest against Communism but who never entered
any house of prayer or praise.

"Had we," he said, "who claim to love God, shown more real love
and understanding, more patience, more trust of others, the churches
would not be vilified as they are today. . . . I have nothing but amazement at the silence of so many of the political leaders of the world. I
have nothing but sadness that our churches have failed so badly to prac-
tise what we preach. May God forgive us all, and may he bring all those
who died so suddenly and unprepared into the light of his glorious presence. Amen."

Later he would call that sermon the "most disastrous" of his entire
ministry, but right then it united us like nothing ever had. *Glued us.*
Now, more than ever, we felt that it was us against the world. Even
Ian Smith had let us down.

The spell of the sermon kept hold of me for a long time afterward and was still in my head that evening when I took the dogs down to the Umfuli.

Mupfuri, the Mashona called the river: "One who passes by."

Were *we* just passing by?

The soil beneath my bare legs was still warm from the heat of the day, and the air was cool and rivery and smoky dense with the fires of the distant compound. The bush glowed gold with the setting sun. And as I sat there watching the dogs snap and snuffle in the shallows and try to hitch rides, the strangest feeling came over me. I felt that, by coming here, by choosing Rainbow's End, we'd stepped knowingly into the fray. And yet I was okay with that. We were in a winnable war. We'd win because right was on our side. Like the song said, we'd keep our land a free land, stop the enemy coming in.

And I felt like everything I'd ever done had been leading me to this point. That I'd sleepwalked through life till now. That this was worth fighting for and, yes, worth dying for.

3

At Rainbow's End, the War was suddenly much nearer than it had been at Giant Estate when soldiers came to drink beer on our veranda. It was actually living inside our house. The War had come here and cut down a family. It had written its name in blood. It was no longer an abstract: a red splash of agony on the evening news. Or the warming community cheer of the farmers' wives ladling *babotie* and fruit salad in the troopie canteen. Or even just the sanitized goodwill of *Forces' Requests* on the radio, with forces' sweetheart Sally Donaldson reading the homesick messages of desperate soldiers and playing their special songs: "If I Said You Had a Beautiful Body Would You Hold It Against Me?"

Now the War was a permanent presence in our lives: an irremovable cloak, a Scarlet Letter—only this one a *W.*

And so we put up our paper-thin defenses. A security fence, which could easily be cut. A pack of useless but vocal dogs. An unarmed night guard, who was always the oldest, least able-bodied man on the farm, the only man who could be spared from the labor force, a man who could be bribed or simply be sleeping. An Agricalert, a two-way radio wired to police headquarters. Failure to report in with your call sign at a specific time every night would result in a truckload of soldiers being dispatched to your farm to check if you were dead or simply forgetful, in which case you'd wish you were dead. A gun cabinet stocked with an FN, a shotgun, a .22 rifle, a revolver, and a couple of grenades. And beside the back gate, a plow disk hanging from a post. In the event of an emergency or terrorist attack, the farmworkers or Maud would beat it with an *ntsimbi* and Dad would run out with his FN.

But these measures were psychological more than anything. They reassured us that, if nothing else, we were delaying the inevitable, and they told the terrorists that there were a few more barriers in place than there had been on the night when they were able to walk unchallenged up to the house and change its history.

My resolve was tested sooner than I might have wished. Within weeks of moving in we discovered that several times a month, and occasionally nightly or even hourly—especially during periods of intense thunderstorm activity, when the house vibrated with colliding-boulder crashes and electric blue forks sizzled around the yard—the picture on the TV would shrink to a gray square and a coal-pit darkness would envelop us.

The first time it happened, Dad said into the blackness: "Oh, hell."

And the spring sweat chilled on my skin.

A power outage meant one of two things: either some gremlin in the elderly, DIY wiring had caused the fuse box to fail, which meant that Dad would have to go to the electricity hut outside the security fence to fix it; or a gang of terrorists had sabotaged it, which meant he'd be walking into an ambush. We lit candles in silence while Dad grabbed his FN and hurriedly put on his *veldskoens*.

Mom said: "Please be careful, Errol."

He went in a rush of night air. Out in the garden, the crickets trilled madly. Mom put a protective arm around Lisa. In the fluttering candlelight, the moths swirled and the shadows boxed and the yellow-fringed blackness weighed heavy on us as we waited, not knowing what we might hear next: Dad's rapid footsteps and smoker's cough, or gunfire. The minutes passed like hours. Then the lights came on and seared our eyes like strobes and the TV's mindless chatter made a nonsense of our fears. We blew out the candles and laughed and pretended that we hadn't been scared, not even for a minute, as the hot wax cooled and the last gray gusts of candle smoke corkscrewed up to the ceiling.

• • •

But if this was our new life, we took it gladly, for the compensations were enormous. On Rainbow's End, nature lent the day a shape it had never had in the city or even at Giant Estate. Dawn arrived in a noisy celebration, with six o'clock sunshine breaking in gilded shafts through the trees and a heart-stopping blue sky and the songbirds competing with the roosters and *pip-pip-uree* of robins and the shouted greetings of Africans arriving for work. Each day came washed clean by the night before. When the laundered smell of morning mingled with the lure of frying bacon, I'd jump out of bed, wash my face, and go to the dining room, where sliced pawpaw and a box of Cerelac, creamy flakes of milky vanilla bliss, waited on the table under the fly net. At that hour of day, Mom and Lisa were usually still sleeping, and Dad was busy in the lands, but Madala was available to take orders. Would I like fried eggs, bacon, tomatoes, and fried banana, or scrambled eggs, tomatoes, fried bread, and *boerewors*? With Daybreak chicory coffee, Cape gooseberry jam on toast made smoky by the woodstove, and fresh-squeezed orange juice from the Etheridges' citrus farm?

After that I'd go riding, returning covered in grass seeds, horse sweat, and dew. I'd rinse it off under the wheezing river-water shower. When the sun rose higher, I'd take my sketchbook or a novel or just a Coke and a stick of biltong and I'd go barefoot, wearing cutoff shorts and a RHODESIA IS SUPER or WE MADE RHODESIA GREAT T-shirt into the game park and paint or draw or commune with the wildlife. In daylight the terrors of war seemed suspended. Whereas in the city my parents might have closeted me and fretted about my safety, here in the place of greatest danger, they handed me my freedom and trusted me to use it wisely. Left to my own devices, I explored abandoned mine shafts, swam with the dogs in the quick currents and bilharzia-ridden depths of the Umfuli River, or lay dreaming on smooth, cold boughs in silent glens, watched by the shy giraffe.

Once when I was leaning against a tree, lost in a book, Jenny came up behind me and put her slender, golden nose around the trunk. I glanced up to see a pair of glossy, long-fringed giraffe eyes level with mine. It's hard to say which of us got more of a fright, and a second later she was crashing away, but the magic of the moment never left me.

But it was the afternoons I loved the best. At the height of summer, the iron scent of rain would come stealing across the land long before the first cloud scudded over the horizon, and the thunder would growl low and soft, like a distant lion. Soon the farm would be plunged into semidarkness, as if in readiness for an eclipse. The defiant sun would infuse everything with saturated color, so that the soil became burnished and the pale, thorny hands of the acacias stood out in sharp relief against the charcoal sky. The first heavy drops would send the picannins running for cover, their pale soles flashing like the underbellies of antelope. The dogs would start and whine as lightning snaked and thunder cracked and the rain arrived in sheets, hissing down white on the brown river and making a muffled pelting on the thatch. I'd open the front door and inhale its mineral blast like a drug.

Then, as quickly as it had begun, the storm would fizzle out, leaving behind it the intoxicating smell of wet earth and soaked vegetation and the less intoxicating smell of wet dog. The trees would return to their full height and lilac-breasted Mzilikazi rollers would balance on dripping telephone wires, twitching water off their backs. More often than not a rainbow would arch over the game park or the river: God's promise. Those were the times when I felt most fully alive, most part of the rhythms and cycles of Africa and our new home.

I felt like we belonged to the land and the land belonged to us.

It was at Rainbow's End I first began to realize my mother was different. Other mothers—even farming mothers—attended PTA meetings or their children's sports days, accompanied their husbands to tobacco sales, went shopping with other farmers' wives in their cream Mercedeses, or spent a lot of time supervising the bottling of preserves or the baking of teas or the preparing of extensive, meaty dinner parties and *braais*; Mom's head was most often in the Himalayas. When she did venture into the kitchen, it was to make a recipe she'd come across on her travels—a delicious Canadian carrot cake or Bumi cheesecake from Kariba (two-thirds of a tin of condensed milk, 284 milliliters cream, the juice of three lemons, or to taste, and a smattering of lemon zest, whipped together on a biscuit base).

If, through part-time work or some other means, she came into a little money, she'd arrive home with shiny coffee table books about Matisse or van Gogh or the ancient Egyptians. Mom had left school at fifteen, and partly because she had a complex about her lack of education and also because she was insatiably curious about other worlds and art and culture, she devoured any information about the treasures of the globe she could get her hands on. The master bedroom was stacked high with *Fair Lady* and other lifestyle magazines in which she'd circled Raffles Hotel in Singapore or Elizabeth Taylor's favorite beauty products and other things she couldn't afford but could aspire to.

But she was sick a lot, and when she was sick, her brilliant light was doused.

When she wasn't in her bedroom or planning her next trip, Mom was directing Gatsi and Medicine to fill the garden with red-hot pokers, Namaqualand daisies, sweet peas, agapanthas, and Watsonian lilies, and to put orange pansies and a magenta bougainvillea by the front door. She planted her favorite rose, a Mr. Lincoln, outside her bedroom window. She went through a sewing phase, and poor Lisa, who had just turned four, was subjected to a wardrobe composed almost entirely of scratchy Victorian doll bonnets and frilly dresses. Before Lisa was born, Mom was always dragging me to the doctor to obtain antibiotics for imaginary illnesses; now my sister had to endure bilharzia tests, sinus probes, and antihistamine shots. Inevitably we both became doctor-phobic.

Away from my mother's clutches, Lisa lived in a world of her own imagination. She was preternaturally bright, with a cherub face and blond ringlets that straightened as her hair grew. She spent a lot of time acting out scenes in front of the bathroom mirror or talking to an imaginary friend. Now that she was older, I was ecstatic to have a kid sister to teach, protect, and tease. I'd put her on Charm and lead her to the barns or bring her pieces of nature—a snakeskin, a seedpod, or a feather—or take her down to the weir with the dogs. I told her that there were fairies in the birdbath and that her dolls came alive at night, but that neither group came out if you were looking, so she'd spend ages trying to sneak up on the birdbath, or lie awake at night peeping through her eyelashes, hoping to see the dolls at play.

Dad's main contribution to the house was to turn the breakfast nook into a bar. All the farming families I knew had designated bar areas in their homes or gardens, just as everyone had at least one calendar in every room and stacks of *Farmers' Weeklies* and Giles comic books beside the toilet, beneath the "Rules of the Loo." RULE NO. 1: STAND CLOSER, IT'S SHORTER THAN YOU THINK. Dad hung a batik of the "Desiderata," a copper mirror, and a Smith's Garage calendar in the bar and lined the pelmet with Grey's Scouts and PATU mugs. The fridge was loaded to capacity with Cokes, mixers, and beers, which Dad and everyone else I knew drank when they were thirsty and not just after eleven o'clock in the morning. The drinking, and the divorce rate, had increased in proportion to the War.

We bought a new stereo, and it was then that I really fell in love with country music. For hours at a stretch I'd sit behind the bar pouring myself copious quantities of Mazoe granadilla juice and singing along with John Denver ("Country Roads"), Juice Newton ("Queen of Hearts"), Kenny Rogers ("Ruby, Don't Take Your Love to Town"), Glen Campbell ("Wichita Lineman"), the Bellamy Brothers ("Let Your Love Flow"), and anything I could find by Olivia Newton-John, with whom I'd become infatuated after seeing *Grease* five times. I made plans to become a singer as well as a vet and a champion rider, and set myself a challenge of learning every lyric on every album I liked. Whole days would disappear as I lifted the stereo needle, wrote laboriously, and put it down again.

I did the same with cassettes in the steaming hot car. I had a word-perfect command of any number of unlikely records, including Marty Robbins's *Gunfighter Ballads* and Olivia's version of Doc Watson's "Banks of the Ohio," the melancholy bleakness of which I found appealing.

> He cried, "My love, don't you murder me
> I'm not pre-pared for eternity."

Cowboy culture fascinated me. I'd read all of Dad's dog-eared Westerns about Sudden the reluctant gunfighter and identified with them far more than I ever did with books or films about Vietnam or any other war. Those depicted a war I didn't recognize, one with tanks and explosions and legions of men being chopped down by the bloody scythe of heavy artillery fire. The war of my experience was more like the battleground of the Old West, where lone ranchers defended themselves against shadowy but well-armed assassins who came in deadly bands of three or six or ten.

I recall almost nothing about my last few terms at junior school. The teacher's face is a blank to me. Male or female, I have no idea. It's as if Bruce Forrester's death cast a pall over the whole year. The only thing that stands out is Bruce Campbell shooting his toe off in a hunting accident, which Juliet, his now girlfriend, was furious about because, she said, he could have died, too. Mr. Clark's temper was worse than ever, and since the Standard Five classroom was situated next door to his office, all day long we heard rants and cries and saw red-faced boys limping past our windows.

I grew straight up like a bean shoot, heading skyward so quickly that growing pains left me writhing. In school photographs I'm always twice the height of every other girl apart from Janet, who walked exclusively on the balls of her feet, like a ballerina on permanent pointe. The unaccustomed length of my limbs made me clumsy and awkward, and that in its turn made me more self-conscious. I was already beginning to realize that I would not be the first, or even necessarily the last, choice of boys like Bruce or Mark. Or anyone else, for that matter. I was turned down for choir, sidelined in tennis and net ball, and relegated to the position of goalkeeper in hockey, and not because I was any good at keeping balls out of the net. The only area where I seemed to pass muster was spelling bees and Allied Arts competitions, for which I wrote overblown poetry proclaiming the wonders of Rhodesia and adjective-laden prose about horses.

For Christmas, I'd received a pink-and-blue battery-operated record player so minute that a vinyl single overlapped its sides by several inches, but in the hospital green corridors of Hartley School its trebly, underwater sound perfectly captured the first stirrings of young love—in my case confined to Charm, Olivia Newton-John, and the odd wistful look at Bruce. Lisa Trumble had "Mandy," someone else had "Sailing," and I had "You Needed Me," and we played those over and over, unless I had a chance to go with Lisa Trumble to one of the cool kids' houses, where we listened to *Breakfast in America* and Foreigner.

But no matter how many ways we tried to lose ourselves in music or screen out the world around us, there was no escaping the realities of the War or its innocent casualties. At the troopie canteen, two sisters-in-law from Gadzema who were on duty there went to the bathroom together for safety's sake. One put a loaded pistol on the shelf above the basin. While she was talking, it slipped off and killed her.

For a lot of Rhodesians, the *Hunyani* Disaster had been the tipping point. Eleven thousand whites had left for safer shores in 1977, and now they were emigrating at a rate of a thousand a month. Some left following the last election because Ian Smith announced that, far from believing the whites should run the country for a "thousand years," he'd been persuaded there should be black majority rule in just two. Which seemed fair enough to me, particularly the part about everyone having a chance to vote, but the people we ran into at the post office or the Farmer's Co-op predicted nothing but doom and disaster. "If you want to know what's going to happen once these *okes* take over, all you have to do is look at the rest of Africa," they'd say. "Look at Zambia—you need a suitcase load of money to buy bread! Look at Mozambique, trashed! *Finished*. Look at Uganda and Idi Amin! No, better we make plans to *hamba lapa* England or South Africa before that day comes."

Since March we'd had a transitional black and white government, with an executive council of Ian Smith, Abel Muzorewa, Ndabaningi Sithole, and Jeremiah Chirau alternating leadership. Far from disintegrating, the country appeared to be working quite fine, but the guerrilla leaders and heads of state across the world considered the government to be an unacceptable compromise or even a sham and wanted the timetable for a one-man, one-vote election speeded up, so the War was intensifying by the day.

Those of us who chose to stay in Rhodesia were engulfed in patriotic fervor. The "Deafening Silence" sermon was released as a record and sold 38,000 copies as we all wept and wrung our hands over it. "Rhodesians Never Die," with its impassioned declaration that we'd "fight through thick and thin" and keep the enemy "north of the Zambezi," was re-released and, as our honorary national anthem, went straight to number one.

Then, on October 19, Rhodesian fighter planes launched an audacious raid on a ZIPRA base in Zambia, during which they killed sixteen hundred terrorists and completely took over Zambian air space. The supercool communications of the air commander, code-named Green Leader, to the Lusaka control tower, were made available on record, and we listened to it and laughed at the sheer daring of it and celebrated it the way people in countries not at war celebrated the World Series or the FA Cup.

That same month Camilla married Billy Miller, the Norton farmer whose wife and daughter had been killed two days before the Rainbow's End attack. They'd met in hospital, where Camilla had been visiting Nigel, whose leg had been shot to pieces, and Billy had been visiting his daughter Victoria, and had slowly, first through a bond of shared grief and later through respect and shared values and mutual admiration, fallen in love. And that, more than anything, showed the extremes and contradictions of the butterfly world we lived in.

Out of gray ugliness and pain, something beautiful had emerged.

4

On hazy Saturday afternoons or Sunday mornings that sparkled like champagne, I went for two- or even three-hour horse rides with Dad. Riding calmed him. Some of the barely suppressed fury that always seemed to boil in him would leave him, and he'd sit tall and relaxed in an Australian stock saddle he'd been given, one hand on the reins, Western-style, the other resting on his thigh. I'd bring up the rear, daydreaming to the comforting creak of saddle leather, watching out for flame lilies in the spun-silk grass, and breathing in the combination of *bushveld* and horse, which was to me the very best perfume in the world. Sometimes a rain shower would come on suddenly and we'd be too far from home to get back, so we and the horses would bow our heads against the cold drenching of it. Or there'd be a Monkey's Wedding, a teasing sprinkle of rain from an incongruously sunny sky, followed by an out-of-context rainbow.

At first, Dad rode his dun mare, Persian Lady, and I was on Charm or one of the Wicklow cattle horses, but then he bought Troubleshooter and I started riding faster horses, and we'd race each other along the long, sandy roads, bending low over our mounts' necks like jockeys and squinting between their ears for signs of land mines. We'd ride the length of Rainbow's End or go over to Stockdale, where there was an ancient trading fort near which the Portuguese and Arabs had reputedly mined for gold centuries earlier. Some mornings we stopped on a kopje and made a small fire and Dad fried up eggs and steak in an old pan and we washed them down with flask coffee. On our way back, we'd sometimes swim the horses in the game park dam, pulling the horses' heads up and pushing them on firmly when their quarters sank and they tried to roll. Afterward we'd loll wearily on the bank and give them a breather, and Dad would smoke while the jacana birds *kwoor, kwoore*d in harsh voices and skipped across the water on pink-starred lily pads, like avian Jesuses.

It was on these rides that Dad began to tell me Army stories he'd previously censored. It started when I came across a bowie knife with an eight-inch blade and a bone handle in one of the boxes we'd brought from Giant.

Dad said casually: "Oh, that, I took it off a dead gook."

It turned out that in the early seventies he'd been on exercise near Mount Darwin with four other white PATU soldiers and a black policeman and been ambushed by nineteen terrorists. Dad and the policeman threw themselves on the ground behind a fig tree, and Dad returned fire as the bullets whined around them. A grenade struck the dirt at Dad's feet, landing with an ominous metallic *thwack*. For a split second he waited to die. But it failed to detonate. The terrorists had forgotten to take the pin out. The policeman, meanwhile, was lying beside him in a fever of fright, his head covered with his hands, his rifle abandoned. With only three men against nineteen (Dad's friend Ozzie had been on a toilet break when the contact started), they were "taking serious strain," as Dad put it, when Ozzie ran across 150 meters of open ground to help them.

They killed three terrorists and captured two. The policeman never fired a single round. When Dad reported him for what he believed was either cowardice or an emotional meltdown that could have resulted in other men being killed, he was summoned to headquarters for a special briefing. The policeman, he was told, was to receive a medal for his bravery. It was very important for the morale of the police force that he be seen as a hero in the record books. Could Dad please change his story? Dad was outraged and initially refused even to entertain the idea, but it was made very clear to him that saying no was not actually an option. He agreed to sign the fabricated report only on condition that Ozzie was also awarded a medal. And that's how the contact was recorded.

I said: "But you should have been given a medal as well."

"No ways, my friend. What did *I* do?"

I looked at the bowie knife in a new light after that, but as it was the only weapon I had ready access to, I put its history out of my head and spirited it away to my room. And from then on I slept with it under my pillow.

Dad told me other things, too. How at the deadliest point of the Mount Darwin contact and when he was in the firefight on the dam wall and at other times when he thought he might die, a serene feeling came over him and sometimes he had the urge to laugh.

How a girl singer had played his favorite song, "Me and Bobby McGee," when he'd requested it one night at the Bulawayo Holiday Inn and then, when he returned weeks later, had halted the band midsong and made his day by singing it for him again.

How a captured terrorist told him conversationally, "The trouble with you people is you like to be clean," explaining that shaving-obsessed or teeth-brushing white soldiers left snowy bubbles in rivers and streams, and mint, sandalwood, or Old Spice lingering in their wake, advertising their position like radar. "We can smell you a mile off," he said, somewhat insultingly, to Dad.

Dad never took war personally. As far as he was concerned, they tried to shoot you and you tried to shoot them: end of story. But he had an old-fashioned perspective on the morality of it. He would lose his temper, even with senior officers, if he felt that prisoners of war or the dying from either side were not accorded the proper respect.

Once, when the Grey's Scouts were on exercise in Wankie National Park, they were called to the aid of a police unit that had been ambushed nearby. A nineteen-year-old policeman had been shot in the neck. He'd died instantly, his face still golden hopeful, his uniform still stiff and new.

The soldiers radioed for a helicopter to collect his body, but none came. The sun burned down and the sky stayed empty and my father fumed and swore—not because of the death but because of what the response to it represented. The boy had died for his country, but his country didn't care for him. It didn't care for him and it didn't care for the morale of the men who'd fought alongside him any more than it had cared for the anonymous men who'd perished in the interests of exploration, tribalism, greed, racism, or colonialism in centuries past. And so there was nothing to do but wait. They zipped him into a body bag and sat with him all day long while the careless sun boiled and the flies collected and the horses grew restless and my father seethed and the boy's blood soaked the soil that he had once lived for.

The horses were not the only ones who liked our new home. The dogs spun in rapturous circles on their way to river swims, and sometimes I'd take the older ones with me when I rode. Kim and Coquette spent their days curled around each other in sunny spots like Siamese wreaths, and Mom's Persian Ming Ming spent hers down at the water hole catching barble—plump catfish that tasted of mud. She brought in a boomslang as a present and deposited it, still very much alive, on the lounge carpet. Cue much comical overreaction as we tried to catch it.

Over the years my vet kit had become progressively well equipped, and it was now stocked with assorted syringes and needles, a scalpel, expired bottles of penicillin, antiseptic and antibiotic lotions, wound power, half a dozen crepe bandages and gauze dressings—everything, I fancied, I'd need should I be called upon to bind broken wings, dress infected wounds, or treat abscesses, which I often was. Rainbow's End was a mecca for the walking wounded. Orphans of every species were carried to our door on a weekly basis, and it was nothing for us to have a baby python in a Tupperware cereal box on the mantelpiece, a duiker in the tack room, and a secretary bird—an eagle-headed, snake-killing bird with long, thin legs like stilts—in the chicken run. With the lessons of experience, plenty of TLC, and a lot of trial and error, we patched things up and sent them on their way.

The only thing my vet box didn't contain was snakebite serum, which was expensive and with which my parents refused to indulge me, despite my snake obsession. Instead I spent hours poring over a book called *Don't Die in the Bundu* (the bush), which chronicled the virtues of urine as an antiseptic and spitting cobra antivenom, and explained why boomslang bites required a tourniquet but binding an adder bite resulted in gangrene.

All this time Cassandra's belly was continuing to expand, and the suspense of waiting for the day when the long-promised Troubleshooter-sired foal would be mine had become harder and harder to bear. When at last it did arrive, it was a stormy December 13. Mom and I were alone at home, Maud and the garden boys having gone for their afternoon break, and she stood at the front door as I ducked out into the rain, her voice a fading echo of warnings about lightning and pneumonia. But there was something else in it, too. Some acknowledgment that this was *my* Himalayas. The bay mare was in the paddock close to the stables. Her eyes were half-shut against the stinging white pellets, against the spasms. I squatted in the mud and stroked her straining abdomen as the thunder cracked and lightning threatened with a forked blue tongue and toffeelike streams formed around us.

When the foal slid out into the inhospitable downpour, I ripped open the moon-colored sac that held it. It was a beige colt. A great star filled his forehead. His tiny nostrils tested the wet air, and his ears flopped under the weight of water. Mom came out with a raincoat for me and cooed over him before fleeing the storm, but I was not about to go anywhere. I knelt in the mud and watched like a proud parent as he made his first, kitten-weak attempts to stand. Before he was an hour old I loved him more completely and unconditionally than I'd ever loved anything or anyone apart from my family.

Two days later he was dead.

He just collapsed without warning and went into a coma. An emergency summons was sent to Eric Staples, who lifted his eyelids to check his responses and declared him "technically dead." He had, the vet said, contracted hepatitis from his mother. His only chance of survival was an immediate blood transfusion, but the odds of it working were minuscule because there was no time to test blood types, and with only two other horses available as donors, the likelihood of a match was slim to none. I was away for the day, and Dad, who knew how much the colt meant to me, was frantic. He told the vet to do whatever it took to save him. Charm was brought forward as a guinea pig, and the transfusion began. Eric Staples held open the lids of the little beige foal again, and afterward Dad was never able to get over the image of his capillaries filling with blood "like lights on a circuit board." Within half an hour the colt was on his feet as if nothing had happened.

For the first few weeks of his existence, he was all knobbly knees, ribs, and star. He and Cass stayed in the garden or near the house, and over the Christmas holidays I spent every available minute playing with him, talking to him, or breathing into his nostrils. It was a wrench to leave him when term started, and one weekend I came home from school to find that, in the space of five days, he appeared to have filled out, turned dark gray, and gained a thin layer of thoroughbred muscle. Gradually the thin layer turned to steely bulk, and he burst with high-octane energy. He would race around the yard, rearing, bucking, and kicking out with such speed and ferocity that people leapt up trees to escape him. But it was all for show. He had Troubleshooter's gentle nature and the same kind eyes.

When his baby fluff dropped away, it revealed, beneath it, a coat of the purest midnight black. In defiance of all natural laws, I had my black stallion. After months of dreaming up exotic, triple-barreled names worthy of his racehorse heritage and his future as a champion three-day eventer, I called him simply Morning Star. It suited him somehow.

5

We learned more about Rainbow's End from Richard Etheridge than from anyone. He knew almost all of the farm's history firsthand or through his father, Eric, who had farmed Stockdale before him, and he had that rarest combination of qualities: a storyteller's eye for detail and near perfect memory for dates. Without reference to notes or diaries, he was able to say with certainty that the Rainbow's End weir was built in 1913 by Charlie Knight, owner of Umvovo, the farm on the opposite side of the river, and that he himself had raised it by a meter in 1963. Tom Beattie would raise it again in 1988, when he bought Umvovo.

The deeds showed the farm as a two-pointed crown of the sort a child might draw, with the house at the very bottom. Between the two points was the southern tip of Giant Estate. Apart from the Etheridges and the Beatties, our neighbors were the Brinks on Aitape and, over the strip road, eccentric Wendy Austin, who ran a cattery. She had scores of pets, and whenever one died she had it stuffed. Their glass eyes glittered eerily at visitors.

Across the weir was Umvovo, now owned by Goldie Knight. She bred chinchillas for their fur and named them, for her amusement, after everyone in the district.

"Let's knock off Kobus tonight," she'd say as she headed out to begin the slaughter.

The Etheridges lived closest to us, and it was they we saw the most.

Richard was stocky, balding, and brash, with a voice that could penetrate the loudest dinner party on earth, and when they'd first met,
twenty years earlier, Dad hadn't been able to stand him. Dad was a big
believer in humility, and even at that stage humility and Richard had
not been on speaking terms for many years.

"If someone said they had a handmade rifle, he'd say, 'I've got two
of those, only they're made in Germany and I've had the stock specially
reconstructed,'" Dad would recall laughingly. "We always thought it was
bulldust, but then we found it was all true. He *did* have the best. The
best furniture, the best original paintings, the best fishing rods. Then
he told us he was marrying this spectacular girl from England. And we
were like, '*Ja, ja.*' Then she came out, and she *was* spectacular. She was
incredibly beautiful. And *nice.* She was the nicest person you could ever
meet. Well, that just killed us."

Now they were the best of friends, because the way Dad saw it,
Richard wasn't arrogant or boastful, he was just truthful. And a truthful
man was a man Dad could respect.

And so we'd go over to the Etheridges' house and sit in their cool,
classy lounge beneath the mounted buffalo heads and David Shepherd
oils of elephants, leopards, and lions, with our feet on their zebra-skin
rug. They had tennis courts and a swimming pool and a lawn that unfurled in Rhodesian flag green right to the edge of the Umfuli. We'd
soak up the unaccustomed luxury. Everything seemed effortless in the
Etheridge house. Everything *was* the best.

The Etheridges had fishing-mad twin boys halfway between Lisa's
age and mine, who were exceptionally well mannered. We'd hang out
under the Kenya coffee tree as the wash of orange sunset turned the
jungly river islands violet-black and Dad flipped the bream on the *braai*
and Richard talked at the top of his voice about how his mother had
grown up with Ian Smith in Selukwe; how Smith had personally rung
to ask him to take P. K. Van der Byl hunting; how his grandfather was a
pioneer of the Klondike and a member of the Pioneer Column, and his
great-great-grandfather was the biggest employer of human beings in
the world—paying ten thousand horsemen in India to look after horses
and haul indigo.

Since there was no topping this or any other claim, and since
Richard was, first and foremost, hilarious, my parents and other visitors
would just settle back and allow themselves to be reduced to helpless

laughter as he told irreverent stories about Gadzema people like the three sisters who managed to bag fifteen husbands, "four of whom died mysteriously." Finally one sister went too far. After being spurned by a prospective suitor, she shot him between the eyes—earning herself ten years in jail for her trouble.

Through Richard's eyes, Gadzema was transformed from a blink-and-you-miss-it dot on the map into a thrilling hamlet rife with adultery, genius, and dark intrigue. Ticking them off on his thick, sun-scarred fingers, he'd say: "Gadzema has produced a priest turned professional boxer, a pro wrestler, a knight, a Wimbledon champion [Donald Black], thieves, millionaires, the most successful stamp collector in Southern Africa, and the owner of the largest collection of Tretchikoff paintings in the world!"

While all of this was going on, Catherine, who had a serene beauty that seemed to come from within, would be watching her husband with a contented, indulgent smile. They'd met in England when Catherine was nineteen and saving every penny to escape to Africa. Richard was there on a farming scholarship. He was the only eligible bachelor she knew. Richard liked to joke: "She married me for my money, I married her for her cooking, and the first meal she cooked me was burnt and our first bank statement was overdrawn."

In his own way Richard was as temperamental as Dad and Tom Beattie, always effing and blinding and ranting about some incompetent, but Catherine pulled him into her peaceful orbit, and somehow the house itself felt calm. Or at least it did until they started talking about hunting. Both Richard and Catherine were accomplished big game hunters with scores of elephant and other hides to show for it, but any objections were crushed by Richard, who knew everything there was to know about wildlife management and could prove the advantages of culling with statistics. But all killing of animals was now anathema to me. One night they showed us a film of their most recent elephant hunt. Footage of majestic bull elephants with long, curving tusks moving in slow motion through the bush was followed by scenes of unimaginable grotesquerie and gore, with slabs of scarlet flesh and rivers of blood and the Etheridges beaming proudly in the middle of it all. I burst into tears and walked out in protest, ignoring Dad's narrowed glare of warning and Mom's appealing: "Honey!" But it was a landmark of sorts: the first time I'd ever stood up to any grown-up.

The first time I'd ever stood up for what I believed in.

What Richard didn't know was that, by curious coincidence, Rainbow's End had been offered to my grandfather in the thirties by his friend William Sidney Senior, then minister of mines and public works. In a letter dated October 27, 1935, "Sunday Morning," their mutual friend Billy Mowbray tells Grampy: "About the Seniors' Gadzema farm, you might take it if only for its name, *Rainbow's End!!!*" But he goes on to warn: "To take a farm on little if any Capital is a big gamble these days; I could not advise you about the Seniors' offer without a thorough knowledge of all the facts about the farm itself and possible markets. There might be something in it but the country itself is not inspiring round about there."

Had he had the capital and not fallen in love with Gabrielle Margaret Joan, the girl who stopped David, Prince of Wales's train, it might have been we who inherited Rainbow's End. Instead Grampy took a job as a cattle buyer with the Cold Storage Commission, Rhodesia's largest slaughterhouse. Before an illness robbed him of his hearing, he'd dreamed of reading English at Cambridge; now he rode a silent, five-hundred-mile route through the African villages and sun-baked savanna around Fort Victoria, alone except for his dog and his horse. His battered diary, black with a gold trim, details his provisions in microscopic handwriting: tea, sugar, milk, coffee, biscuits, cheese, potatoes, onions, polony, tobacco, cigarettes, hurricane lamp, one bottle paraffin, soap, SSG cartridges, No. 5 cartridges. His motto, a Neville Chamberlain quotation, is written at the front of it: "Failure only begins when you leave off trying."

Bill Senior was the first owner of the land he called Rainbow's End. He paid 371 pounds and four shillings for 464 morgen (980 acres) and water rights on September 27, 1923, not because he had any interest in farming but because he wanted unrestricted access to the water he needed for his mines in Gadzema. Senior was a visionary. An Englishman who'd followed his parents out to Rhodesia at the turn of the century, he had exceptional business and personal skills, highly prized by companies like Lohnro and De Beers. When he began prospecting independently, those skills brought him success with mines like the Seigneury—scene of a spectacular recovery of a lost reef—as well as Giant and others in Gadzema.

While in office in the thirties, he brought power to the country by founding the Electricity Supply Commission, bridged the Umfuli, and drafted and passed through Parliament so many crucial bills to do with roads, railways, and mining that he was awarded the Companion of the Order of St. Michael and St. George (CMG) by the king. He already had the Military Cross, earned during the Great War on the battlefields of Egypt, Palestine, and France.

His great love was flying, and it was that which killed him. On a fine, clear day in December 1938, his Hornet Moth experienced engine trouble and he crashed into the railway line near Makwiro, sixty-six miles from Salisbury. He was found dead in the cockpit. He left a wife and four children. He'd lived, the Rhodesian *Herald* obituary said, a "life of some austerity, devoting a great deal of time to study, and in his personal and public life was conscientious and efficient."

Following Senior's death, a fabulous cast of eccentrics had either leased Rainbow's End from the Seigneury Trust for agriculture or mined the seam that had given the farm its name—a seam so rich it was said to have yielded 880 ounces of gold from a single ton of ore. One family, the Downs, worked the Waterlily Mine in the early forties. They had four children with the unlikely names of Ida Down, Ben Down, Neil Down, and Sid Down. One of Richard's more bizarre claims was that they were the first family in the country to import a Persian carpet. "They lived in a bloody hovel, but they had a Persian carpet on the floor!"

After the Second World War, the Waterlily was taken over by Sir Hugh Grenville Williams, sixth Baronet, and his second wife, Maud Beatrice Fraser Marie, daughter of Compte de Marillac St. Julien. For years they camped on Rainbow's End in a caravan that had been custom built to house Lady Williams's grand piano. They kept a pet baboon on a string. I liked to imagine it cocking its head in delight on moonlit nights as the symphonies of Bach or Mozart rose above the savanna. Sir Williams was a tall, lean man, who by all accounts had taken to heart the family motto: "Strong and Crafty." His baronetcy originated in Bodelwyddan, Flintshire, and he'd served in the European War, 1914–19, where he was mentioned in dispatches. He was, Richard said, a gambler "of note." "He always, *always* had the fastest horse, the fastest women, the fastest dog, the fastest whiskey. . . . If you lent him money it would be on the fastest horse that weekend."

The Williamses were still camping on Rainbow's End in the late forties, when Thomas Agorastos Plagis, whose family were Greek, leased the farm from the Seigneury Trust. Tommy employed a nineteen-year-old Irish farm manager by the name of Mike Swan, paying him five pounds a month to grow sixty acres of tobacco. It was Swan who built the four barns, using ant-heap clay and Kimberley brick. Despite his youth and inexperience, Swan had three successful seasons, but it was not the quality of the tobacco that made him fall in love with the area, it was the quality of the women. "In the fifties Gadzema had more available girls than any town in Africa," he claimed nostalgically.

Tommy had five siblings, who moved on and off Rainbow's End as the mood took them. Among them was RAF Wing Commander Ioannis Agorastos "John" Plagis, a war hero who'd "saved Malta" in savage dog-fights and been awarded the Distinguished Flying Cross. In 1944 he'd been shot down over Arnhem but escaped with minor injuries. He returned to Rainbow's End four years later and built a house in Salisbury, where a street—John Plagis Avenue—was named after him. But he struggled to readjust to civilian life and later committed suicide.

Not all of the Plagises had the stellar reputations of John. Old Mrs. Plagis scandalized the neighborhood by running off with Mr. Passaportis, who owned the Gadzema Hotel, and having another five children.

In 1957 Bill Senior's only son, John, for whom the farm was being held in trust, died, like his father, when his light aircraft crashed. For three years the only residents of Rainbow's End were a Canadian geologist and a couple of managers, but then along came Dr. Claude "Champagne Charlie" Chiltern, who'd bought the farm from the Seigneury Trust. Chiltern was married to Elizabeth, one of Bill Senior's daughters. She was a gifted anesthetist and would later become head of anaesthetics at the Princess Alice Orthopaedic Hospital (which is linked to the world-famous Groote Schuur Hospital) in Cape Town, South Africa. Champagne Charlie, though, was just a playboy. He fancied himself a millionaire and was a fixture at Gadzema Club, ordering magnum after magnum of champagne. He even entertained the idea of building a nightclub on the island at Rainbow's End. He appointed himself general manager of Giant Mine, in which he had a controlling interest, but was banned from visiting it after taking a bottle of champagne underground.

Conditions were shabby, and there was a bad accident at Giant on his watch. The mine went bust as a result of mismanagement and neglect and never really operated again.

At the age of fifty-five Charlie took up dentistry, because as he unabashedly told a contemptuous Richard: "'It's the least amount of work.' That's what he bragged about."

In all, the Chilterns lived on Rainbow's End for around five years, after which the farm was vacant or run by managers until 1976, when Richard oversaw the sale of it, for $25,000, to Ben Forrester. And so the die was cast.

6

The part about war that nobody ever mentions is how quickly it assimilates into everyday life. After a while it seemed as if there'd never been a time when we didn't scour the farm roads for land mines or steel ourselves for bullets through the windshield as we drove into town. As if there had never been an evening when my father didn't strip and clean his guns after dinner or count his ammunition.

As if there had always been people waiting in the darkness to kill us.

For the first time I was semientrusted with a gun. On car journeys with my mother, it lay on my lap like a deadweight, a black .38 revolver in a brown leather holster. If we were ambushed, I would in theory have to try to pass it to her, but repeated visits to the firing range with an Uzi submachine gun had not made her any less timid around weapons, and I was secretly confident that, even without training, I would save the day.

To some extent, the continuance of normal life relied on the willing suspension of disbelief. On the day of the Rainbow's End murders, Richard had taken a party of friends around the game park and had seen a group of "four or five *munts*" washing clothes in the river near the old fish eagle cage. It was only afterward he realized that he'd probably been looking at the terrorists. So although I was well aware that the terrors of war did *not* vanish in daylight, that any time I was alone in the hundred wild acres of the game reserve, which was off-limits to everyone except the game boy and therefore deserted apart from the wildlife, the terrs could be watching me and planning to cut off my lips and ears and feed them to me, I chose to believe they went away. Which is why, when I set off into the sunset on Charm, my rucksack clinking with the pot, plate, and other utensils necessary to make myself an early evening *braai* of steak sandwich, fried bananas, and flask coffee, I did so optimistically, with a feeling of adventure.

Things went well only insofar as we managed to reach our destination, the old mine workings in a pretty, hilly copse at the farthest corner of the game park. I tethered Charm to a tree and began to prepare my fire. As dusk moved in, the copse lost its prettiness and became downright spooky. Charm felt the same way. When the out-of-sight impalas made their nervous barks, she threw up her head and trotted in circles around the tree. I had to keep getting up to disentangle her. Charm's fear communicated itself to me. The crudely covered mine shafts seemed too close for comfort, and the agitation of the impalas unnerved me. I squinted through the trees and tried to see what they could see. Finally Charm broke her reins and tore away home, leaving me to walk through two miles of twilight and darkness on my own, sustained only by dry bread and a bruised banana—an easy target if there ever was one.

This latest Charm fiasco convinced me that I'd need an interim horse until Morning Star was of an age to ride. The obvious one was Cassandra, but there was a problem. Cassandra hated me and I wasn't crazy about her. She'd come to us traumatized from her experiences in the Grey's Scouts, but although she still distrusted people and was nervous of them, I was the only one she seemed actively to loathe. At first I put it down to jealousy, because I spent hours of every day cuddling her foal or playing with him. But then it started to irritate me. I felt an almost spiritual connection with horses and prided myself on my affinity with them, and yet, if I walked past Cass's stable, her ears went back and she tried to bite me. If I reprimanded her, she was worse. It became a sort of feud between us.

Then Dad asked me to exercise her. I wasn't about to admit that I was scared of her, so the next morning I saddled her up in a businesslike fashion and rode her nervously up to the lands. I discovered straightaway that, unlike Charm, who was deaf to the loudest appeal to go faster and whose fat insulated her against kicking, a word or a nudge or a tiny movement of the reins was all Cass required to go from a standstill to a flat-out gallop.

Just past the compound, she bolted. I tried and failed to stop her. I remembered Butcher Boy and thought: I'm not going to fight her. She can run herself out. I leaned forward and her black mane whipped back and stung my face and the sandy road slipped beneath her flying, dark legs and the wind was as loud as a sea gale in my ears. Her stride was smooth and light and effortless. It was like riding a dolphin. When we neared the lands, I said softly, without using the reins, "Steady, girl, whoa," and she slowed of her own accord. Her ears pricked. I could tell by the rhythm of her that she was enjoying herself. She practically danced along the shimmering plum grass. Right then, I fell in love with her.

Dad was standing shoulder-high in green tobacco, etched against the blue sky, rooted to the land—earthed almost—as if he were growing out of it. He detached himself from his gang. They were scattered around him, a ragged, candy-colored crew, some of whom paused in their work to say *"Mangwanani, mamuka sei!"* (Good morning, how did you sleep?) or *"Kunjani?"* (How are you?) with white, uneven smiles. Dad was in his uniform of khaki pants, a thin, much-mended khaki shirt with a Parker pen and a packet of Madisons (his new brand) in the pocket, a floppy khaki hat, and *veldskoens*.

He said: "Hello, my friend. Is she going well for you, is she?"

"Dad, she's amazing. She's so fast and she's so willing."

He laughed. "Come and say hello to Kenneth."

Kenneth was the Boss Boy. He was a neat, courteous man with a serious air about him who always dressed in blue pants, gum boots, a checked shirt, carefully rolled up at the sleeves. He always came over, shook my hand, and asked me in English how I was doing, and I asked him in English about his family and children and congratulated him on the condition of the crops, and then we either thanked God for the rain or complained about the lack of it.

Kenneth shared Dad's philosophy on farm labor, which was that you had to work at least as hard as the people beneath you and never ask anyone to do anything that you were not prepared to do yourself. However, Dad went that much further because he took a perverse, almost masochistic delight in doing things he would never dream of asking anyone else to do.

On crop-spraying days, when farmworkers dotted the vivid green tobacco in bright yellow rain jackets and plastic hats, like so many sunflowers, Dad could be seen leaning casually against his truck in his cotton khakis, smoking a Madison, poison raining down on his head. If there were lethal chemicals to be mixed, Dad would be the one sloshing toxic solutions around drums checkered with skulls and crossbones and red Xs with his bare hands and arms, waving away the assistance of workers correctly attired in gloves, protective clothing, and gum boots.

Not surprisingly, he ended up pouring methyl bromide, a highly toxic fumigant, into his *veldskoens*. He was administering it to his tobacco seedbeds and failed to notice that the applicator hose had sprung a leak. When it did come to his attention, he was too busy to do anything other than give his sock and shoe a cursory wash under a cold tap. By lunchtime the methyl bromide had scorched a sizable portion of his skin. "Crikey Moses," he exclaimed when he awoke in the early hours of the morning to find a monstrous yellow blister, like an alien toadstool, covering the entire upper surface of his foot.

Then he burst out laughing.

Everything ever written on the subject of methyl bromide warns that inadvertent inhalation or absorption through skin can have a devastating effect on the central nervous system, resulting in chemical pneumonia, severe kidney damage, mental confusion, double vision, tremors, and death, but Dad waved away Mom's pleas for him to see a doctor. She didn't pressure him because she'd long ago concluded that, when it came to medical matters, he was a martyr. So Dad swallowed Disprins by the handful and applied farm animal wound treatments to his foot until it looked gangrenous. Even then he merely winced when he eased the seeping mess into a Slip Slop and limped off to his truck to continue working.

We were on our way to the South African coast when the agony became too much even for him. In Louis Trichardt we searched out a doctor, who took one look at Dad and, doubtless recognizing the type, advised him that seawater was the best possible medicine for it. Dad emerged from the surgery with an ear-to-ear smile and an aura of smugness. He felt completely vindicated. To him, this outcome offered final proof that refusing to seek medical attention had been the right course of action all along because the cure was, in fact, a natural one.

In between trips and hospital visits, Mom floated round the garden like some Hollywood star from the Golden Era. She'd lie out by the rondavel, a thatched summer house she'd had the farm builders construct on an anthill overlooking the river, wearing sunglasses and a sarong and reading *Fair Lady* or *A Passage to India*, while Maud delivered cups of Tanganda tea and thick-buttered date loaf on a tray. The garden boys knew that at those times they should work at the other end of the yard. In the afternoons, when they went off for lunch and what I thought of as their siesta period, Mom would put on her bikini and bake in the sun.

Fragrant farmers' wives like Anne Ford and Catherine Etheridge would come to take tea with her—teas I seldom attended, although I did like to stop by on Cassandra, say hello politely, and then, with no discernible movement or change of expression, leave the scene at a flat-out gallop, like a cowboy in a bad Western.

Years later the Etheridges summarized their memories of us as follows: I was quiet and shy and "fanatical about horses and Olivia Newton-John," my sister was "always crying," my mother was "glamorous and always holidaying," and my father was "always manic-busy, always rushing. He was never in the house; he was always in the lands."

Which, by my recollection, is entirely accurate about everyone except Lisa, who had by now grown into a relatively sunny, albeit overprotected, child.

"Your dad," Catherine said, "always, always cooked the meat at *braais*. He was always the helpful one. If there was a boat to be launched, he was there."

Without realizing it, we all started to lead separate lives. Perhaps we always had. When my friends came to stay, they could never get over the lack of parental supervision in our house, how at the height of the War, I could disappear into the bush for hours at a stretch on foot or on my horse without anyone ever asking where I was going or what I was doing. I'd wave to Mom as I set off into the game park or down to the weir, and although she'd look up from her magazine with some well-worn note of caution—"Wear a hat or you'll get sunstroke" or "Don't go near the water, you'll get bilharzia" or "Please no stunts if you're going riding" or "Put shoes on or you'll be bitten by a snake"—a grin and an "Okay, Mom" would be enough to distract her and I could continue on as before.

At Giant I'd spent so much time reading in my tree house or shut away at Hartley School doing homework that people still occasionally asked me if I was anemic, but now I was tanned and strong and fit, a fully-fledged tomboy. When the Cranswick twins—swarthy farm boys with flashing grins and hairy, bare chests—came over for a *braai*, they asked Dad: "Don't you sometimes wish you had a son, Errol?"

And Dad just laughed and said: "No *ways*. Why would I want a son? My elder daughter's as good as any boy."

That did not go down well with Mom, who told me I walked like a boxer. To compensate, she treated Lisa like a china doll, fussing over her, prettying up her hair, and scolding her if she got mud on her frilly dresses. She took Lisa with her wherever she went, parading her like a beauty pageant winner before the other farmers' wives or driving her to Salisbury to see Granny, her friends, the First Street shops, and her long-time physician, Dr. Kantor, who poked wooden spatulas down Lisa's throat and cold metal mirrors into her ears.

Even on holidays, the separation among us all continued. The previous year, when we were in Spain on what was supposed to be a "family holiday," Mom had broken the news to Dad that he and I were going to Switzerland alone while she and Lisa went to England without us. Not only that, but she and Lisa were planning to stay on in England long after Dad and I had returned to the farm. What it boiled down to was that sanctions restrictions did not permit me to enter England on a Rhodesian passport, and she didn't see why she and my then three-year-old sister, who had British and South African passports respectively, should miss out on visiting London. Dad hit the roof, but Mom had no regrets. Traveling had become like a drug to her, and she didn't always care how it happened, so long as it happened.

"What possible difference can it make to you whether we're in England or on the farm?" she reasoned when Dad had stopped ranting. "You'll be busy with the farm or in the Army, and Kari-bai"—she'd taken to calling me Kari-bai, an Indian term of endearment—"will be in school. Besides, I thought it would be nice for the two of you to spend time together."

So I and a fuming Dad had gone to the Alps on our own and had climbed a mountain in *veldskoens* and *takkies* and cotton clothing and been caught in a sleet shower on the way down and been unable to grip and, in a very real way, had contemplated falling to our deaths in the icy river several hundred feet below for more hours than I care to remember.

Mom's travels took her away for a month or more at a time, and she'd return with hair-raising stories about being chloroformed in an Austrian hotel or suffering dysentery in Delhi or watching her life flash before her eyes during nightmare journeys with deranged taxi drivers in Bangkok or inadvertently eating marijuana-laced cookies in Katmandu.

Local gossips cornered me to ask: "Don't you think it's *terrible*, your mother leaving you and your sister and your father *all alone?*"

In fact, I thought it was fantastic. My mother went traveling, my father went to war, and I went to boarding school. It was the natural order of things.

When we did come together, we bonded most often over animals, and the woman at the local SPCA rejoiced every time we visited the attached veterinary surgery, knowing full well that we were sure to be persuaded to cart away some sad, unwanted ridgeback or even a budgie or two. That's how we came to be driving back to Rainbow's End with Goat, a white male goat with a collar and lead who was under the impression he was a dog. He was affectionate and smart and loved to go for walks. He lived in the garden until he started eating the laundry, at which time he was banished to the game park or out with the sheep. He appointed himself leader of the herd and guided his docile companions into the barns on rainy days.

We'd go over to visit Dad's friend Chris van Rooyen, who had fifty baby elephants saved from culls, which he planned to ship around the world to zoos. I didn't approve of the culling or the zoos, but the little elephants were magical. I sat on the corral fence and tried to touch their rough, prickly gray hides and laughed at their attempts to manage their flopping trunks and cartoonish legs, which seemed to fold and give way when they were least expecting it, like faulty trestle tables. Their eyelashes were film star luxuriant, but their eyes were mournful, as if they'd known way too much anguish, way too young.

A year or so after we moved to Rainbow's End, Chris acquired a voluptuous, husky-voiced girlfriend with a red kiss of mouth and two lion cubs, and I liked those even better than the elephants. At barely two months old, their topaz eyes were watchful and hungry, and there was something coiled about their body language, even at play, as though they were only biding their time until they were old enough to feast on you. Had horses been compatible with lions, I would have wanted one desperately. Their fur was coarse with tawny dapples, and their heavy paws were pink padded and disproportionately huge.

The game park was a strong draw for visitors, and the giraffe, playful impalas, and bad-tempered ostriches added a picturesque element to our *braais*. Shaded by the msasas and acrikapas, eyes aching with smoke, mouth watering at the meaty aroma, I'd help Dad turn the sizzling fare on the plow disks, which were suspended on a metal rod above the fire. The *boerewors*, steak, chicken, or fish went on the top two disks, both of which had holes in them so that the juices drizzled down to the solid bottom disk and added to the flavor of the gravy of onions, beef tomatoes, and beer.

Rhodesian social gatherings were characterized by a relaxed, easygoing vibe and generosity of spirit: everyone came with smiles and armfuls of fresh veggies, or bottled fruit, or fish caught with pride in Kariba. The kindness of people was extraordinary. And we would return the favor with prickly pears or eggs or even huge, heavy gray "sausages" from the sausage trees in the game park, which farmers with red crusts of skin cancer on their arms swore by, crushing the stringy, melonlike flesh and applying it topically each morning. Another, less positive, aspect of these gatherings was that they always divided along gender lines. The women—crisply ironed, perfumed, and made up to within an inch of their lives—hovered over the puddings or salads or sat around the garden table talking about the men, the best Salisbury shopping, and who was having an affair with whom, while the men stood in tough-guy stances near the fire, discussing the War, weather, crops, and cattle, brown beer bottles piling up at their feet.

The kids knew enough to stay out of sight, be polite, and entertain themselves.

The servants, disempowered, fretted on the fringes.

Some weekends we trawled for bream on the olive river or just drifted on the current past the mysterious island, while kingfishers dived and snakes slipped from the reeds in S-shaped ripples. Often we took Goat, who was a natural-born sailor, much better behaved than the dogs, and didn't shake gritty mud all over us. Goat adored the boat. He'd put his hooves on the prow like some character from "The Owl and the Pussycat," and his white beard would part before the wind as we cut a foaming swathe down the river. And if all we were doing was reading or relaxing, he'd stare for ages at the blue sky arching over us, while the water soothed us with its rhythmic *slap, slap, slap* on the sides of the little boat.

Uncle James came to visit from Fort Victoria, and Lis and I volunteered to take him out on the boat, with Goat, to find artistic bits of driftwood and fuel for another *braai*. It was a mission that had more to do with showing off than with pragmatism, but James was young and vague and easily persuaded to go along with our madcap schemes. Out on the river, we entertained him by feeding Goat cigarettes. Goat chewed them up with gusto, and fragments of tobacco fell from his lips and collected in his beard like gold leaf. Not surprisingly, there was little in the way of firewood or driftwood on the green expanse of water, but at last we found what we deemed to be the perfect tree: a silver skeleton just yards from the Etheridges' front garden (but still in the river and thus in neutral territory). James was standing with his legs spread wide to steady himself against the rocking of the boat, hacking away at it, when Richard came storming out.

He did a double take at our eccentric party—one genial uncle with an ax, two scruffy children, and a white goat with a cigarette in its mouth, in a boat. "What the hell do you think you're doing?" he thundered. Indignation radiated from him.

"I, we . . ." Suddenly I had no idea what the hell we thought we were doing. "We're having a *braai*," I said lamely.

"Well, why don't you go and cut down a tree in your own bloody garden!"

7

When my parents were out, I colluded with Maud and the garden boys to steal from the pantry the ingredients of *muputahayi*, an unleavened African bread made from *mielie-meal*, flour, sugar, and salt. Gatsi mixed it up in a bucket and shaped it into a flat rectangle, which he wrapped in banana leaves, put between two sheets of iron, and buried in the coals of the boiler. He'd bring it to me steaming and black around the edges. It tasted of burned, bittersweet *sadza*. Lisa and I would break off crispy chunks and sit around eating them with Maud and Madala and the garden boys on the paddock fence or the furnace-heated steps of the boiler and achieve, briefly, what we couldn't achieve any other way: something akin to companionship.

For reasons I didn't really analyze, I worked hard to make them like me. I gave Maud little gifts or played her our Wrex Tarr Chilapalapa record as an expression of solidarity (with what I wasn't sure) or propped myself against the lime-washed laundry wall when she did the ironing in the afternoons and told her stories about school or things I'd seen on the TV as her rough, dark hands paused to sprinkle water across the fabric, the better to eliminate creases. The scent of hot cotton would fill the air around us.

I hung around the garden talking to Gatsi, whom I liked because he was warm, always laughing, and full of unexpected kindnesses, like making me a miniature wooden guitar with fishing gut for strings or bringing me a nest of baby mice or slashing the hard shells from sticks of sugarcane with a *bemba* and giving me the juicy, sweet cores. I liked him, too, because he had a real affection for animals and appreciated their individual personalities, which was unusual in African culture. Luka just watched us a lot and didn't say much, and it was impossible to tell what he was thinking.

When I rode my horse past the compound, the picannins would run out from behind the neat rows of mud huts and chicken coops and pathways swept tidily with twig brooms—a watercolor in taupe and brown— and wave or perform somersaults or scream a musical approximation of my name, which made me feel benevolent, popular, and a bit like royalty, but also slightly disconcerted, because as soon as I waved back, they'd run away giggling behind their hands, laughing at some private joke.

I fancied us as liberals because Mom had always said we were and I'd read *Roots* and cried and because we thought of Maud as family and liked black people in a general way (Dad was excluded from this because he was a soldier battling black terrorists and a farmer battling idleness and the elements, and we hadn't walked in his soldier or farmer shoes) and because, apart from anything else, so many Africans were on our side in the War. That, Mom said, was obvious, because only whites, Coloureds, and Asians were conscripted, and yet two-thirds of our Army was black.

Also, nearly 3,500 black civilians had died in the War the previous year, and if it was a war about color, why would the terrorists be killing their own people?

"It's black and white fighting side by side against Communism," I explained to my South African cousins and others who appeared confused about why we were still at war, especially now that we had a black and white government. The really evil people, I told them, were the Russians, Chinese, and Cubans who, in the name of Marxism, were training, arming, and sponsoring the terrorists who'd burned twenty-three African villagers alive, cut off the lips of dozens of informants, and regularly tortured, shot, or bayoneted to death babies, pregnant women, nuns, doctors, missionaries, and priests.

This view was supported daily on the news and in *The Herald*. In *Contact*, a 1973 book detailing military records and accounts of battle, our then president, J. J. Wrathall, had written: "What is not so well appreciated outside the country, however is that the war [our soldiers] are waging is not one between black and white—Africans and Europeans serve side by side against a common enemy—but between East and West."

The only time it became clear that there was an unspoken wall between me and the Africans was if they were on a break and I disturbed them. They'd be cement-mixing tea and jam and brick-size lumps of Lobels' bread, which they bought from the farm store, and talking in low voices, and if I walked past or stopped to ask a question, they'd hastily rearrange their expressions, which were either brooding and serious or relaxed with a free kind of laughter, and although they'd look up or answer pleasantly enough, there'd be an undercurrent of resentment or something challenging in their tone—particularly Maud's. I thought of it as a kind of showing off and put it down to them not wanting to appear servile in front of their peers. However, moments like that pointed up the subtle divide between us and reminded me that, although not all black people were terrorists, all terrorists were black.

One morning as Dad was gulping down his black coffee, a cry of *"Nyoka! Nyoka!"* went up and the dogs started barking their snake bark. We ran out through the kitchen. Two farmworkers were digging in the French drains beside the boiler, and Eutom, a burly Mashona, had uncovered a nest of baby night adders. He and his workmate were smashing them over the head with shovels and tossing them, still writhing, into the furnace. The sound of their wet flesh on the coals—a kind of *tssss*—made my skin crawl.

Dad, who couldn't stand snakes to be killed unless they presented a clear and present threat—which, he grudgingly conceded, they did in this case—grew more irritated by the second. His own unique approach to snake handling had led him to have unrealistic expectations when it came to the conduct of others in the same situation. Finally he ordered Eutom back into the seeping pit. Eutom complied without a word, pausing only to scoop out the remaining night adder from beneath a flat stone. His face was expressionless.

That was the moment it became cemented in my mind that they were stronger than we were. More resilient, more courageous, more resistant to pain. Madala regularly lifted roasting pans or sizzling pots of "corrifrower cheesey" in and out of the oven without gloves (I teased him that he had asbestos hands), but if I so much as went to touch a warmed plate without a napkin, he'd shriek, *"Basopa, Picannin Missis, yena tshisa stelek!"* which on the one hand was protective but on the other betrayed the fact that he considered me a weakling. In the lands and in the compound, people were frequently being bitten by adders or suffering complications while giving birth, and although they were rushed to hospital, mostly by Dad, eye-rolling all the way, they were back at work a few days later.

But it was emotionally, I felt, that they really had the upper hand. Parents regularly spent months apart from their children and husbands apart from their wives, for a variety of reasons to do with lack of accommodation or money or problems within the marriage or instructions from a witch doctor. Children or partners would be sent away to live in a single mud hut with grandparents or other relatives in the Tribal Trust Lands, sometimes hundreds of miles from their loved ones, and yet the front the Africans presented to us was largely stoic. If I tried to commiserate with Madala about his far-distant wife, he'd wave me away with a chuckle, saying: "I'm used to it. I'm used to it. Don't worry for that."

Less stoic blacks tended to be branded by their employers as malingerers or accused of inventing reasons to visit relatives on daylong bus journeys away in the Tribal Trust Lands, or of inventing relatives.

Which, like any group of employees, some were and some did.

Maud revealed herself more often than most. At Giant, when I was still too young to have learned about the grievous wounds grown-ups are capable of inflicting on each other, I'd come across her alone in the garden, looking so gray and distressed that at first I thought she had malaria. With a candidness no white adult of my acquaintance would have been capable of, she told me that a friend of hers had been caught cheating by her husband. He'd drenched a plastic bag in petrol, shoved it inside her vagina, and set it on fire.

I cried horrified tears; Maud didn't. It was only now, thinking back on her reaction, that I realized it was not that she didn't feel what I did; very obviously she felt a lot more. It was just that she, Eutom, and Madala were better at holding it in.

They buried pain the way Mom had buried the pain of her lost babies.

As the war swirled around us and the country reeled from the shooting down, in February, of a second Air Rhodesia passenger Viscount, resulting in the deaths of all fifty-nine passengers, followed by the dissolution of the Rhodesian Parliament, officially ending eighty-eight years of white rule, Maud came to Mom to ask for extended leave. Her estranged husband, whom she referred to as a *skelem*, a rascal, lived in the Tribal Trust Lands. The chief of her village had ordered her to live with him for six months before he would consider granting her a divorce.

To replace her, Maud recommended Agnes, a tall Ndebele in her early twenties. She had an open, pretty face, across which shy smiles and giggles broke like sunshine, and she was keen and hardworking and fun to have around. Maud had a dry humor and laughed a lot, but she also had a cynical streak and was inclined to be moody. Agnes was easygoing, warm, and motherly. You wanted to be enveloped in the folds of her apron. Within days Mom was so enamored with Agnes that she was fervently hoping Maud would be reconciled with her husband. A month on and she'd forgotten about Maud altogether.

It was the police who came to tell us that Agnes was dead, murdered by terrorists in an attack on Rainbow's End's second compound, which was across the strip road near Blue Rock Mine. Mom was shattered. Of all the senseless atrocities of the war, the killing of Agnes would always be, to her, among the most heinous.

"That beautiful, smiling girl," she kept saying. "She was like an angel. How could anyone hurt her?"

But they had. Others had been beaten, but it was Agnes who'd been singled out and murdered as a sellout. They'd tortured her and shot her in a compound only a few hundred yards from the entrance to Rainbow's End when they could, just as easily, have walked down our road and done the same to us. So once again we were spared.

"I don't know about you," Mom said darkly, "but I see it as a warning."

8

When you grow up in a war, war defines you. When you fully expect a grenade attack at any moment, when every good-bye could be your last, when you ride into town behind the armored vehicle carrying your freshly killed maid to the morgue, her white-*takkied* feet bobbing around on the back, every thought, every decision, and every emotion is colored by those things. Death, fear, heroism, and loss shape your days, as well as your responses.

One evening my mother answered the telephone to hear a voice ask: *"Do you know what heppened to the people who used to live in your house?"*

"Who is this?" she demanded with false bravery, hoping, even as the blood squelched to a halt in her veins, that someone had dialed a wrong number. That she hadn't answered the phone, expecting to hear a dinner invitation from a friend, only to find herself talking to one of the men responsible for murdering four people within feet of where she was standing.

"Do you know what heppened to the people who used to live in your house?"

"Yes," she whispered.

"This is a warning. You must get off your farm or the same thing will heppen to you. The only reason we are giving you a warning is because your husband is good to his labor, but we will not talk to you again. Go now, otherwise you will all be killed."

But we stayed. We stayed knowing that there were only four things between us and the men who would do to us in a heartbeat what they had done to the family before us: our dogs, our guns, our security fence, and our Agricalert.

The Forresters had had three of them.

And so, when the dogs went crazy at night, I was instantly bolt upright, this-is-it-we're-probably-going-to-die awake. I trained myself to become fully alert in seconds. Sometimes the terror I felt at a single threatening growl was so intense that it hit me in the solar plexus like a physical blow and left me gasping and nauseated.

I became obsessed with contingency plans. If we were attacked and my whole family was killed, could I escape by pulling myself through the trapdoor in the passage ceiling? And if so, how would I hide the chair I'd need to get up there? How long could I remain in the roof undetected, and what would I do if they set fire to the house to smoke me out? And what if they shot me and I wasn't really dead but just pretending, how long could I hold my breath if someone was standing over me? And what if my family were mortally wounded and the telephone lines were cut and it was up to me to go for help, would I be able to hike through the bush to Hartley or Salisbury without being seen by the terrorists?

I collected survival tips the way other kids collect stamps. The opening chapter of *Don't Die in the Bundu* was a fictional account of a plane crash followed by detailed information on recognizing edible plants, building a lean-to, finding directions using the stars or sun, and collecting rainwater. Because there seemed a very real chance of being shot down in a Viscount, I committed as many instructions as I could to memory.

The nights I dreaded most were the blackout ones, or those when Dad was away at War, or the reaping season, when Dad checked the tobacco barns every few hours until morning, leaving us exposed in his absence. Sometimes I'd go along, just so I'd be safe with him, clutching at the tails of his khaki shirt as we cut through the darkness on his motorbike. The barn boys, smoky from their fires, would start forward with evening greetings and lever open the clanking metal doors, engulf-

ing us in the dragon breath of the barns. I'd step inside and inhale a lung-
ful of steamy air. Something about the leafy perfume of the curing
tobacco, the rippling heat of the scalding flues, and the murmurs of
African voices, soothing and reassuring as they discussed barn tempera-
tures with Dad, was infinitely comforting.

At other times I'd hear the faint squeak of the gate and know that
Dad was going down to the compound with his FN. He'd creep as close
as he could to the peaked silhouettes of mud huts and the dying fires
and watch for signs that terrorists were being harbored there.

Lying in the darkness, not knowing what I might hear next, my
father's footsteps or AK47 fire, I'd console myself with the stories of
angels that were doing the rounds in Rhodesia. The ones about captured terrorists relaying how they'd been unable to attack farmhouses
because they were surrounded by giant soldiers dressed in white; about
missionaries reading the Bible with the men who had come to kill
them; about swarms of bees descending out of nowhere to chase away
attackers. But when I talked to God myself, it was like a long-distance
call that never quite connects. I listened but heard no answer. I believed
that God was out there and trusted him to look after us. I just didn't see
why I, particularly, should be spared.

Agnes hadn't been.

Late one afternoon Dad brought me an orphaned Mashona-Sussex
calf. I named her Mindy. She was two days old, weak and feverish, and
to my mind, dying of a broken heart. Her eyelashes sagged wetly
against her chestnut cheeks, and moisture beaded on her Milo-colored
nose. In her calf way she was weeping, and I wept with her. I made her
a nest of hessian in the passage outside Lisa's bedroom and nursed her
throughout the evening, and long after midnight I was still lying with
my arms wrapped round the cotton-soft folds of her, trying to will her
to live, to keep her alive with my own body warmth. Only when she
stopped shivering did I go back to my own bed.

I was in the initial, dreamlike layer of half sleep when the dogs
started barking in a keening, hysterical way. I shot up in bed, ready to
run, hide, pray—or all three. The darkness was like a hood, blinding and
claustrophobic. Dad, a pouncing shadow, rushed into the room.

"Come, kids, get your mattresses and lie in the passage. Don't turn
on any lights. Don't move unless we say so."

I grabbed my blankets, pillows, and mattress and heaved them into the passage beside the wide-eyed calf, then half-carried, half-dragged my six-year-old sister out of bed.

"I'm *sleeping*," she hissed crossly. I ignored her and began building a cocoon of blankets and pillows around us. If there was a grenade or mortar attack, these were the things, so we were told, that would save us. Bricks, feathers, and initiative. If the terrorists made it to the house, none of these things would be any use at all. We'd be slaughtered in a carnage of blood and bone just like the Forresters before us.

"Lisa?"

Her eyes opened half-mast, and she glared at me. *"What?"*

"We're being attacked. There's terrs outside. We could all be killed."

She stared blankly at me. Her eyelids drooped and her breathing slowed. The calf had gone back to sleep. Her milky, baby animal smell filled the passage. Out in the garden, the dogs were snarling and fighting as if they were ripping the flesh from the hounds of hell, but the house itself was silent. I was alone with my fears.

The immense vulnerability of our position on this moonless night— an isolated farmhouse on the banks of an oil black river, the only obstacle between the terrorists and their crossing point, the weir—hit me. Surely it wasn't a case of *if* we were killed but *when*. I thought about death. Did you see it approaching? Did God spare you the final, unendurable seconds? Did he halt the pain when it became too great? Did you slide without suffering toward the white light, comforted by angels, or did you live every minute in a paroxysm of agony until the lonely darkness came crashing down and the maggots started inching toward you?

"Lisa!"

"Mmm."

"Aren't you afraid of dying?"

"Tch! Why don't you just shut up and go back to sleep?"

The lounge light came on, and Dad appeared at the top of the passage. He was laughing, the way he does when he's on an adrenaline high. He was calm and cheerful, the way he always is in a crisis.

"Sorry, everyone, false alarm."

"But the dogs . . . ?"

"My friend, if there was someone out there, they've gone now. Come, kids, try to get some sleep."

But I knew and Dad knew that there had been someone out there, and I knew and he knew that they were only biding their time.

To us, though, death was only the downside of war. War also brought heightened joys, daily excitement, and unexpected heroes. It brought troopie canteens full of laughter and camaraderie, and squads of soldiers drinking Lion beers in our living room, radiant with sweat, the bush, and adventure. It tested our hearts, our nerve, and our loyalties. It brought pride, patriotic songs, unbreakable bonds, and a warm, cocooning community spirit. It gave us identity and a sense of belonging.

Of course, none of these things could be explained to the BBC men who ambushed Mom and me on our way back to Rainbow's End. They were standing in a lacy fringe of acacia shade when they flagged us down, and after we pulled over, they stepped into the glare with reluctance. There were two of them—a cameraman and a reporter. The reporter introduced himself as Ian Smith, "like your prime minister."

"Oh!" Mom said. "That's nice!" She gave him her best smile.

He wanted to know, was she a farmer's wife, and if so, what did she think of the people attacking the farms? Did she sympathize at all with their cause?

An image of Agnes, her treacle black blood smeared in spidery patterns across the back of the police vehicle, flashed celluloidlike across Mom's face, and she said harshly: "I don't believe they've got an ideological bone in their bodies. They're just a bunch of murdering thugs."

The BBC man nodded like he couldn't agree more, but I knew because Mom was always saying so that the British were "treacherous" when it came to politics, and something told me that he wasn't necessarily a friend. I rehearsed what I'd say if he spoke to me. I wanted to tell him how much I loved the War, the constant, heart-stopping adrenaline of it. That I was prepared to die for my country, even though I might be frightened to death doing it.

The fluffy boom poked through my window. "And how," Ian Smith asked gravely, "do *you* feel about the War?"

I squirmed in my seat, hot with shyness. "It's fine," I said. "I don't really mind it."

His face fell. "But—"

Mom interjected: "Why don't you guys come to our farm for some tea or a cold beer or something to eat? We only live a couple of miles down the road." And I could tell that she had jumped ahead—past a slot on the BBC evening news—and was already imagining us as the stars of some tragic documentary, smiling bravely through the tears, while a newly divorced Maud served up Tanganda tea and Highlanders shortbread on the front lawn.

"I was hoping that they'd come back to the house," she said disappointedly as we drove away, sans camera crew. "I thought they could film you riding your horse."

I was disappointed myself because I wouldn't, after all, be famous on the British news, and I said frustratedly: "I wanted to tell him that I love the War."

Mom made a face. "Well, I don't know about 'love,' but I always say to people, 'We'll miss it when it's gone.' There *is* something addictive about living on the edge."

9

In some ways, I occupied two parallel universes. At weekends and school holidays, I spent the nights when my father was away on call-up mentally guarding my mother and sister, convinced that if the house was attacked I'd rescue them with one of my contingency plans. I entered the second universe during term time, when I was sent away to boarding school in Salisbury, 120 kilometers away. At 1:00 p.m. every Friday, Mom or one of the other farmer parents would collect me and deliver me to Rainbow's End, and at dawn on Monday or late Sunday afternoon they'd return me, whipping along the Bulawayo Road, where pink and white cosmos blossoms lined our route, nodding against the blue summer sky. Those sixty-minute drives always seemed endless, so I'd doze in the backseat, counting off landmarks.

After Hartley was Selous, a patchwork of farms with one store, a toilet-size post office, and a grubby motel you could check into but probably never leave. Listing, pollution-spewing long-distance buses hissed to a halt opposite, their roof racks stacked high with gray-dust-coated *kutundu*—cardboard suitcases, bags of *mielie-meal*, protesting poultry, and cheap furniture. Crowds of Africans spilled from them, stiff from their cramped, stinking journeys. They bartered at the roadside stall for red pyramids of tomatoes and yellow-black hands of bananas and green heaps of rape to eat with snowy balls of *sadza*. The nutty smell of fire-blackened maize followed us down the road.

Then came miles of mopani-dotted bush, broken up by cattle, fork-tailed drongo birds on telephone wires, and vibrant lands of tobacco, cotton, and irrigated wheat; then Norton, another garage-and-tearoom-with-milk-shakes speck on the map, then the Lion & Cheetah Park, where you could snuggle up with lion cubs, the Snake Park, the hills of Lake McIllwaine, and a showcase dairy farm, where black-and-white Friesians nibbled at rich emerald pastures.

As you neared the tree-stripped *vleis* on the outskirts of Salisbury, there were glimpses of high-density housing and the occasional mud hut or shanty thrown up without the pride of those in the rural districts, followed by suburbs of small, beige houses, where the Coloureds and Indians lived, and the grander spreads of the mainly white areas, where garden boys tended to perfect beds of flowers and children splashed in sparkly aquamarine pools.

The city center had wide, clean streets and an old-fashioned feel to it. There were parks with fountains with winking copper coins in them and flower sellers with brilliantly hued red-hot pokers, and roses and sweet peas exuding the most incredible perfume. In spring jacaranda trees cloaked every avenue in mauve blossoms. First Street, the main shopping area, was partly pedestrianized, and if you started at Jameson Avenue, you'd pass Truworths and Edgars, homes to the latest fashions, the pile-'em-high, sell-'em-cheap emporium of OK Bazaars, a Wimpy, various banks and steak houses, Sanders luxury department store, where the blue-rinsed posh staff were like cast members of *Are You Being Served?* and, finally, Barbours department store, which was on the corner of Stanley Avenue.

Barbours was the place where Mom went to spray herself with Anaïs Anaïs and gift hunters went to find elephant-hide footstools or massive copper pictures with three-dimensional buffalo charging out of them and I went to get school uniforms or listen to Dionne Warwick in the record section or covet the airbrushed Sara Moon posters in the picture booth. Then we took the gliding, operator-controlled lift to the top floor for pastries, gâteaux, or crème caramel in the restaurant, or milk shakes and Brown Cows (Coke and ice cream) in the palm-fringed open-air café. Barbours was filled with people like us, people who smelled of Lux soap, and when you stepped through its portals you felt safe from the War and the heaving masses disgorging, with their *kutundu*, from the carbon monoxide–issuing buses at the Union Avenue depot just a few streets away.

Safe from the Great Unwashed.

Roosevelt was in Eastlea, a leafy, middle-class suburb, fifteen minutes' drive from the town center. It was an all-girls government school with two boarding hostels, and I was in the newer one, Delano, a flat-roofed glass-and-brick building. The dormitories were partitioned into six cubicles with three or four beds in each. There were private cubicles for two prefects at one end and toilets and showers at the other. In summer, the smell of sanitary pads smoldering in the bathroom incinerators floated unpleasantly through the dorms, offset by ozone-depleting quantities of Impulse spray deodorant, Charlie perfume, and Clearasil acne medication.

Even here we couldn't escape the War entirely, and we had regular emergency drills. Once the alarm went off in the middle of the night, and we thought we were under attack, and we all huddled together in the matrons' quarters and contemplated dying far from our families, and some girls sobbed about their boyfriends: "I'm never going to see Frankie *again!*"

For the most part, hostel life was a world gloriously free from adult supervision. The matrons checked on the dormitories only rarely, and it was left to the prefects to watch over us—a job for which they had little appetite, although they did enjoy enslaving us. First-year girls were known as Sprogs and expected to skivvy for them in innumerable ways, involving bed making, shoe polishing, and tea and coffee brewing. However, once they discovered I made execrable coffee and was almost completely useless at other chores, I was quickly relieved of most of my duties and they settled for tormenting me, usually by making me stand on a chair in the dining room while they mocked me and the rest of the girls stamped their feet.

Luckily I had plenty of allies, starting with Jean, a freckled farm kid from Umvukwes with laughing brown eyes and railway-track braces. She and I had been mutually bad at the sex quiz conducted by the prefects on our first night in Delano.

"What's cunnilingus?" we were asked.

"What's a condom?"

"What's another word for blow job?"

Jean and I had absolutely no idea. I'd only recently learned what French kissing was, thanks to a junior school friend who had demonstrated it at length when I was staying at her house. She assured me that I wouldn't survive high school without it. She never explained what the word for two girls kissing was, but the sex quiz helpfully supplied it. When Merina and I became friends, we ran around the hostel with the odd, repugnant term rolling around our mouths and jokingly directed it at people like Bruna, a strapping Afrikaner girl with flushed cheeks, crinkly raven hair, and gray-blue eyes, which she fastened on Merina during evening prep. We giggled to each other over Bruna's tendencies, but we didn't really believe that she might actually be of questionable sexual orientation. As far as we knew, there were no gay people in Rhodesia.

Merina had grown up in Zambia, where she'd led a relatively sheltered life with much loved but much older parents, and when she came to Roosevelt she had a vulnerable, gawky, alone look I had long since recognized in myself. We were both outsiders. In time we became part of a big social group, but we always remained slightly separate from it. We were too gauche, too ungainly, and too dreamy ever to really fit in; but more than that, we didn't *want* to fit in. Fitting in implied conformity and conformity implied normality and the surrender of dreams, which led—inexorably, as we saw it—to a suffocating destiny of office jobs, scheduled holidays, marriage to a tobacco farmer in some godforsaken rural location, stretch marks, and death.

From the day that we became friends—a date we solemnly marked while on shoe-cleaning duty by pricking our fingers and vowing to be blood sisters—Merina and I had only two obsessions, and neither of them involved study. We wanted to become pop singers, and we wanted to escape from our boardinghouse, a fortress with an alarmed and guarded perimeter fence. To those ends, we operated a series of scams that kept us busy for most of our school days. As a result, while our classmates were locked away in dreary afternoon prep sessions, Merina and I spent our time swimming with boys, watching *The Blue Lagoon*, and eating pineapple and cream gâteaux at Barbours department store.

Toward the end of our first year, our biology teacher let slip that if we volunteered to clean the cages of the laboratory rats, we wouldn't be required to attend afternoon prep, a stupefying homework session lasting two and a half hours. Lining the cages with newspaper, refilling food and water bowls, and playing with the rats took us under twenty minutes, leaving us with over two hours of freedom, in which we could work on our tans, practice gymnastics, or discuss what to name our band when we became pop singers.

When, after a few weeks, our charges went away (we hoped to a better life but more probably to the dissecting table), we saw no reason to mention that fact to the matrons who signed us out each afternoon. They'd already nicknamed us "The Ratters." For the next three years, we left the hostel religiously at three o'clock each afternoon, sometimes to clean the cages of nonexistent rats, sometimes to clean the tanks of nonexistent fish, and sometimes to jog. The jogging club was a short-lived but genius invention that allowed us to jog around the block to the home of a friend of a friend, who had a swimming pool and a son with lots of mates. We had a wonderful time raiding the fridge and lolling about the poolside with various boys until someone (probably the friend) reported us and the fun came to an end.

When we weren't escaping or practicing singing, our time was taken up with trying to improve our looks, which, infuriatingly, had gone into decline at the exact stage we'd started to care about them. Acne bloomed, hair became lank and greasy, and cellulite became a regular topic of conversation in our group. I couldn't understand why my family's good genes had not been passed down to me. At high school, a new set of children had been introduced to my parents and been suitably impressed. "Are those your *folks*? Your old queen looks more like your sister! Your old man looks like a movie star!"

And though I was proud and secretly agreed, I felt more than ever like a duck delivered to two swans.

For help we turned to Miss Zeederberg, our English teacher, who also took us for guidance. There were three dominant forces at Roosevelt. There was the headmistress, Miss Robinson, who arrived on an archaic bicycle each morning, skirts billowing up over sausagey ripples of cellulite, and then there was the real power behind the throne: the deputy head, Miss Saunders, nicknamed "Bubbles." It was said that she'd been a gifted ballerina before injury robbed her of a career, and she was now as wide as she was high. But she was tremendously dedicated, and it was obvious that it was her energy and integrity that drove school policy. She had a way of teaching geography that permanently ingrained in your mind the methods that the Eskimos employed to build igloos and the contents of the caribou's stomach.

Bubbles and Miss Robinson and some of the other maiden-aunt teachers cast disapproving or envious glances at the third force, Miss

Zeederberg, who was attractive, exuberant, and immensely popular. She had curly hair and glasses and was stylish in a cool way. Miss Zeederberg held guidance classes in which she gave advice on skin and hair care, diet, and relationships—most obtained from *Cosmopolitan*—which we boarding school girls, who didn't have access to such things, treated as gospel. She had a Question Box, into which you could pop anonymous questions you couldn't possibly ask your parents and were too shy to ask your friends, and she'd read them out and answer them with perfect frankness.

After her classes we'd beg ingredients off our matron, Mrs. Cook, who was tall and angular, with grooved smoker's skin and a cruise-liner nose. She walked as if she was leaning into a tornado. She and her dachsunds could have been triplets. She called me and Merina "The Gannets" because we were always starving and scrounging for food. She'd supply us with cookies and what she could in the way of beauty aids, and we'd steam our faces over the basins, exfoliate them with *mielie-meal,* and apply oatmeal or egg-white masks. At home, we conditioned our hair with beer and egg yolk and bleached it in the sun with lemon juice.

The guidance advice was great, but it was Miss Zeederberg's English lessons that I lived for, probably because she singled me out and made me feel like I was special in some way. The attention embarrassed me almost as much as it inspired me, but it also made me feel as if becoming a writer might be my goal, too. I worked for her, trusted her, and tried for her in a way I'd never done for anyone else. On the day that she left, I cried. We stood on the tiny landing outside her classroom, and she said to me: "You'll have written a book by the time you're eighteen."

I was shocked and a little flattered, but mostly I thought she was just being kind. "No, I won't," I said, thinking, I won't if you go. I won't if I don't have you to believe in me.

She hugged me. "Believe in yourself," she told me. "You will."

Periodically my universes collided when my friends came to visit Rainbow's End. Jean was a rough-and-tumble farm kid, so she and I climbed trees and explored the game park, but Merina liked to go on careful horse rides or to sit on the weir wall and fish for bream, which

Madala would then fry up for us, dusting the fillets lightly with flour and tossing them into a pan of boiling Sunflower oil. When they were golden, we'd drench the white flesh with garden lemon juice and eat them with lots of salt.

Merina lived in suburban Bindura in a house so spotless you had to remove the candlewick cover if you wanted to sit on the bed. She had a fantastic, elegant mother who smoked cigarettes with a long holder and had furrowed creases of laughter at the corners of her eyes, and a Scottish miner father who brewed up mulberry wine, could recite twenty-five-verse poems, and was irrepressibly happy. At Merina's house we ate epic brunches and climbed nearby kopjes in search of flame lilies, but at Rainbow's End we were preoccupied with music. We sang along with Dolly Parton, Kenny Rogers, Barbra Streisand, and Olivia, and fantasized that we were already famous and in rehearsal for a show.

Afterward we'd go in search of the horses. Once, a storm rolled in over the jagged outline of compound huts and caught us unawares. It rained so hard that the drops stung our faces like beaded glass, and we ran from the theatrical menace of it and the horses with their wet, darkened flanks. At the tobacco barns, the nearest shelter, we ducked into the grading sheds. The air in the sheds was humid and smelled of hessian and tobacco scrap. We wrung out our clothes and found a bale to shiver on while the rain drummed a noisy African rhythm on the corrugated-iron roof. There was something safe and still about the big, echoing space. We sang a song or two to experiment with the acoustics.

When the storm passed, we walked home through puddles, kicking water and throwing mud pies until our limbs were streaked with dirt, our hair hanging in gritty rats' tails. We filled the tub in the pawpaw bathroom and peeled off our filthy clothes. Underneath, our skin was goose-bump rough and so white with cold that as we sank beneath the bubbles, the water had a peppery scald to it. We wallowed in it like scrawny mermaids and warmed our bones with steaming mugs of malty Milo. We felt invincible.

Later, when my world was imploding, I'd remember that day and others like it, and it was those that became my retreat.

Those that gave me something to hold on to.

10

The War was getting to everyone. Dad was gone for long stretches in the PATU and rebelled against the shackles of domesticity after the hard-drinking, death-dicing, macho extremes of the Army; and the warning call from the terrorists had taken its toll on my mother. She was diagnosed with a heart murmur and prescribed a small pharmacy of pills. She looked pale and drawn, her hands shaky. She and Dad began to fight like they hadn't fought since Cape Town, and I ran from the house to escape the things they said. I ran to be with Star or Cassandra or in the dappled glens with Jenny. I took Lisa, and we hid down by the river and let the peaceful constancy of it—the plodding-sheep clouds and the sky mirrored in its green depths; the bright blurred wings and chirrups of red bishops, wax-bills, and pied and malachite kingfishers—shut away the hurtful echoes.

After their rows, Mom referred to Dad as "Your Father" and he called her "Your Mother."

As in: "I don't understand why Your Father has to snarl at me all the time."

As in: "I'll never understand Your Mother."

Nothing strained relations more than a trip to Hartley Club, which had changed little since Billy Mowbray's comment to Grampy in his 1935 letter about there being "far too much scandal and gossip and drink" on the Hartley Gatooma scene, "though no doubt there are nice people if you look for them."

The club still gave me the same afraid feeling it had when I was eight. For Lee and Carol Walters, the Keevil kids, and others who came from happy, sporty families, the club was presumably a haven of tennis, golf, rugby, and squash, where healthy parents in whites and bobby socks served up aces with orange slices and birdies with lime-decorated G & Ts. But the rest of us loathed it in varying degrees. A night at the club meant the men sitting at the bar talking about the floppies and the *kaffirs* and "The Situation," and the women sitting separately on the veranda with the babies, and Lis and me being sent away with Cokes, Turkish delights, and packets of Willards tomato sauce chips to sleep in the car, or hang around the floodlit car park with all the other cold, overtired, bored-half-to-death, and eaten-alive-by-mosquitoes children awaiting parents the worse for wear.

If some kid was crying or had hurt themself and you made the mistake of actually taking them into the club, gamma rays of disapproval came your way, and your mother or theirs tried to hush you up and dismiss you as rapidly as possible with even more cool drinks and sweets, although occasionally a beer-bellied farmer ran drink-brightened eyes over you and tried to haul you onto his knee, or commented in a low voice intended for your ears only: "You can put your shoes under my bed anytime."

Some of these club nights were preceded by afternoons of rugby, and those were even more hellish, because afterward the testosterone-addled men lined up beers on the bar and there was no telling when they'd be ready to leave. Mom, who didn't drink much and didn't belong to any clique, once became weary of the girlie banter of the wives and tried to join my father at the bar. That led to Armageddon on the road to Rainbow's End because, Dad said through his teeth: "All the other *decent* women sit on the veranda but not *my* wife. No, my wife wants to sit at the bar with all the men."

So Lis and I were unsure which was worse, the wait or the aftermath. When, after an eternity, it came time to leave, Dad was always laughing too loudly, and Mom, who'd grown to hate the club "like poison," looked pained or in pain, and then they fought over the car keys and, all the way home, headlights zigzagging madly along the strip road, about Dad's fitness to drive.

Then an intruder got into the yard when my mother and sister were alone at Rainbow's End. Mom awoke to the sound of the dogs attacking someone or something. Lisa was sleeping in the bed beside her, as she always did when Dad was away, and at first Mom was too petrified to move. But as the snarling moved closer and closer to the house, she forced herself to leap out of bed, fetch her pistol, and radio for help on the Agricalert.

The woman who answered was an old witch from Mom's factory days at David Whitehead. She said in a nasal drawl: "Are you suuure it's a terrorist?"

"Obviously I can't *see* if it's a terrorist . . ." Mom was almost sobbing she was so frightened. "It's pitch-black outside. But there's definitely a person out there. The dogs are going mad."

The controller said in the same patronizing tone: "Look, we're dealing with a lot of emergencies here. Do we *really* have to send someone?"

And Mom, because she was sensitive and prone to self-sabotage, practically shouted, "Don't bother."

The hysterical dogs were right outside her bedroom. Mom fired one shot out of the bathroom window before the gun jammed. Lisa came to life with the bang, confused and mumbling, but soon went back to sleep. And for the rest of the night Mom leaned petrified against the bedroom door, convinced that a killer was on his way to break it down. When dawn came like a salve, she found a line of bloody footprints traversing the flower bed outside her bedroom window.

In Hartley, she met a farmer who told her that he and his friends had heard her desperate call on the Agricalert. Aghast, Mom asked: "Then why didn't you help me?"

He looked at his shoes. "You don't understand, our wives wouldn't let us."

That's when it struck her that she was Gadzema's *femme fatale*.

"Even though," she told me later, "I've *done* absolutely nothing."

The intruder was the final straw. Dad had several long call-ups in the works, and he didn't want Mom and Lisa on the farm on their own. So Mom rented a flat in Salisbury for three months and took a temp job with an accountancy firm. I remained at boarding school, and we all drove back to Rainbow's End at weekends when Dad was there. The flat was dusky rose and faux Moroccan, and while Mom was there a young American came to visit and told me that he wanted to marry Mom and take her away to his grandfather's Morgan stud farm in Fort Worth, Texas, which since Morgans were my favorite breed of horse and Dad and Mom were not getting along very well, seemed an excellent idea. But Mom dispatched him, saying she was only in love with Dad. Plus, she said, he was too young.

Another time her boss came around when she was out and I was looking after Lisa and tried his best to lure me away to the park. But I'd watched him climb the stairs from the kitchen window, and it was obvious that he was rolling drunk, so I opened the door on the chain and showed him the pot of boiling water that I'd be pouring on him if he didn't leave me and my sister alone. For twenty minutes he pleaded and wheedled, and then he repaired to the car park, where he accosted Mom when she returned after dark and tried to get *her* to go somewhere with him. They had a heated discussion and the following morning, when she came out to go to work, she discovered he'd let down her tires.

Once again I had the feeling that everything in our lives was not exactly as it seemed.

When her lease expired, Mom moved not, as expected, back to Rainbow's End but into a larger flat in the same complex. It was just for another three months, she said, just until the farm was safer, but privately I thought she was enjoying the Salisbury life too much to leave. In those days Mom seemed like a remote, beautiful stranger. She took on a Career Girl glamour, and she embraced her newfound independence with ladies' lunches of fish au gratin in the Birdcage Restaurant at Sanders, a blue-tiled roof garden with tinkling fountains, fake canaries in gold-painted cages, and expansive pools of sunlight. Lisa was in nursery school by then, and Granny and I (in the school holidays) were available as babysitters, so Mom was out a lot and never appeared to notice if I attempted to copy what Maud did on the farm and cleaned and polished the flat and made the beds and washed the clothes in the bath.

But behind the façade, Mom was filled with the same simmering anger that had always boiled in Dad. I noticed it in the little things. Twice she lost her temper with me because my hair was a "horrible bird's nest," and she insisted on wrenching at it so brutally with the comb that I cried out with pain, and then she didn't care and didn't say sorry.

With all of this going on, it was hard to take in the seismic shifts in the political landscape. At Roosevelt we were allowed to watch TV only once during the week, and that was a special concession granted to us on a Wednesday evening to allow us to see the sequined, bitchy, shoulder-padded extravaganza that was *Dallas*, to which we were addicted.

I rarely saw the news or read a paper, so the changes as they came presented themselves to me as a series of visuals. Long lines of jubilant black voters, snaking through the savanna and up to dusty polling stations in the April elections. Images of Bishop Muzorewa, a smiling, benevolent figure in the robes of his Methodist faith, accepting the keys of prime ministerial office from Ian Smith, who now looked pale and drawn, his body language increasingly defeated. All of our fears about the chaos that might follow the election of a black prime minister proved groundless because Abel Muzorewa turned out to be extremely nice and everything continued as normal. The only real difference was that Rhodesia was renamed Zimbabwe-Rhodesia and—in a poignant, richly symbolic ceremony—our green-and-white Rhodesian flag, which had always seemed to me to be the very best on the face of the earth, was lowered for the last time in September.

Unfortunately, the outside world was still displeased with us because they saw Muzorewa as a puppet of the whites, and the War was as deadly as ever. So that same month, even as our security forces launched raids on Frelimo (Front for the Liberation of Mozambique) and ZANLA (Zimbabwe African National Liberation Army) bases in Mozambique's Gaza Province, Ian Smith and Muzorewa prepared to sit at the negotiating table with the guerrilla leaders at the British-hosted Lancaster House Conference in London.

Whatever the politics of it, Rainbow's End had never felt more dangerous, and every good-bye still felt like the last. Dad put himself in the line of fire so often that it was hard not to wonder if he had a death wish. In late 1979, when our friends Bev and Fred Bradnick (in whose garden Lisa had once found a live grenade) were firebombed by terrorists on their farm on the Lowood Road, Dad was first on the scene. He'd expected shooting or scenes of devastation, but there was silence. The only sounds were the doves and the faint crackle of thatch. Dad used a garden hose to dampen the cinders, and then he climbed through a window with his FN. He feared a bloodbath. He walked from room to room, checking possible hiding places for terrorists or children. But the house was empty. Fred was a Selous Scout, and he'd used his skills to save his family.

Later, when Dad told the Bradnicks what he'd done, the blood drained from Fred's face. He'd booby-trapped the house as he left it so that any terrorists attempting to loot the family's belongings would be blown to pieces if they opened a cupboard.

"Hell, Errol," he said, "it's a miracle you weren't killed."

Dad grinned as he relayed the story to us afterward. "If I had opened the wrong cupboard I'd have had my chips," he said. For some reason he found the idea funny.

We were a family again at Christmas, but although we made our annual outing to see the lights on First Street—the giant flame lily winking jewel-like in the night rain—the overall atmosphere of the festivities convinced Lisa that Christmas was the worst day of the year because "it always rains or a dog dies or we have a big family fight." One Christmas we even had to interrupt our lunch to put a shotgun pellet in the hood of a massive Egyptian cobra with a white rat in its mouth (it was outside Maud's *kaya*, and for once she and Dad concurred completely and insisted: "We have to kill it before it kills someone!") despite my pleas for clemency so that it could enjoy its own Christmas dinner.

In the New Year, Mom returned to her flat in Salisbury, and it became apparent that she and Dad were undergoing a trial separation. Muzorewa had stepped down after a night of prayer, a new election was planned, and a cease-fire had supposedly come into effect at the end of December, so the War was no longer an excuse. But Mom kept going back and forth to the farm to try to work it out.

By the end of March, she and Dad were reconciled and had decided that all of their problems could be solved at a stroke if we just moved to Australia and started afresh. That suited me, because it would mean being closer to Olivia, with whom I was at least partially in love (platonically), and Dad liked the idea of working on a cattle station. So Mom assigned herself the task of researching the possibility of us living in Queensland. She deposited Lisa at Granny and Grampy's African violet–filled flat for a month and flew off to explore the beaches and tropical rain forests of Australia.

The sweeping changes going on in the rest of the country—the pouring toward us, like lava, of black Africa in all of its musical, magical, violent, untamed, unpredictable glory—were reflected in our dormitories at school. Delano filled up with the progeny of ministers, former guerrillas, and businessmen. When the first black girl had moved into our dormitory the previous year, we'd welcomed her and made a big fuss over her and done our best to include her, but the new girls had plenty of friends and made it clear they no longer had any need of our magnanimity. They occupied one section of our dormitory and we occupied the other. They tried to come to terms with our long blond hairs in the basins, sickly white-girl potions, and unwieldy knives and forks, and we tried to get used to their short, springy hairs, special wooden combs, and penchant for eating with their hands.

In the first week of March, our dormitory reverberated with the music of Oliver Mtukudzi, the Harare Mambos, and Bob Marley & the Wailers as the Africans monitored the progress of the elections on their radios. While the white girls watched, subdued and even depressed, the black girls rushed around in a high state of jubilation, their strong, chocolate arms pumping the air, their womanly bodies straining against their turquoise uniforms, and when the results were announced, they whooped and screamed and jumped on their beds, and whirled around hugging each other and tribal-danced along the parquet corridor in an ecstasy of celebration.

"Mugabe, Moo-gar-bear," they chanted.

Jean and I looked at each other. *"Who?"* we said.

But what was quite clear was that they were all black and we were all white and it was like a party we hadn't been invited to.

Independence
1980–1983

Wicklow School kids

1

I can pinpoint the exact moment when I knew that the War was over and it had taken something with it. I was in a lift at Barbours. The doors slid shut on the dazzle of copper buffalo, carved ivory tusks, and game-skin belly-button warmers "For the Man Who Has Everything!" and we rose in a seasick jolt. It was a weekday lunch hour, and the lift was stuffed with Salisbury secretaries and farmers' wives in cotton sundresses (sunspots like brown animal prints on their tanned shoulders), plus one or two awkward farmers in khaki, and absolutely nobody was looking at anyone else. And I had the strongest, saddest sense that the glue that had bound us together—*through thick and thin*—had come undone.

After that, every time we stopped at Hartley Post Office or the Farmers' Co-op, someone was leaving. It was like a pandemic, like the Great Flu sweeping people away, like a photo where someone had airbrushed out all the white faces. They were going to Australia, New Zealand, South Africa, America, Canada, and the U.K. They were going with mixed emotions. Some went with gladness, some with regret, some, especially those who'd lost loved ones, with hatred, and some with doom-laden prophesies: "*Ag*, you know, it's *mush* [great] in the bush, but with these *okes* running things, this country is going to go one way. One way."

Others said: "The writing's on the wall."

And others—those who were staying, like my mother—said we'd been sold down the river by the British and the South Africans, who had engineered Robert Mugabe, the former guerrilla leader of ZANLA, into power, if only by turning a blind eye. Although the Commonwealth observers had declared the elections to be free and fair, there'd been widespread reports of voter intimidation by Mugabe's supporters. But everyone knew that, regardless of how it had come about, it was the right result.

The result that the majority of the country wanted.

With a suddenness more frightening than anything that had led up to it, the War was over. The country that we'd fought for, lost limbs for, died and put our lives on the line for was no longer our country. Zimbabwe-Rhodesia became plain but glorious Zimbabwe, a Karanga term probably meaning "House of Stone," and Rhodesia became a dirty word. History books depicting Colonialists like Cecil John Rhodes and David Livingstone as visionary heroes were burned, statues were taken down, and any street or town that paid tribute to the British "invaders" renamed: Hartley became Chegutu, Salisbury was now Harare, and Gatooma, where I was born, Kadoma. Avenues like Jameson and Rhodes were named after African leaders like Samora Machel and Kenneth Kaunda or former guerrilla commanders like Josiah Tongogara.

The communism that we'd always been taught to fear and despise was suddenly everywhere, albeit in the garb of socialism. Banners advertising the Palestine Liberation Organization were draped over fences on Second Avenue. Grainy black-and-white propaganda films about the Soviet Union and China clogged up peak viewing time on the television. Mugabe was not just Prime Minister Mugabe (later he would make himself president "for life") but *Comrade* Robert Mugabe, and everyone else in the government and civil service was Comrade, too, and at school the children of the new ruling elite called each other and sometimes me Comrade in a way that suggested I was anything but.

Owning war memorabilia of any kind or weapons that weren't licensed strictly for the purpose of hunting or protecting crops from wild pigs and other animals became an offense too grave to risk. My WE MADE RHODESIA GREAT T-shirt, Dad's Grey's Scout mugs, and records like *Troopie Songs*, "Green Leader," and "The Deafening Silence" had to go. So did Dad's camouflage, webbing, grenades, rifles, Army sleeping bag, and other kit. We destroyed what we could and dumped the rest down mine shafts or disused wells at the ends of overgrown dirt tracks, transporting it furtively like it was porn or dangerous subversion.

• • •

But these things were nothing compared with the death of the War.

The war I loved.

The cease-fire had come into effect at the end of 1979. Within hours of the announcement, grimy, war-weary guerrillas had started turning up at assembly points to surrender their weapons to men like Dad, who just days earlier would have shot them without blinking but were now, thanks to the Games Politicians Play, simply logging their AK47s and bayonets methodically. Some, but by no means all, Rhodesian soldiers had returned to their bases. So effective was the killing machine that had been the Selous Scouts and so audacious some of their missions—which included the infamous 1976 raid into Mozambique in which seventy-seven Scouts disguised as guerrillas had driven into the heart of a ZANLA camp in a sort of Trojan Horse tactic and, after being greeted as returning heroes, killed more than twelve hundred guerrillas with not one of their own lost—that many of them chose to slip quietly over the border into South Africa, taking their weapons with them.

Overnight our way of life ended. The culture that had grown up around the War—the nightly check-ins on the Agricalert; the convoys, curfews, and songs; the bonds born out of terror—was eradicated in an instant, and all that was left was a dawning realization of what had taken place. It was like going to sleep in Jamaica and waking up in the pages of *1984*.

All my life I'd been taught to value and hold sacred the name of Rhodesia and the history and blood ties that bonded me to it. I'd been raised on the belief that ours was the very best country on earth, with the best climate under God's sun, and that everything about it was special: our landscape, our wildlife, our green-and-white flag, the living flame that was our national flower, the flame lily, our national anthem, set to Beethoven's "Ode to Joy." And that because these things were so special, they were worth fighting for and worth dying for. Even our war was better than anyone else's war because we had the best songs and the most cheerful troopie canteens and the bravest, most dedicated soldiers. And because we were told these things so often and saw all of this beauty and courage and magnificence with our own eyes, our land became our life, our nationality our identity.

Now my identity was gone, and the shock was overwhelming.

The euphoria that erupted on Independence Day in April 1980, when Bob Marley rocked Harare with his anthem "Zimbabwe," was like nothing I'd ever seen before. It was as if Africa had been given permission to be Africa. The whooping women and drum-pounding men who had performed for so long behind the midnight silhouette of huts at Rainbow's End were now out in the open, celebrating on the streets, their music thudding insistently at the walls of your chest. It was the sound of a releasing, the sound of pure, untrammeled joy. You could see it in the smiles and newly direct gazes of everyone from the petrol pump attendants to the picannins who sold fishing worms on the roadside near Lake McIllwaine (soon to be renamed Lake Chivero). You could see it in the way that restaurants and department stores like Barbours suddenly filled up with black businessmen in smart suits accompanied by sophisticated women in vibrant traditional dress or designer outfits from London. You could see it in the surging confidence of the children, the wealthier of whom no longer had to walk six miles to school and whose work ethic could now bear fruit. You could see it in the previously banned novels of writers like Chenjerai Hove, which appeared as if from nowhere on the bookshelves.

I thought, incredulously, *Where* have all these people been? These dynamic businessmen and their head-turning partners, these artists and writers, these accomplished lawyers, journalists, and politicians? It was almost as if they'd been waiting in the wings of some vast discriminatory theater production. But I wasn't able to allow the thought to become fully formed because it was too much to take in, that we, the white Rhodesians, might in some way have been responsible for their nonappearance on the stage.

Of course, not every African was purely joyful. Some people felt that destiny had treated them unfairly or even wickedly, and they wanted immediate reparation. Some felt a sudden discontent with their lot. The Maud who'd returned, divorced, from the Tribal Trust Lands, was surly. Her old lightness had gone. When the new Zimbabwe fifty-dollar note was released and Dad went to pay her wages with it, she held it up so that the sun illuminated its battleground red and said accusingly: "The color of our *blood*."

He was incensed. He'd always distrusted her, always thought she was "spoiled," and now he had incontrovertible proof of her treachery.

Mom, to whom Maud was chicken soup, a surrogate mother, and a security blanket all in one, was really shocked. "I truly didn't know she felt like that," she said. "Truly I didn't."

For me it was the euphoria that was the giveaway. That and the fact that I'd only recently registered the name of Mugabe, and yet every black person in Zimbabwe seemed to have known about him for years and, depending on whether they were from the Mashona tribe like Mugabe or Ndebele like Nkomo, either held him in iconic status or entertained strong views on him. But it was the euphoria that told me that the war of freedom, which in my childish innocence I had believed we were fighting against Communism, had turned out to be someone else's war of freedom. *We* were the terrorists. Our heroes were not heroes at all, they were evil racists. Only black people were allowed to be heroes.

The sense of disillusionment I felt was total. The country I had loved so much that at times I almost wished I could die for it was not the country I had thought it was. We had repressed people, oppressed people, tortured people, and murdered people for the worst of possible reasons: the color of their skin. Twenty thousand people had died in our war, apparently for nothing.

I felt like an earthquake had taken place in my head. Because although at thirteen I cared nothing for, and understood nothing about, politics, the effects of Independence were everywhere to see, and I couldn't square those with history as it had been told to me, or come to terms with the idea that so much pain and suffering and brutality could have been caused to so many innocent victims just because we didn't want black people to have the vote, just because we thought we had a superior ability to run the country. And if it was really a war about race and votes, why were the Communists involved? All I'd ever heard about China and the Soviet Union had been their horrifying human rights records. It wasn't as if they had the ordinary people of Zimbabwe's best interests at heart. So I couldn't understand if what I thought was true was true or if there was more to the story. And I couldn't accept, *wouldn't* accept, that twenty thousand people might have died in vain or with dishonor. And it was made very clear to us that it was in vain and with dishonor because when Mugabe asked the Koreans to build Heroes' Acre, a memorial site to honor the fallen of the Second Chimurenga, as our war was now known, only former "freedom fighters" were buried or remembered there. The remains or pictures of the black soldiers who had volunteered to fight against them in such numbers that they made up two-thirds of the Rhodesian Army were not welcome. And yet, if they hadn't died with honor for their country, for whom and to what purpose had they died?

And how could the world be so upside down that Joshua Nkomo, who'd laughed after his fighters hacked to death the survivors of the *Hunyani* crash, and whose ZIPRA forces had been responsible for the murders at Rainbow's End (the attack had been found detailed in their diaries when they were caught), was now our minister of home affairs and was seen as a moderate and a Good Man and we were glad to have him in power?

How could these things be possible?

What justification could anyone have had for taking the life of an eleven-year-old boy with nature in his eyes and the freedom of falcons in his heart?

What right did they have to torture and murder Agnes, an innocent, loving young woman with her whole life before her?

And what of the atrocities the Rhodesians had committed? How could the War have been sold to us in such a way as to make it not only desirable but a matter of pride to drive into a camp of what we now understood to be African nationalists fighting for the right to be treated equally in their own country and slaughter every living soul, twelve hundred people, leaving ten times their number in bereaved and broken relatives?

How could we have celebrated the deaths of a similar number of nationalists in the "Green Leader" mission in Zambia as if we were cheering the results of a football match?

And how could that be right on the day that they were terrorists and wrong on the next, when they were freedom fighters?

I had no answers for these or any other questions. Lying on my bunk at Rainbow's End, my stomach twisting into habitual knots every time the dogs barked, the only thing I knew for sure was that fear and the warm glow of fighting for what I believed to be a worthy cause had been constants in my life for so long that I missed those feelings—*ached* for them—when they were gone.

The War had held everyone and everything together and helped save as many marriages as it destroyed, but now couples who'd spent a good part of the last decade trying to stay alive suddenly realized that survival was the only thing they had in common. Men who'd seen things they didn't want to see drank too much. Others found that they had lost their whole reason for existence, that they no longer knew who they were. Wives found it hard to adjust to having their rarely seen husbands pacing the house again, interfering in the running of the home, trying to wrest back control. As a child of non-divorced, though definitely not harmoniously married, parents, I was in a minority in my class.

The person most sanguine about the end of the War was Dad. He was a little disappointed that things had not worked out differently, that we weren't going to be running the country after all, but mainly he was just relieved the fighting was finished.

"*Ag*, it's almost like it was a losing battle from the beginning," he said philosophically.

For the most part, the "Rhodies," as the whites were nicknamed, were so accustomed to adapting, to surviving sanctions with deals on the black market, to "Making a Plan," that they just adapted once again. They accepted, sometimes grudgingly, sometimes with a shrug, the new black government and the changes as they came—the new town names and the right of Africans to access all areas—and if they didn't accept them they used humor to cope, making "Banana Republic" jokes about our new president, Canaan Banana. Some things, such as the moral right of individuals to interracial relationships, would take longer to swallow, and those were best ignored or regarded with pity for the time being.

Once they found that life could, in essence, continue as before, the Rhodies returned to their booze cruises on the Zambezi and to Lake Kariba with its fighting silver tiger fish and epic red sunsets parodied in a thousand gruesome paintings. They went on shooting elephant, fly-fishing in Inyanga, plying their beer bellies with Castle lagers and T-bone steaks, and dividing along gender lines at generous-spirited, camaraderie-warmed *braais*. They replaced their RHODESIA IS SUPER shirts with ZIMBABWE baseball caps, and the country became a sunny paradise again. And if now there were more black faces in restaurants, on golf courses, and at holiday resorts than there were white, well, that made it even more of a paradise because it had become an inclusive paradise—although obviously a percentage of Rhodies would continue to talk about floppies and *kaffirs* and how they wished we'd won the War.

And, of course, we had our own personal paradise at Rainbow's End—the only problem being that Mom herself had been airbrushed out of it. When she'd stepped off the plane from Australia at the end of April, arms laden with I LOVE AUSTRALIA T-shirts and toy koalas, having missed Independence entirely, Dad had decided that not only did he have no intention of leaving Africa but he had no intention of remaining married. So Mom moved in with Uncle James in what was now Harare until she could talk sense into my father. She found work with a company supplying the government with materials to build new villages for people displaced by the War, and Lisa went to a school down the road from James's house.

So our paradise was, in a sense, a fool's paradise.

But I chose not to think that way, or at any rate to believe that any glitch in our happiness was temporary, because Mom and Dad had always fought and made up, and Mom had always been off somewhere else, doing something else, and we'd always all been separate, and the fundamentals of my existence—Morning Star, who at nearly eighteen months old had a glossy, arching neck and a shock of black mane; my forays into the game park with Jenny; and my long Sunday rides with my father—were still the same.

And maybe Mom could tell that, because right before she left the farm, when I was relaxing on her cool eiderdown, chatting to her, she suddenly said to me: "Nothing ever fazes you, does it?"

I grinned lazily. "Nuh-uh," I murmured, and it was only later, replaying the question in my head, that I felt a pang in my chest, a catch, and realized that there had been a warning in the words that felt like a premonition.

2

In Africa, paradise is finite. As Karen Blixen, Beryl Markham, Rian Malan, and Kuki Gallmann all discovered, it doesn't belong to outsiders, to the people who have lived there for centuries, or even to those people who love it best. The past has a stranglehold on it. The immutable laws of survival, of death and renewal, follow a cycle that takes no account of the emotion invested into it or the blood shed for it.

I can still remember the day that paradise as I knew it ended. It was May 1980, and Dad had come to James's house. The lawn was yellow-dry with the winter sun, and there were cats basking in among the rocks and aloes, and bees floating in the birdbath, and a bay horse temporarily living out on the dirt area by the *kaya*. I can picture Dad standing by the pool in his town clothes and thinking that they weren't him. That in them he was something of a stranger. That, detached from the land, from nature, he always seemed less than the sum of his parts, his stomach too large, his hair too neat, his hands embarrassed and in his pockets or even trembling slightly while shielding a flaring match from the wind.

He was there for five minutes. No sooner had I flown into his arms for a hug and cried: "How's the farm, Dad? How are all my babies?" to which he replied: "No, my friend, everything's fine," than Mom came out of the house looking like an invalid to see him, yawning, without makeup, still in her nightie and dressing gown.

I was furious with her for not making an effort. How could she hope to win him back looking like that? Evidently Dad thought the same thing because after a brief screaming match, he departed. I followed him to his truck, panic burning in my chest. I pleaded with him to stay, but he shook me off with a curt "Talk to your mother."

Inside the house, Mom was running a bath. The luminous rush of jade water made mirror-ball light patterns on the ceiling and old enamel.

I burst in as she was about to get undressed. "What's wrong with you?" I cried. "Why are you always so horrible to him? He tries so hard with you, and you're always pushing him away and criticizing him and being mean to him, and now he's gone and it's *your* fault. I wanted to see him. I wanted to spend time with him."

Mom said coldly: "If you knew the truth about him, you'd never speak to him again."

I caught my breath, sniffed, and said slowly: "What do you mean?" And even as I asked the question, I was as sure as I'd ever been about anything in my short life that I shouldn't know the answer.

I sat down on the edge of the bath.

It felt like a precipice.

The roar of the taps shut off. In the sudden silence, the metronome echo of the final few drips was like the countdown to an execution. Mine.

Then, one by one, the building blocks of my life were taken apart.

The next time I saw my father I saw him from a long way away. In between, random incidents had been recast in a grim new light, and they reared from my memory like murderers from a fog. Wasn't it only yesterday that I'd parted the yellow curtains of the double-story to see him reeling in and out of the shadows, fists flailing, shielding himself against the unpracticed punches of the stranger in the office shirt? And wasn't it ironic that it was in that house I'd spent hours singing along to "D-I-V-O-R-C-E" and "I Don't Wanna Play House," not understanding the words but taking on, in a kid's way, their mantle of unbearable sadness: "Me and li-i-ttle J-O-E . . . Will be goin' away . . ."

But that was only one of a million memories to sift through. There were looks, there were laughs, there were rows and unexplained absences; there were suspicious phone calls and terms of endearment. Which were real and which weren't? All of our moves lost their innocence and became instead futile—piteous even—attempts to wipe the slate clean.

Once he knew that I knew, Dad was full of theories and excuses. It had to do with the Army, the War, the family holiday when Mom and Lisa had gone to England without us. It was proof of what he'd known all along, that you should never marry above your class. Not that there was any class difference between them, but because Dad's background was relentlessly blue-collar, and Mom was "cultured" and liked the finer things in life, he'd put her on a pedestal and convinced himself there was one. And that was what hurt the most, because I knew it was the one thing he truly believed, and I hated him for saying it out loud; for allowing himself to think, even for a second, that something as shallow and subjective as class could ever come between a family like us, an ordinary family who loved one another.

Where once I'd seen only strength, now I saw a wide streak of weakness. Even his voice, raised in guilty anger, seemed tremulous and his cries of protest hollow, and he was defending himself against the indefensible.

With Mom gone and Lisa too young to understand (though one desperate night, in bitter confusion, I tried to make her), I was alone with my anger, with my unreliable memories. At mealtimes, I sat at the dining table turning food over in my mouth and studied my father through a veil of betrayal. I felt as much at his mercy as I had the day I washed toward him on the current at Shamrock—only this time the current was wrenching me away and I was gone, downstream, and he was watching from a distance.

Then Mom went back to him, which felt like a double betrayal.

That was the beginning of the time when we all pretended everything was normal. That some natural catastrophe had occurred which had definitely damaged us but was outside of us and apart from us, like a hurricane seen from the windows of a moving train.

Mom returned to Rainbow's End in late July with an even more idyllic picture in her head than the one before and set about re-creating it. The farm builders were brought in, and they knocked down the carport, which, its throw of coral creeper aside, she'd always detested, and built an extension on the house: a big, light bedroom for her and Dad. Lisa got the two back bedrooms to herself, and a pocket-size room was created for me above the hallway, a narrow space with thatch so low that I could touch the beams with my fingertips if I sat up on my top bunk. It had outside steps, there being no space for an indoor staircase.

In the new room I was up in the msasa tree with the birds—practically in the branches. I could lie in bed and watch the sun's vermilion ball climb above mist-veiled trees on the early morning river, or the black streak of Star tearing through a spray of mauve jacaranda blossoms, or just lie back and breathe in the thatch, which to me was almost the smell of the bush. And in the evenings I could sit on the top step outside my door and watch Jenny and the impalas gather at the water hole through the amber filter of sunset.

It was there in that room that my dreams started in earnest. I began to write songs both as escapism and as a means of escaping in years to come. The way I saw it, the sooner I became a singer or a famous rider, the sooner I'd be out of here. The sooner I'd be free from adults, with their secrets and lies and false trails and hidden agendas. Free from everything. Free.

And so I wrote songs with titles like "Breakdown" and "The Game Is Up," some of which were full of teenage angst, some of which spoke of things I knew nothing about.

> *As daylight lifts our cover*
> *At any moment we could be discovered*
> *And held before society*
> *Then unwritten laws of what's meant to be*
> *Will put the blame on you and me*

Only one thing happened to interrupt the haven that was the new room. It was a languid afternoon at the time, and I was on my bunk reading. Kim was dozing beside me. Suddenly his blue eyes snapped open, and he leapt up and started hissing and spitting at the blank wall opposite, his creamy Siamese fur bottle-brush stiff. For several long seconds he raged at nothing, and then he sprang off the bed and bolted out the door.

I did the same. The ghosts at Rainbow's End may well have been happy, but I sure as hell didn't want to encounter one.

That was also the beginning of the period when I spent a lot of time in Mom's bedroom while she held court. Mom had always conducted much of her life from her bed the way that some families conduct their lives from the kitchen table, usually because she was recuperating from an illness or jet lag or because the bed was heaped with so many newspapers, art books, and maps of the world it was impractical to move them. But now it became her sanctuary, her hiding place from the world. And because she wanted company and I was in on her secret and Lisa, at five, was too little to be in on it, too, I was summoned to be in there with her. It drove Merina mad when she came to stay. She'd spend hours staring at the gray mare with the chestnut colt over the fireplace, unable to understand what I could be doing or why she wasn't allowed to share in it.

Lisa enrolled in her third education facility in her first year of kindergarten, Chegutu (former Hartley) School, where Mr. Clark was still operating a reign of terror. There were days when I resented her for not being able to interpret the subtle ways in which grown-ups tortured one another, for not being old enough to be Mom's confidante and share the burden, and on one of those days I informed her that Father Christmas, the Easter Bunny, and fairies didn't exist. After which she told me I was a "destroyer of childhood dreams." Her sole contribution to the 1980 Chegutu Primary yearbook was a simple "My sister hates me."

That was sobering, so from then on I went to huge lengths to show her I loved her and to have her love me back. I made her two picture books in art class with little windows that opened up to reveal cute animals, and there were drawings of grinning family members. For her birthday, Lis had been given a microscope, and it had sparked her interest in all things scientific or natural. She collected revolting things from around the garden, and I helped her squish them between glass slides and examine them under the lens. We gathered the zebra bones that were heaped near the old mine workings, and she took them to school for a nature project. Her room filled up with dolphin posters and SAVE THE WHALES stickers.

But we both spent a lot of time alone. With the War over, the separation among us all was even more pronounced because there was no longer any excuse for it. We still came together in the evenings and on Sundays. At those times Mom and Dad made a determined effort and we managed to laugh quite a lot and my parents were lovey-dovey in a sickly but restrained way. Like many Zimbabwean men, Dad had a chauvinistic prudishness. There was no worse crime Mom could commit than to go out in a dress that was in any way revealing. She said his list of rules was endless. No short dresses, no tight dresses, no low-necked dresses, no dresses with big armholes. For years she wasn't allowed to wear nail polish because that's what prostitutes did. The same strictures applied to sex in books and films. At thirteen, I was only grudgingly allowed to read Wilbur Smith, and if a couple on the television did anything more amorous than hold hands, the TV went off or I was sent to bed.

Dad and I skirted each other warily and dishonestly. We went on few rides, and if we did go on them, there were long silences. Something had broken and we both knew it might never be fixed. To lighten the mood, he tried to tease me, particularly about subjects he knew I was sensitive about, like Star, whom he constantly referred to as a "donkey." And if I was wounded or didn't get the joke, he blew up much more quickly than he had in the past and was much sorrier afterward.

He and Mom decided yet again that the fault lines in our lives could be magically smoothed over if we just moved away to Australia. Dad applied for a job, and Mom organized immigration papers and studied the rental market in Queensland. I carried on as usual. They changed their minds so often these days it was not worth getting involved. I just lay in the cradle of the mulberry tree reading books and tried not to think too much.

In her absence, Mom had been tried and found wanting by the cliques at Hartley Club. Men were almost always given the benefit of the doubt in these situations. It was the women who led them astray, the women who were sluts, the women who failed in their duty. When one farmer had an affair and broke up his marriage for his young, blond mistress, it was his wife who was condemned because, it was said, she'd become a religious nut. She was always in church. What could she expect? Two known pedophiles in the area were not child molesters but simply men "with a funny thing about young girls."

So Mom, who'd blatantly "dolled herself up" and sat with the men at the bar, who'd unapologetically left her own husband and children year after year to go globe-trotting, faced a gradual closing of ranks.

After the intruder incident, she'd become much more cynical. Whereas before she'd had a childlike faith in the essential goodness of human nature and had taken everyone at face value, now she judged them as harshly as she felt they'd judged her.

About one wife who stayed with her wealthy but abusive husband, she said: "It's called Cupboard Love."

About another, she said: "She married a lifestyle, dear."

But at heart Mom was an irrepressible optimist, particularly if she had the prospect of money and a holiday to buoy her spirits, and when the company she'd worked for earlier in the year offered her a contract to supply them with thatching grass, she forgave and forgot and approached every farming family we knew for hay. For several months she was as ferociously energetic as a hamster on a wheel. After years of trying, she'd found a winning lottery ticket.

However, money couldn't buy her health, and as soon as the contract was completed she was back in hospital for another operation.

To celebrate her recovery, her thatching grass success, and our reunion as a family, we went on a holiday around Zimbabwe, my first since visits at age four or five to Inyanga, although we had been to the beach in South Africa and Mom and Dad often went to Kariba and other places without us. Dad didn't like holidays and could never really relax, but he did his best.

In the vast wilderness of Hwange (formerly Wankie) National Park, I experienced the profound spiritual silence of nature left alone to be nature. A soul-healing silence. By day we went out on open-topped Land Rovers and were awed by the scarred golden flanks and killer glares of the dominant lions; by the ancient silhouettes of the baobab trees, with their lacy headdresses of leaves; by the slow-motion getaways of great herds of giraffes. We were mock-charged by elephants, gray ears flapping, dust roiling up from their feet.

At night, constellation overlaid constellation in such a crowded and haphazard fashion that it was as if an angel had stumbled while setting the stars out for the evening and spilled ten times their usual number. I lay on the grass outside the Safari Lodge and stared up at them. I felt like I was falling into a sea of diamonds, into Mars's red glow. The paranoid shrieks of the hyenas and the lions' murderous roars provided an eerie sound track.

At Victoria Falls, we took refuge from the humid, clinging heat in the mists of the rain forest, breathing in the scent of moist wood and laughing at the antics of the mischievous monkeys swinging overhead. To Mom's distress, Lis and I stood in the wet, green grass on the very edge of the canyon and were hypnotized by the miracle of water that the Makalolo people call *Mosi-oa-Tunya*, "the Smoke That Thunders." The forceful spray from it was as sweet and drenching as rain. The white, crashing walls of it filled your vision on an epic scale, and the sound of it pummeled at your eardrums and made you feel as if you could, at any second, be sucked over the black granite cliffs and into its vortex. A rainbow, lit as if by a divine light, arched over the whole spectacle. We also stared down into the Boiling Pot, where the currents of the Zambezi and tidal fallout from the foaming excesses of the falls met in a deadly whirlpool. Mom claimed that some great-uncle ancestor of ours had fallen in there and become one of the only people ever to survive.

Afterward we hiked up the steep trail to the Victoria Falls Hotel, collecting red velvet rain spiders (heavenly creatures bearing no resemblance to actual spiders) along the way. We stood on the lawn in front of the steps and majestic white columns of one of colonialism's most magnificent buildings and looked past the warthogs grazing on their knees and the baboons sucking mangoes and sassing one another, at a view hardly changed since the time of Livingstone. The suggestion of a rainbow and a line of spray rising like rebel smoke from a slash in a thickly forested valley were all that was evident of the falls at this distance. At the end of the manicured grounds, bisecting the scene with its stark white, was a flagpole. A year ago it would have proudly flown the Green and White. Today it flew the colors of the country we'd betrayed and which had betrayed us.

• • •

Hardly had we unpacked our bags at Rainbow's End than Mom booked herself a round-the-world ticket and disappeared for nearly three months. While she was away, I contracted gastric enteritis. I didn't tell Dad because I shared many of his ideas on doctors and because I was so angry with him that the last thing I wanted was his advice or his help, but at 3:00 a.m., staggering jaundice-pale from the bathroom, I found him sitting up waiting for me, the smoke from his Madison rising in curlicues around him.

"You're very sick, my baby" was all he said.

He hauled me, protesting, to the Polish doctor who'd replaced Dr. Bouwer, a brusque man whose bedside manner, if he'd ever had one, had been amputated in the Eastern Bloc. He stabbed me in the right buttock with a long needle, and the shock to my system was so great that as I left his office I pitched forward in a dead faint.

And my father, whom I no longer trusted to catch me, caught me.

3

In early August 1980, when Merina and I were bored out of our minds in Delano, where we'd been abandoned by our parents to spend a stupefying weekend (Mom had only recently gone back to Dad and was still organizing herself at Rainbow's End), the matrons came looking for volunteers to go and wave to Samora Machel, the president of Mozambique, who was coming to Zimbabwe for a state visit. Any chance to get out of the school grounds provided an opportunity to escape and meet boys, so we were in the first wave of volunteers. We put on our school uniforms and "bashers," much-loathed straw boaters, which we'd crushed until they were soft like Stetsons, and rushed out to the waiting buses.

It wasn't until we'd been deposited on the roadside near State House, Mugabe's residence, that we realized we'd made a colossal error of judgment. Boarding school was dull, but this was a thousand times worse. We had no money and there were no shops nearby anyway and no one could tell us how long we were expected to stand there. Other bused-in wavers unfurled in festive, mainly black lines as far as the eye could see in either direction, their splashes of color rippling like inky mirages in the heat.

As the sun rose, the skin of the five or six white girls started to burn. We grew thirsty and hungry and cast envious glances at the thirty or so African girls, whose skin was impervious to the unrelenting rays and who *had* thought to bring money and who gathered laughing around the blue-and-white cooler of the ice-cream vendor and guzzled down orange juice and fruity ice lollies and Choc 99 cones, licking chocolate from their red-chocolate lips. My blood sugar plummeted and I felt weak and feeble and it went through my head that I'd been right all along: they *were* tougher than we were, and smarter in all the ways that mattered.

Far from feeling like we belonged to the land and the land belonged to us, I felt like an alien in my own country.

Sated, they turned their attention on us. One by one they cornered us and surrounded us, like bees engulfing wilting flowers, pressing their voluptuous, warm flesh against us and then, if we shifted away, saying: "What's the matter? Don't you like black skin?"

We tried our best to say, actually, we liked it quite fine, we were just hot and tired and didn't want anyone pressed up against us, but urged on by an aggressively confident girl named Pleasant, they called us racists and honkies and goaded us and took turns at touching us or pulling our ponytails and just generally behaved like the winners of a fight—a fight from which they knew we could claim nothing, not even the moral high ground.

It was hours before Samora Machel arrived to cheers and whoops from the crowd, his bulletproof black limousine flanked by a mounted escort, and then it was at least another hour before anyone came to take us away. By that time it was late afternoon and we'd been without food or water for seven or eight hours and I felt dizzy and headachy and my chest was tight with tension.

We were walking through the gates of the hostel when I heard Pleasant, who was in the group of girls behind me, shout out another insulting remark. That was when I lost my temper. I swung round and said: "Why don't you just fuck off?"

I never saw her cross the ground between us. All I was conscious of was a dark blur and an explosion of pain in my head and then I was up against the fence and the wire was slicing into my cheek and lips and the metallic taste of blood was in my mouth. Pleasant was yelling something that I couldn't take in or understand, and even when I turned to face her, her words continued to pound me like blows. Her fists were up and her eyes had an animal wildness to them. My soul shriveled under the onslaught of her rage. Not an ounce of me wanted to retaliate in any way, not verbally and not physically. Her hands dropped to her sides and she laughed contemptuously and then she and her friends walked away whooping, their arms wrapped around one another.

And after she'd gone I sobbed with fury, because even though I hated her, I couldn't blame her.

The hardest part about the phone call home was admitting to my parents that I'd sworn at her.

"You said *what?*"

Dad never said anything stronger than *bloody*, and I could hear the disappointment in his tone.

"I told her to fuck off."

On the advice of the matron, and since we were only days from the end of term, Mom came down to Harare to take me home to recover. One look at my mashed lips, black eye, and purple, swollen face, and she was ready to press charges, but Miss Robinson and I talked her out of it. We had a long, uncomfortable journey back to Rainbow's End, with Mom irritating me by fussing too much about my ruined face and possible scarring and going on and on about how sorry she felt for me and what a wicked, monstrous girl Pleasant must be, while I stared unseeingly at the citrus light that always made brilliant the green commercial farmlands that lined the road home. When we reached the house, Maud, Gatsi, and Medicine ah! ah! ah-ed! about my wounds, and I let Mom do the talking about how some horrible girl had inflicted them, although of course, she didn't mention the girl's color or the story of how they'd come about.

Over the next few days, I watched from behind my mask of plum bruises as my father went about his work with all the cheerfulness of the just and Gatsi mowed the lawn with smiling enthusiasm, and concluded that my whole life was a lie. I'd been brainwashed politically and blind in almost every other way, and I had to reprocess everything from that position.

The trouble with having your eyes forcibly opened is that there's no way of closing them again. I felt like I'd been snapped from a happy dream, from a beautiful illusion, as if a crevasse had opened up underfoot. I began to take stock of my life, and I didn't like what I saw. Absorbed in the narrow focus of my dreams, cocooned by my friends and my life at Rainbow's End, I'd gone along in a daze. Not only had I not seen what was going on in my own home but I'd lived alongside or been in very close proximity to Africans all my life and yet we'd led completely separate lives. What did I really know of them or their struggles beyond a checklist of generalizations?

Sure, I knew the customs they'd shared with me and those I'd learned in school. I knew the feel of their skin—sometimes rough and cool, sometimes buttery and hot—and the scent of their soap and sweat. I knew the sound of their shouted gossip and their deep-throated expressions of fright and the sometimes menacing beat of their compound drums. I knew the clean, porridge taste of *sadza* and how they trapped and fried flying ants. I knew the advantages of crafting huts with mud and dung, the disadvantages of their slash-and-burn method of agriculture, and the principles of *lobola* (the marriage dowry). I'd incorporated bits of their languages into my own (cows were *mombies* and medicine *muti*) and I'd mimicked and made fun of their turns of phrase: "It is not my fawlt! I em not the one!" I knew all the shades of Maud's moods and expressions and how to make her laugh.

But I didn't really *know* them. Maud had fed me, ironed my clothes, withstood my tantrums, scolded me, consoled me, and shaken her head over Lisa's brattishness or my parents' fights. She'd seen almost every nuance of my growing up. But I'd never sat down to a meal in Maud's *kaya*. I'd never talked to her about her childhood in Malawi, about how she'd met her husband, about how she felt about being away from her children in the months they spent in the Tribal Trust Lands. I didn't know how many, or even if any, of Gatsi's relatives had been in "protected villages" during the War, locked away under curfew every night, supposedly for their own good. The system had seen to it that we were kept apart.

Over the years I'd looked across the border at the South Africans and thought of *them* as racists because *they* had discrimination enshrined in their constitution; *they* had separate and usually foul-smelling toilets for black people; *their* police had *sjamboks* made from rhinoceros hide, which they used to lash rioters in hellhole townships like Soweto; *they* had a way of talking of Africans as "Blacks," as if they were a disease. But I'd thought of us, the Rhodesians, as being different. I'd thought of our police as polite, nice men who lived by the law and beat people only if they really deserved it, and then only with a thin wooden truncheon. I'd read the bold quotation in Mom's Rhodesian Front (Ian Smith's party)

brochure, "You and Your Future in Rhodesia": THE RHODESIAN FRONT IS
THE ONLY PARTY THAT CAN GUARANTEE THE WELL-BEING OF ALL RACES IN
THIS LAND OF OURS, RHODESIA, and I'd taken it at face value.

I'd read *Roots* and wept over Kunta Kinte and the inhumane treatment of the slaves and reacted just as intensely to the plight of the Jews
in *Exodus*, Leon Uris's best-seller on the birth of Israel. It had given me
a physical pain in my throat that people could be persecuted, tormented, and killed on account of their race or religion. And if there
were parts in the narrative of *Roots*, to do with the treatment of farm or
domestic labor or the referral to grandmothers and old men as "girls" or
"boys," that hit uncomfortably close to home, I shut them out. I didn't
want to acknowledge any parallels.

At the same time, I'd turned away, embarrassed, when I'd seen
white farmers randomly stop black men who were crossing their land or
riding their bicycles innocently along on the strip road—men often
bowed and snow-haired and unlikely to be terrorists—and aggressively
demand their *stoepas*, their identity papers. I'd tried not to hear the stut-
tering replies of terror or see the shaking hands that held out the
sweaty, crumpled cards. It hadn't even entered my head to wonder why
it was that Africans had identity cards when we didn't and why they
had to produce them on request as if we were the Gestapo.

I'd squashed down the uncomfortable feeling it always gave me
when, after long, merry dinner parties, I'd go into the kitchen to find
Madala, whose duties were long since over, standing at the sink, bleary-
eyed with tiredness, waiting to be dismissed. I'd accepted without question that the farmworkers used long drops rather than flushing toilets.
I'd referred to the Africans as *munts* (though not to their faces) even
though I knew on some level that they considered the term derogatory
or insulting. I'd never spent even a minute considering why it was that
the Tribal Trust Lands, the areas of land held in trust for Africans, were
often in the driest or least arable areas of the country. Until the schools
were integrated, I'd been perfectly content, and even glad, that there
were no blacks in our schools, and I'd never questioned that either, only
vaguely imagined they were too poor to afford school. And now I knew
that there was only one way I could have accepted any of those things
and that was because I thought of Africans as second-class citizens. And
that made me a racist.

A child and a product of my environment, yes, but still a racist.

I wondered if it was too late to make amends with people like

Gatsi, Maud, and Luka beyond being as good to them as possible. How could I now, in conscience and in decency, say to them, You've worked for us all this time and I've no idea what your thoughts, fears, and dreams are, and I'm hazy on the numbers of your children?

Yet I could think of no other way to move forward.

And so I opened my ears and my heart and, not without trepidation, let Africa come flooding in.

My first introduction to our new government was when the Ministry of the Environment sent a shiny, black car to Roosevelt to collect Merina and me and we were chauffeured away, with the matrons, prefects, and our friends staring after us in disbelief, to see the minister himself. We'd written to him telling him we were determined to Save the Rhino. And he'd written straight back, inviting us to visit him. Of course, Merina and I were more interested in pop singing than in fund-raising, and not having expected a reply, we had only a passionate defense of the rhino and few feeble suggestions of cake sales and sponsored swims to offer the minister, but he made a church and steeple of his fingers and gave us his undivided and unpatronizing attention, and we all smiled at one another under an unsmiling portrait of Mugabe. Then we returned to the hostel and never thought about the rhino again.

Merina had spent her formative years in Zambia in a mixed-race school with black toddler friends, so she had no real journey to make when it came to color, and I spoke to no one about my own journey—which had to do with trying to comprehend the past and working out how to negotiate the future—because I could hardly articulate it to myself. But it was a road with many obstacles and contradictions.

At Roosevelt there were daily tensions, many of which had to do with discipline. Because the African girls had been discriminated against or been lesser citizens all their lives, and because many of them had been held back by the previous educational system, which had seen to it that white children received free secondary school education but black children didn't—a fact I'd been blissfully unaware of—and were much older than their white classmates, they were sensitive to slights. If a white teacher or a prefect shouted at them or ordered them around, it was often interpreted as racist. That led to problems, because discipline at Roosevelt was rigorously enforced. Even smoking could lead to expulsion. The white girls had to adjust to the idea that they were now sleeping in the beds beside the daughters of many of the men they'd been afraid of since birth, men who'd possibly murdered or terrorized their relatives. And the black girls had to do the same.

On the face of it, the education we received was largely the same after Independence as it was before because we were working to syllabi provided by British Examining Boards. The only real difference was that we now had African teachers and matrons, and Shona lessons were compulsory. Class sizes also increased, and parents of white girls in coed school had nightmares about their peach-perfect twelve-year-olds having to fend off the advances of the twenty-one-year-old black boys with whom they now shared their classrooms.

At Roosevelt, the friendships and bonds that were built were slow and tentative ones. They came with little shocks, too, to do with how similar we were rather than how different, and that itself made me feel guilty. The fact that I was surprised they had the same insecurities we did regarding weight or boys or looks, for example. Or that they were incredibly funny in a droll or dry way. Or that we all fancied Michael Jackson.

The only person I wasn't about to become bosom buddies with was Pleasant. I was going through a teenage phase in which everyone who annoyed me or got on my nerves in any way—including Merina from time to time, the bossier prefects, Miss Robinson, Bubbles when she made us weed the grounds on detention, and our French teacher—was a "bitch," at least for ten minutes, so I'd decided that Pleasant was a "bitch," too, and not just because she'd hit me. She had decided more or less the same thing about me, so we pointedly ignored each other for a couple of weeks, and then we lost interest in the whole thing and just got on with being insecure, music- and boy-obsessed teenagers, the only difference being that Pleasant didn't wear her insecurities on her muscle-bound sleeve.

School was one thing, but there was a whole country out there and not everyone was on the same page all at once. When Diana Ross appeared on *SOS (Sounds on Saturday)*, Dad referred to her as a "nanny," albeit in a complimentary way.

As in: "*My* goodness, that nanny's got a beautiful voice."

At *braais* it made me cringe to hear whites making racist remarks while they were in the presence of, or being served by, a black person. Some had retreated into Rhodie enclaves, from the safety of which they made jokes about the *jongwe* (cock) symbol of Mugabe's ZANU-PF party or the likely effect of the Rhodesians' interrogatory procedures on Mugabe when he was in jail. Others declared themselves fans of post-Independence TV programs about affluent, wisecracking black Americans like *The Jeffersons* and *Diff'rent Strokes* and enthusiastically welcomed Zimbabwe's new multiculturalism but, after years of social conditioning, found it tricky to do this in a way that didn't come over as patronizing.

"She's a super girl, Beauty," a woman might say affectionately of her maid. "I really don't know what I'd do without her. Aren't you, Beauty? You're a gem."

"Ah, *medem*!"

And I was probably a bit the same way, because I was so childishly eager to please and fix the past, to try to undo what had been done. Like every white kid, I knew I'd always dismissed commercial African music as "all sounding the same" (ironically, most of our favorite artists at that time were African-Americans like Donna Summer, Kool & the Gang, Stevie Wonder, Michael Jackson, George Benson, Dionne Warwick, Diana Ross, and Lionel Richie), but now I carried the radio through to the kitchen so that Maud could hear the jangly guitars and infectious beat of the new black stations and artists like the Harare Mambos and the Four Brothers, and in the process I found myself liking the music more and more. I'd belatedly discovered that Chilapalapa was resented by many Africans as a language created by oppressors and that Wrex Tarr's records had racist undertones, and was trying to make her forget about the times I'd played them for her.

Maud went back to her old mix of caring and cynicism, and she helped me with my Shona homework and I made her smile with a pastel portrait of her. She showed it to me on the bedside table in her *kaya*, which I was touched by, although after years of being tacitly discouraged from entering *kayas* or playing with picannins, I still felt like I was violating some code or overstepping some deeply entrenched boundary to go into her home. Many *kayas* consisted of little more than a one-room mud hut. Maud's whitewashed house had only two small bedrooms and a toilet. The walls were speckled with soot, and the air was

potent with smoke and cheap perfume and cold *sadza*, but apart from
a Bible and the booklets of her Jehovah's Witness faith, which she read
slowly and carefully, there was little of her in it.

Hers seemed like a life half-lived.

No doubt she looked at me and, for different reasons, thought the
same thing.

4

The country's transformation from pariah state to Pride of Africa had a revolutionary effect on the national mood. For years I'd always fancied that the minute you crossed the border into Zimbabwe, the light seemed different somehow. I thought of it as *sponspek* light: honeydew melon light. Everywhere you went, whether it was the mountains of Inyanga or canoeing between hippos on the Zambezi, the landscape was bathed in the same honeyed glow, as if an angelic, teapot-shaped filter were fitted over each (the outline of Zimbabwe is said to resemble a teapot). Now that positive glow was visible in every area of life. Sanctions had been lifted, and records that weren't country collections and books that weren't Wilbur Smith and chocolates that tasted of real cocoa poured into the shops. Rock stars like Bruce Springsteen and UB40 came to visit us. Areas of town that had once seemed foreign and mysterious and off-limits were now available to be explored. We could squeeze between the bright reams in curry- and cardamom-scented Indian shops and buy silk braids for our hair and scraps of fabric for headbands. We could walk through the noisy throngs disembarking from the belching buses at the depot and browse through the albums in the secondhand shops behind it, while Thomas Mapfumo & the Sounds of Africa blared, and pavement-lounging picannins snacked on charred maize, and black black-belts did roundhouse kicks at the karate school overhead.

Rainbow's End was safe again—from terrorists, if not from snakes and crocodiles—and we could try things we would never have risked during the War.

"Wouldn't it be great if we built a raft," I suggested to Merina, "and sailed it across to the island at midnight?"

Despite the transparent lunacy of launching a homemade craft on a crocodile-inhabited river and sailing by flashlight to a jungle-covered sandbank populated exclusively by mambas, boomslangs, and baboon spiders, Merina was fully onboard from the start. We spent a busy day procuring planks and bits of rope and wire from various outbuildings on the farm and lashing them to two rusty oil drums. When we had something loosely resembling a raft, we carried it, with difficulty, down to the river's edge and hid it in the long grass. I had my reservations that it was seaworthy, but it was too late to turn back now.

That night we lay on my bunk talking and waiting for midnight. One of the strange laws of the universe is that when you have to stay awake you crave sleep so desperately you would practically kill for it. Few experiences were more tortuous than midnight feasts at boarding school. You'd be woken by your friends and dragged in a drugged stupor to the bathroom, where you'd have to sit on the cold, tiled floor and pretend to be enjoying a sickly feast of marshmallows, jelly babies, corn curls, cake, and Rosemary Creams, all washed down with cream soda. And every single minute you'd just be praying for sleep.

That was how it was on the night of the raft adventure. We stared out the window at the black, unfriendly night and listened to a storm brew and thunder crackle, and wished and prayed for sleep, and then when the rain finally came just before eleven, making a satisfactory launch of our vessel impossible and providing us with a face-saving opt-out clause, we fell onto our pillows with relief. The next morning we attempted the journey in daylight. Unhelpfully assisted by the dogs, we pushed the raft offshore and clambered aboard. Halfway to the island, it disintegrated into a dozen pieces, some of which sank without trace and some of which floated away on a brisk current. Merina and I and all the dogs swam as fast as we could until we were out of range of crocodiles, and then we stood up to our waists in green water and laughed until we cried. Then we made plans for our next scheme.

When we first arrived at Roosevelt, Merina, Jean, and I had more interest in horses than in boys, but that soon passed, and the walls of our dormitory filled up with posters of insipid white stars like Shaun Cassidy, Leif Garrett, and Andy Gibb, and Michael Jackson, who was still a handsome black man. We planned on saving our virginities for marriage, but that didn't mean we couldn't enjoy a few fantasies in the meantime.

Jean spent every waking moment reading Mills & Boon romances, and it didn't take me long to pick up the habit. We read by flashlight, we read in evening prep, we read in our breaks, and we read below our desks through every math and French class for almost five years of high school. No matter how many times we were swept away by near-identical story lines about rugged, dark strangers with a façade of arrogant indifference getting their hard hearts melted by pretty, unassuming young women, the formula never failed to enchant us.

In the late seventies and early eighties, Mills & Boons were annoyingly smut-free, and we prided ourselves on being able to identify at a glance those authors who went further than the rest. "Try Ann Rule," Jean would say. "She's very, very . . ." and she'd blush. Apart from Wilbur Smith books, which had the odd racy scene among the lion hunts and deaths from blackwater fever, my only access to "porn" of any sort had been the occasional Jackie Collins, and so I'd snatch the precious contraband and hurry it away to my metal bed, with its paper-thin mattress and government-issue brown blankets. There I'd picture myself being crushed to the chest of a hitherto indifferent doctor called Ryan Hunter or Conrad Knight, who'd kiss me hard and whisper hoarsely: "You little fool! Don't you know I can't live without you?"

Twice a year, our boardinghouse organized disco dances and invited a couple of boys' schools; and four or five times a year, the boys' schools returned the favor. We were not allowed to attend until we were fourteen or fifteen and in our third year, and as our first dance approached, Merina and I, as the resident boardinghouse freaks, found ourselves the butts of the prefects' worst jokes. They'd ask us incomprehensible questions about sex or make horrible sucking noises while pretending to be snogging their palms.

Determined to prove them wrong, we went all out to transform our appearances. We begged our parents for Farrah Fawcett-Majors–style perms, which were in vogue at the time. After suffering through several hours of burning scalp and sulfuric stench and emerging triumphant and slightly Beverly D'Angelo–like, we discovered that, unless you had access to a hair dryer, a roller brush, and some heavy-duty mousse, one splash of water turned you into an electrified version of Roger Daltrey.

Undaunted, we went shopping for dance dresses. My mother took me to Honors in Chegutu, which catered primarily to conservative farmers' wives and churchgoing grandmothers. Because it was a special occasion and because I had nothing in my wardrobe besides torn jeans, indecently frayed shorts, and stretched T-shirts, I was allowed to choose two dresses. I selected a white nylon calf-length one with a gold tinsel trim, which made me resemble a Christmas tree angel, and a stretchy white dress patterned with garish pink, black, and jade green triangles, which Mom trimmed into a miniskirt when the fashions changed. It came with its own cummerbund, and cummerbunds were in so far as I knew. I wasn't a fan of stilettos, so I was allowed to buy boots. I chose a metallic-hued pair of Robin Hood boots in copper, one size too small. Thus armed, I prepared for my first disco.

That Saturday, thirty girls in towels rushed shrieking around the dorm competing for the use of a single dryer. It was a two-pronged dryer without an adapter, but we made it work by sticking a plastic comb in the third hole of the electrical socket. Most of our friends were unworldly farm kids, and few had any experience with makeup or high heels. Mascara wands were poked into streaming eyes, and borrowed foundation was squirted liberally over spots. Strawberry-scented lip gloss was passed around, and we chewed grape Bubble-Yum for good measure. Once dressed, we turned the dormitory corridor into a cat-walk and tottered up and down in our blister-inducing new shoes like a fashion parade of fledgling transvestites.

When the distinctive keyboard intro of George Benson's "Give Me the Night" boogied its way up the stairs, we proceeded nervously to the dining room, which had been converted into a dance hall for the evening. The walls were draped in tinsel, lights in primary colors flashed, and a mirror ball twirled slowly on the ceiling. A DJ spun hits from Kool & the Gang, Diana Ross, ABBA, Air Supply ("All Out of Love"), and *Saturday Night Fever* as the boys from Prince Edward, the invited school, drifted in self-consciously. The black boys had a sexual confidence that we, as committed virgins, found disturbing. The Indian boys, who were always immaculately dressed, with smooth, golden skin and stylishly gelled hair, seldom looked at us. The white boys sat alongside them on one side of the room and picked at their spots and whispered to one another and gave us sly grins. We sat on the opposite side of the room like traumatized lemmings. It was like a scene from the fifties. The thing we dreaded more than anything else was being a wallflower.

Predictably, I was among the last to be asked to dance, and then it was by a bony blond boy named Neil whose nickname was "Scarecrow." On fast numbers he shuffled his school shoes lethargically on the floor and did everything possible to avoid my gaze. On slow songs he breathed hotly down my neck and swamped me with Old Spice, while stabbing me intermittently with his erection. When he grew tired of dancing, he took me by the hand and led me behind a hedge in the courtyard, where he thrust a long, smoke-flavored tongue into my mouth. Relieved to have been saved from being a wallflower, I returned his kiss with enthusiasm. It was not of the standard I might have expected from Ryan Hunter or Conrad Knight, and there wasn't much conversation, but at least he was alive and not a girl.

Unfortunately, when we emerged from behind the hedge, Neil's fly was undone. Far from proving, as I'd hoped, that I was a success with boys, the hedge incident made me the subject of much merrymaking for years to come.

The pressure to find a boyfriend didn't end with dances. Every afternoon the matrons would place our post on a tray beside the tea and sandwiches. The letters from boys were always on blue or white paper, with squashed, uneven penmanship, and reeked—intoxicatingly, we felt—of Old Spice. Receiving one turned you into something of a star for the hour and meant that some boy somewhere was thinking of you. It didn't matter if he was called "Scarecrow" or was geeky or weird or had acne, as long as he was thinking of you. We replied fondly on pink or cream stationery purchased at Barbours that had moody photographs in the corners depicting lovers kissing on Caribbean beaches or strolling hand in hand into Florida sunsets. These missives we placed tenderly in matching envelopes and sprayed with Charlie perfume. Then we carved the boys' initials into our school desks with compasses and bit our nails every day until a response finally came and we could prove, once again, that we were In a Romance and someone cared.

We had a series of tried and trusted excuses to get out of school grounds in the afternoons, but it was not until our chain-smoking Czechoslovakian art teacher, Mrs. Krog, decided we were gifted artists that we managed to get out of lessons as well. Then we could legitimately tell our math and French teachers that we were doing art projects, crawl through the fence onto Chapman golf course, and devote several blissful hours to tanning our legs in the sun and ten minutes to some impressionistic painting with which to present a beaming Mrs. Krog.

In pursuit of further freedoms, we signed up for singing lessons. Our singing teacher was a former cabaret artist from Berlin who favored full-length fishnet body stockings, black bras, and G-strings before they were fashionable. She was enormously tall with blue-white skin, frizzy chocolate hair, and a slash of crimson lipstick. Her name was Magda. Magda would demonstrate breathing exercises and then lead us into scales. "Ah, Ahh, Ahhh, Ah-hhh, Ahh, Ahhh, Aahh, Ah-ahhhhh! Maw air, Mireenaaaah, maw air-r-r HAHHHHH!"

We arrived for our third lesson to find Magda's stereo stolen and a detective in the studio. It was obvious that it was taking all his powers of concentration to keep his eyes averted from the fishnet body stocking and his ears on Magda's theories about the break-in. He followed her over to the window for a reenactment of the moment when the burglars forced the clasp.

"I'm sure zis is ver zey entered, no?" she speculated. She bent double, and her G-string disappeared from view. "Look, and here you haff ze flingerplints!"

The detective gave up the struggle for propriety and bent over himself. "Yes," he breathed. "Yes, I see what you mean."

Magda gave the lyrics of a song of mine to a dreadlocked student of hers named Ashante, and it made me feel proud and quite revolutionary myself when Ashante set "The Juggler" to reggae music and played it at beer halls and Rastafarian gigs around town. After half a dozen lessons Merina decided that she'd learned all Magda could teach her, and I was too shy to continue on my own. However, by now the matrons were accustomed to signing us out of the grounds for singing lessons, and we saw no reason to disabuse them of the notion that we were budding sopranos. From then on, we left the hostel at lunchtime every Thursday and caught the bus into town for nonexistent music lessons, a crime for which the punishment was instant expulsion. Since neither of us ever had a cent to our name, we'd spend the morning collecting small change from day pupils whose parents gave them lunch money. "That's great," we'd say. "Man, you're nice. We're short of twenty cents for our bus fare."

Weighed down by coppers, we'd spend the afternoon watching 16-certificate movies like *Endless Love*, which we'd been expressly banned from seeing; or eating gigantic slabs of cream gâteaux heaped with fresh strawberries or chunks of pineapple, in the top-floor restaurant at Barbours. There among the smart black businessmen and fragrant farmers' wives, we'd be convinced we'd found nirvana.

5

Mom came back from her Round-the-World trip in mid-1981 alive and glowing in the way that only travel ever made her, her eyes full of Venetian gondolas and San Francisco's Golden Gate Bridge. Winter was on its way, and on cold, clear nights I stared into the dancing flames in the hearth at Rainbow's End, listening to the crackle and pop of the moisture in the fragrant gum logs and the endless song of the crickets and frogs, which was never interrupted, no matter how much agony life inflicted on the humans inside the house. I *braaied* cubes of steak for myself and tried to toast marshmallows, which kept melting and falling into the coals.

We were having discussions about Australia, where we were moving because Dad had been offered a job and some doctor friend of Mom's had offered us accommodation, and because everything would be put right and be like it was before.

I asked: "How is Star getting there?" I imagined him traveling by ship, like the black stallion in the novels.

They replied together: "Star's not coming."

I said flatly: "Well, then I'm not going."

Soon afterward Dad decided that there was no way he was leaving Africa, which he loved with every sinew of his being, and the question of Australia was off the menu forever.

Mom was furious at his intransigency. She was sure that Zimbabwe was going to go the way of Zambia and Mozambique. That we'd soon be buying bread with suitcases full of money, and all the essential services—she was thinking of the hospitals—would collapse. "You know what they say," she told him. "'When the Jews go, it's time to leave. When the Asians go, it's too late.' What time will it be when you decide to pack your bags?"

Despite the current stalemate in our relationship, she was convinced that Dad and I were somehow in league. Over the years his last-minute U-turns, the way he could passionately advocate one course of action at night and then just as passionately reject it the following morning, had nearly driven her demented. He gave the impression that he thought destiny was grimly preordained and nothing but heartache lay in store for those who tried to climb above their station. But underneath he was a born dreamer.

"You're not the only one who has dreams," he told me testily one day. "When I was your age, I used to want to be a singer, too."

I was skeptical, but he jumped up and went to his spartan bedside drawers—the opposite of my mother's, which spewed Suits-by-Sylvia, Liberty scarves, magazine clippings, and jewelery boxes coughing up strings of fake pearls, antique brooches, and Indian lapis lazuli—returning with a spiral-bound notebook, its pages rippled with age. He'd had it since he was a teenager. Inside he'd lovingly transcribed the lyrics of dozens of songs from his era, just as I did now, and a couple of poems. I couldn't believe it. For years all I'd talked about was music and singing, and yet he'd kept the notebook a secret, his childhood hopes private. For a moment I had an image of him as he must have been at that time, carefree, matinee-idol handsome, sitting by a campfire with a guitar. But he wasn't that person any longer. Now he looked like the Marlboro Man after too many cigarettes, too many beers, and too many worries.

Now he was yoked by circumstance to African reality.

The success of Mom's thatching grass enterprise did enable Dad to achieve one long-held goal, and that was to buy his own cattle. So far Independence had brought largely positive changes to the country, enough for him to believe that it had a bright future. The main gripe of the farmers had to do with tax hikes and the introduction by the government of a minimum wage for farmworkers. Most had no problem with the wage itself, which was fair, but Dad and many other farmers I knew thought that the extra money would, ironically, leave the farmworkers worse off, because it was to be given in lieu of "rations"—which on Rainbow's End was a monthly supply of one kilogram of meat and 14 kilograms of *mielie-meal*, plus Nyemo beans if they were available per person (many farmworkers were also given farm seed, fertilizer, and a plot of land to grow their own maize)—and they were cynically certain that the majority would not spend the cash on food but would fritter it away on women and Chibuku beer.

None of these things diverted Dad from his goal, and in September 1981 he leased a remote, lovely farm called Chikanga out on the Lowood Road near Shamrock and stocked it with his favorite Brahman-cross cattle. Chikanga had shaggy, wild kopjes, where leopards crouched in dank caves, and when he took possession of it, Dad, flush with the feeling of semiownership, took the dogs and his .22 rifle and went out hunting for them.

"Thank goodness I didn't find them," he said later, when the inadvisability of facing down one of Africa's most lethal predators with a light rifle and a couple of cowardly fox terriers struck him. "I wouldn't be here now. It was *suicide*. Absolute suicide."

Chikanga also had light, sandy soil, perfect for growing tobacco, and after a year or so Dad decided he should buy it and finally become a landowner. A *real* farmer. At night he sat up smoking and writing figures on the backs of cigarette packets. It was going to be amazing. We'd be wealthy. He'd grow this many hectares of tobacco and have this many cattle and they'd all be Brahman-crosses. We were all encouraged to take emotional shares in his plan.

Then, just as suddenly, it was over.

It was the best thing he ever did, he told us, not taking it. He'd nearly had a nervous breakdown over it. Could we imagine what would have happened if it had been a bad season or some plague had taken hold of his tobacco or cattle or it hadn't rained and he hadn't been able to repay his loan and had been faced with a huge tax bill?

"I'd have been finished, absolutely finished."

After that, every negative event was grist for that particular mill. In 1983, when there actually was a drought, all we heard about was the blessing that had been his decision not to take Chikanga.

It was things like that which convinced me to write out a list of my goals. It seemed to me that adults either surrendered their dreams or the trials of life made them forget them. If I wrote mine down, I reasoned, that was less likely to happen. When I was fourteen, my Ambition List read:

1. Become a pop singer and write a hit record
2. Write a book and get it published
3. Show-jump at A-Grade level and win a medal for cross-country eventing
4. Become a vet
5. Win an award for painting
6. Act in a play or a movie

Consequently I was constantly on the lookout for opportunities that might lead to a rapid rise in one of my desired professions. My main aim was to quit school as soon as possible. Once, I was flipping through the Sunday paper when I came across an audition notice for *Cinderella*. The only qualification was the ability to sing songs like "Hopelessly Devoted to You." I interpreted this as a sign. Mom was overseas, so I appealed to Dad to forgo his roast lunch in order to drive me to Harare.

At Reps Theatre, they asked me to read a few lines and parade up and down the stage in shorts (Dandini had to have good legs, apparently). I raised several eyebrows with my performance, and a woman with a clipboard rushed over and took my name and contact details. Then came the singing. I watched indulgently as several puppy-fat-challenged and acne-blighted teens stumbled their way through a horrible show tune I'd never heard before called "Bye Bye Blackbird," played, without sentiment, by the theater pianist. While I waited, I recalled with pleasure the many hours I'd spent singing along with Olivia. Dedication, I mused, was its own reward.

"Next!" boomed the woman with the clipboard.

"I'll sing 'Hopelessly Devoted to You,'" I informed her.

"You'll sing the song you've been given," she retorted.

I had no option but to launch into an unrehearsed version of "Bye Bye Blackbird." After numerous false starts, not helped by the fact that I could see Dad at the back of the auditorium covering his face with the audition flyer, I was unceremoniously dispatched. I left the theater relieved I had so many other careers from which to choose.

If something good could be said to have come out of the gulf between me and Dad, which existed even on days like that, it was that it brought me closer to my mother, who for years had drifted in and out of my life like an exotic butterfly. In light of her revelations about my father, the mother-daughter barriers dropped away and we became friends. I realized that she was extraordinary. I was becoming interested in art and culture and travel, and Mom read more and was more curious about the world than anyone I knew. She was also an expert on style. Thrilled that I might be emerging from my tomboy phase, she had a burst of sewing, running up dance dresses and knickerbockers for me as the fashions changed. I in turn was fiercely loyal to and supportive of her. Whereas before I'd do anything to avoid attending the teas she loved or being dragged around the shops, now I went relatively willingly.

Of the friends who still spoke to her following her split with my father and the years she'd spent scandalizing the district, my favorites were Anne and Mike Ford. Anne was a tall, vital Englishwoman who wore floaty silks and linens in cream and pale blue and served teas no restaurant or hotel in Zimbabwe could have hoped to match. When sanctions were in force, you could go to the Fords' and enjoy silver platters laden with rare delights such as tuna fish or prawns in mayonnaise, as well as flaky homemade sausage rolls or vol-au-vents, or a bouncy sponge cake with a heady aroma of vanilla, farm cream, and garden strawberries.

Anne spoke perfect Shona with a cut-glass English accent and kept a totem to ward off the dwarf water-sprite Tokoloshe above the kitchen door. Some Africans are so mortally afraid of the evil Tokoloshe, which is said to have an overlong penis, prey on women, and carry a magical pebble in its mouth to help it disappear, that they sleep with their beds elevated on bricks so as to be out of the dwarf's reach.

Mike Ford was a workaholic, devoted to farming. He and Anne conducted their relationship in eye rolls, but they couldn't disguise the immense love and respect they had for each other. They had two children with model looks, Lisa and Jeremy, and lived in a house that was classically Zimbabwean in design—massive, airy rooms with concrete floors, whitewashed walls, a high, thatched roof, and exposed beams. It was so inviting you wanted to move in at once. In the background was a paddockful of horses in pastel colors: strawberry roans, duns, and dapple grays.

Anne took a real interest in my dreams and talked to me about some of her own, which were all to do with visiting England. She was

the most generous person on earth. It was impossible to leave the Fords'
house without bulging bags of award-quality produce, baked goods, and
preserves. She bred fat white ducks for eating, and we almost always left
with a prepared bird. Mom didn't have the heart to tell her that Dad
refused to let Madala cook them because he claimed to have seen what
they ate.

"Horrible birds," he'd say with a shudder. He considered eating
weaknesses in animals to be indictments of their character, as though, if
they had any strength of spirit whatsoever, they would not stoop to eating horse manure or rotting leftovers.

It was their dining habits that formed the basis of Dad's grievance
against Patches and Pebbles. With the exception of the fox terriers,
which had been a gift, every breed of dog my father ever bought was the
best in the world until proven otherwise, and then it became the worst
and he denied there ever having been a time when he thought differently. The more he tried to get a *real* dog, a dog like Jock or leopard-
fighting Muffy, a dog with the requisite manliness and courage and with
no interest in human food, the more he attracted cringing curs, or dogs
that ate cats or fawned all over the servants and thus could not be relied
upon to be good guard dogs, or planted muddy paws on his thighs when
he was smartly dressed to go into town, or watched him dolefully
through the bars of the garden chairs while he tried to relax with a beer
and a chicken drumstick until he let out a growl that was not dissimilar
to theirs, only many decibels louder: "GET AWAY, YOU BLOODY
SCAVENGER!"

Thanks to the SPCA and Dad's quest for the perfect canine, bea-
gles, rottweilers, and Rhodesian ridgebacks came and went, and our
dogs grew in number until we had eight. When I whistled for them, the
ground vibrated with the thunder of their paws. Even after Jock died,
Dad had never lost his passion for dogs, but unless they met his exacting expectations, he gave them only limited attention, as a consequence
of which, like the victims of unrequited love, their ardour increased ten-
fold. Nowhere was this more obvious than in the fox terriers. One non-
committal pat from him was worth more to them than all the hours
Lisa and I spent ratting with them or taking them down to the river, and

yet they were a source of daily disappointment to him. Their neediness drove him crazy. His fervent hope, frequently expressed, was that they'd die relatively early of natural causes, possibly by stopping to scratch a flea when he was reversing his truck out of the yard. As if in silent reproach against these harsh sentiments, Pebbles and Patches spent their days rolling in carrion or eating the feces of the game animals, two pastimes guaranteed to send Dad running down the passage to hurl, pausing only to yell: "GET AWAY, YOU BLOODY SCAVENGER!"

The teas with the Fords and *braais* with the Etheridges and the fluctuations in our menagerie showed that, superficially at least, life continued as before. *Before I knew the truth about my father. Before I knew the truth about the War.* Like couples who imagine a new baby will save a crumbling marriage, we were continually acquiring new pets, because they required a long-term commitment and shored up our status as a picturesque family living in a picturesque house with a garden and game park full of picturesque pets. For me especially, they provided a welcome distraction from the emotional undertow that sometimes threatened to drown me. One day, Mom came home with a chestnut pom-pom. Somebody had put it in her trolley at Schofield's supermarket. At least I thought it was a pom-pom until it started moving. That was when Mom said: "It's a present for you. A Pomeranian!"

Like Dad, I felt that dogs should be feisty and adventurous and full of personality, and the last thing I wanted was a Pomeranian, which was not exactly a farm dog. But thirty seconds after being introduced to Tiger, I was smitten. As he grew, he became the boldest and most like Jock of any of our dogs, and he was always the first in the river and the first to defend me against every possible threat. When I came home from school, he'd take a flying leap of faith right into my arms. No matter where I went or what I did, he was at my side or at my feet—a furry red bodyguard, always watching me with a kind of half smile.

Tiger started a positive trend in our menagerie and was followed by a wonderful blue heeler cattle dog, Skippy, and two warthogs, Miss Piggy and Bacon.

At its height, when we had a base population of eight horses, eight dogs, and six cats, plus Goat, Mindy the cow, two unstable ostriches, a giraffe, and two warthogs, an element of farce entered our daily lives at

Rainbow's End. When a tobacco rep came to see Dad, Star greeted him by putting a hoof on the hood of his Mercedes. Despite that, the rep unwisely continued indoors without winding up his window, so Star chewed up his leather seats and distributed his labels and documents around the yard. Star also liked to drink Coke from the bottle and come into the lounge—right onto the carpet—for slices of Tomazo's bread.

When she was about a year old, we decided to lock Miss Piggy in the outside storeroom where we kept horse feed, saddles, and bridles, because Anne Ford was coming over. Miss Piggy was the most loving warthog in the world, but she did like to show her affection with mud, and not every visitor appreciated her special qualities. Anne was sitting at the rondavel with Mom, sipping tea and saying in her posh English accent: "Oh, I never get tired of the view at Rainbow's End," when there was an explosion of splintering wood and a warthog-size hole appeared in the storeroom door.

Even as they pondered this development, Miss Piggy pounced on Anne from behind, rapturously rubbing her legs, ankles, and any part of her baby blue linen skirt she could reach with a snout load of fresh mud. Anne took it in good spirit, but when Miss Piggy's tusks reached the size where her affection was starting to become dangerous, we decided to release her into the wild in the larger game reserve of Mike Campbell (Bruce Campbell's father). On a subsequent visit we found that she'd met a friend and had a fleet of stiff-tailed babies.

Ever since Charm had run away and left me in the game park, I'd ridden her only rarely, but Cassandra was in foal to a chestnut Arab from Kadoma and I didn't have a choice. Although we had eight horses, they were all too young, too old, or too pregnant to ride. By now, however, I was addicted to jumping. Cass had turned out to be a superb gymkhana horse and show jumper, and my bedroom wall was covered in rosettes. With Cass out of action, I brought Charm out of retirement. When Jean came to stay, I decided to demonstrate Charm's skills as a dressage horse by trotting her over a line of *cavaletti* (low jumps used as schooling aids) I'd erected in a newly burned field—so newly burned it was still smoking. Charm managed to get her hoof caught on the last one and send us both crashing to the ground. By the time I crawled out from underneath her, I looked like I'd spent a month in a coal mine.

That was a weekend of double humiliation because Mindy, the orphaned Mashona-Sussex cross I'd kept alive in the first few nights of her existence with my own body warmth, decided to attack me.

For reasons that probably had to do with colostrum, the immune-boosting ingredient found in new mothers' milk, which she had been denied, Mindy had never grown taller than a six-month-old calf. When she was old enough to be weaned, she moved into the field behind the house, where she ate and ate until she was the size of an adult rhinoceros, only shorter. At a certain point, she began to show signs of madness and was sent to live in the game park with Cheeky and a Brahman bull that had become too vicious to handle. It was there that I first noticed her watching us strangely from the bushes. Jean and I were deep in conversation at the time, perched on the edge of a gully, legs swinging happily, and it took a while for me to register that Mindy was pawing the ground like a wounded bull elephant. By then, she was already in full charge.

Jean let out a shriek and cleared the gully like a champion hurdler. I decided to sprint away through the trees. It didn't for a second occur to me that Mindy was serious. After all, I'd taken her in when her own mother rejected her. I had even cleaned her bottom. Sadly, gratitude was not in Mindy's vocabulary. She pounded toward me with a commitment that was truly terrifying. Her eyes were red and she was panting and dribbling. It was like something out of a horror film. I ran and ran until I could run no more, past herds of astonished impalas and the wide-eyed wildebeest. Finally I reached the dam at the edge of the game park. There I crumbled exhaustedly to the ground, sobbing with tiredness and rage.

"*Bitch!*" I panted weakly. "*Cow!*"

Mindy bounced to a surprised halt. An expression of benign innocence came over her face. Keeping one eye firmly fixed on my forlorn figure, she poked out a gray tongue and sampled the leaves on the tree above her head. She chewed on them reflectively, as if uncertain how best to proceed. After a few minutes, she strolled down to the edge of the dam and took a long, cool drink. The game, she'd decided, was over.

6

In February 1982, it started raining and didn't stop. Day after day, the sodden giraffe sheltered under the mountain acacias and the rain gauge filled up faster than Dad could empty it. The weir became Victoria Falls in miniature; the river rose in alarming increments.

First to be flooded out were the Burrows family, two or three miles upstream. We stood in our front yard and watched their deep freeze twirl by on the current. The Etheridges were next to leave, fleeing the muddy tide with their David Shepherd originals and mounted ivory tusks. By then the water was lapping at our security fence, and our beehive, a present from James, had gone the way of the Burrowses' comestibles. Mom's charity newsletters had filled her head with images of Bangladesh-style disasters, and she was desperate to follow the Etheridges' example and decamp with all possible haste, but the proximity of disaster had imbued Dad with his usual confident positivity.

"No *ways* will it reach the house," he asserted as the rondavel on the anthill, thatch sagging under the weight of the rain, became an island in a coffee-colored sea. "*Never.* Never in a million years."

Mom became increasingly hysterical. "Do you want your children to drown?" she demanded. "Is that what you want?"

But Dad insisted he was monitoring the situation. He claimed to have a tractor and trailer and a team of men (none of whom were immediately evident) standing by to whisk us to safety, and he put sticks in the lawn, one foot apart, to track the water's progress. Every night he'd shake his head at the clouds scudding across the television weather report and say: "I can't see this continuing much longer. I just can't see it myself."

I began to feel relieved that my bedroom was on the second floor.

Twenty-eight years earlier, the time of the last great flood at Rainbow's End, the young Irish manager, Mike Swan, was woken by his farmworkers in the dead of night. He'd emerged, blinking, to find a black lake moving in on the tobacco barns. Only some quick thinking, hard labor, and a wall of *mielie-meal* sacks saved them.

That was also the year that Cameron "Cam" Meredith and Nobbie Clark, two local boys, decided they weren't going to let a little thing like a flood prevent them from visiting their girlfriends in Gwelo. On the day that his father took ownership of a brand-new Humber Super Snipe, Nobbie Clark persuaded him to hand over the keys, and he and a very excited Cam set off on their road trip. When they reached the Umfuli, they found the bridge underwater. In time-honored Gadzema tradition, they refused to countenance failure and "made a plan." Why, they reasoned, couldn't they use the railway bridge? There it was, just a few hundred yards upstream, standing proudly above the current.

Having been assured that the trains were canceled because of the floods, the boys and some hastily recruited volunteers set to work. Boards were fetched and placed on the tracks, and the car was driven onto them. Once the rear wheels had passed over the back boards, these were carried forward and the car was moved again. In this way they inched toward the opposite shore, cheered on by a growing crowd.

They were almost there when a plume of smoke floated over the tree line. Pandemonium ensued. How could they save the car? But it quickly became obvious that the best they could hope for was to save their own skins, and they sprinted down the tracks and dived over the side just as the train, packed full of passengers, burst into view. There was not the smallest chance of it stopping. With a scream of its whistle, it slammed into the hood of the Humber Super Snipe, scooping it up on one side of the bridge and propelling it clean across to the other, whereupon it left the rails like a departing Boeing. When gravity intervened, the car smashed down onto the bank and slid into the mud and reeds. There it lay for the next decade—a rusting blue reminder of the dangers of allowing passion to cloud reason.

At Rainbow's End, the river was two feet from our front door when the rain finally let up. By then Mom was preparing to pack her suitcases, gather up Lis and me, and leave.

Again.

"It's one thing him taking a chance with our lives—we don't matter. But I won't have him endangering you children.

"And," she added pointedly, "it's not the first time he's done *that*."

But Dad was unrepentant. He'd told us the water wouldn't reach the house, and he'd been proved right. Thanks to him, we'd been spared the hassle of moving.

"No, we're quite fine," he told people when they phoned to check if we'd drowned or been swept away to Kariba. "Quite fine. *Ag*, you know, it came as far as the garden, but it was never really a problem."

When the waters receded, there were no longer two crocodiles sunning themselves on the sandbank being flossed by the egrets. One had disappeared.

"I'm very worried about it," my mother said on the phone to Richard Etheridge. "Maybe it drowned."

"May, crocodiles don't drown!" roared Richard down the line. "I shot it and turned it into a handbag for Catherine."

In hindsight, the flood was an omen of what was to come, but I didn't recognize it as one. Instead I sent Morning Star, who'd come of age, flying around the cross-country course the carpenter had erected for me in the game park, splashing through water jumps and galloping up treacherous muddy banks as if we were at Badminton, frightening Jenny and the impalas.

Only a few weeks earlier Star had been diagnosed as "mentally ill" by a woman trainer who'd reputedly been a stunt rider in a James Bond film. I'd trained Star myself and ridden him quite happily around the farm, but because I wanted him to be a champion, I'd sent him to her for an extra polish. On his first day in her yard, he'd smashed through a stable roof and tried to kick to death a couple of grooms. It had taken her a week to get him under control, and then she'd managed to ride him only by roping him between two horses and using a severe bridle.

Afterward she'd devastated me with the "mentally ill" comment and told me that, although I'd be able to ride him, I'd never be able to trust him. One day when I least expected it, she warned, he could go berserk and kill me.

Needless to say, on Star's return to Rainbow's End I went to ride him as nervously as I'd once prepared to ride Cassandra. But he was the same way he'd always been, fiery but sweet-natured. I rode him in a soft rubber bit, but he hardly needed even that. Like Cass, he went from a full gallop to a stop or vice versa on voice commands alone. We were cantering home through the bush and I was wondering how the trainer could have been so mistaken about him when a kudu bull sprang up out of the long grass underneath us.

Star reared. His black hooves scissored at the air, and his mane slapped my face as I leaned into him. When he touched down again, his quarters bunched, and I felt the immense power of him beneath me as he propelled himself forward and bolted.

I thought quite calmly: This is it. This is the moment when he goes berserk and kills me.

But he didn't. He didn't then and he didn't for the whole twenty-three years of his life (during which I went back to Zimbabwe at least once a year for up to two months at a time), never hurting me or harming me in any way, never being anything other than gentle with me. He simply galloped a couple of strides and then he wheeled and stood still, snorting, and we both watched as the kudu, one of nature's most perfect creations, loped away through the flaxen grass, spiral horns tipped back.

And so Star and Cass and I went to shows together, and I practiced singing in the cathedral vastness of the barns and cut my hair short and combined aerobics with gymnastics and Royal Canadian Air Force exercises in an effort to look like Olivia on the cover of *Physical* and bought a guitar that I wasn't able to tune, and in between I studied my little stack of albums or the novels on my bookshelf and wondered how I'd ever cross the gulf between me and the people who created them. How anyone *ever* escaped the railway tracks of destiny, the small-town thing that locked you down, sealed you in, trapped you forever in a web of your own making.

I'd go to Mom for advice because she was a world-class escape artist, even though she hadn't managed to escape this—a life she hadn't wanted. Soon she'd be telling Lisa: "Never marry a farmer and never become a secretary."

Mom agreed with me that a significant bar to success of any kind was our unpronounceable Dutch surname, and it was she who decided I should change my name to Lauren St John. She, Dad, and Lisa took steps to alter their names by deed poll as well, but since we couldn't find a mutually acceptable option, we all ended up with different surnames. Regarding the logistics of becoming famous when my starting point was Gadzema, Mom repeated like a mantra: "You can have anything you want if you just want it badly enough. It doesn't matter if it's a Rolls-Royce or a castle on a hill or if you want to be a pop singer. Everything is possible. You just have to want it enough."

And so I'd lean against a tree in the game park and watch the giraffe and yearn until my veins seemed to overflow with wanting, but it didn't resolve the conflict. The bush and the animals were my life, and Africa was in my blood. How would I ever live without it?

My new loyalty to Mom added to the friction at home, and Dad told me I was the cause of all the trouble in the house. I couldn't see how I could possibly be the cause of the rows that turned the dinner table into a war zone at which Lisa sat wide-eyed with alarm and I tried not to cry, because if I cried I was screamed at and if Mom cried she was screamed at and that always made Lisa cry, too. But it was there in my diary:

> May 3, 1982: Dad told me I caused all the trouble in the house. So I said I was leaving home. We said sorry though.
> May 5: Mom is going overseas soon. She's going to London, Portugal, Switzerland and Holland.
> May 29: Got a postcard from Mom. She was in Lisbon and had a crash-landing because her plane burst a tyre.

While she was away, Dad dragged me to the Suri Suri Club out on the Chakari Road. The clubhouse was rustic and thatched with a slate floor, and it overlooked a pretty dam with a lush fringe of reeds. There he played tennis and drank, and not necessarily in that order.

He and his tennis partner, Betty B, laughed a lot on the court, and anytime he wasn't playing, there was a smiling circle around him because he was naturally sociable and always in the best of possible humors in these settings and very popular because he was funny, self-deprecating, and anxious to please, and always incredibly polite.

Bored and resentful, I glowered on the sidelines until my friend Lisa arrived to cheer me up. She introduced me to Nick, who was dark and bare-chested and in his late teens or early twenties, wearing safari green OK Bazaar shorts. One of his legs was tanned and muscular; the other was a stump, blown off in the War. His nickname was Skippy.

Toward evening I ended up in a haystack with him. When I kissed him, I felt like I was healing him, like I was making up for the War years, for everything he'd lost. The arching sky was overcast, and the air felt close and sticky. A film of sweat lent Skippy's skin a bronze shimmer. We kissed until the sun set over the dam in a muted quilt of pillowy clouds laced with halfhearted pinks. After a while we just lay there in silence, and I rested my cheek against his brown chest.

Dad's voice boomed into our love nest.

"Come on, my friend, let's go now, see."

I scrambled out of the hollow in the bales, pulling hay from my hair, hot with humiliation. Dad said nothing. He just strode to the car, weaving slightly, and focused on getting the key into the lock. When I dared to glance back, Skippy was sitting up grinning. He was waist-deep in hay. He looked whole.

> June 27: Dad watched cricket all day and then got
> smashed (drunk) and pranged the truck on a police road-
> block. He might lose his license.

Mom was back from her travels by then, and she drove to the police station along dark farm roads to collect him. The only damage done to his blue pickup was a broken headlight, but coming so soon after he'd crashed our new Renault at the end of another drinking session—arriving home not with an apology but with a warning to Mom: "Don't say a word. Not *one* word"—it led to furious rows. He went to court and was heavily fined but didn't—to his relief and ours, because it would have cost him his job—lose his license.

I spent as little time in or near the house as possible. I rode Cass along the strip road to my friend Dee Burrows's house, and we went out on the old green railway bridge where Cam and Nobbie had killed the Humber Super Snipe and I flirted with my own mortality by hanging upside down by my knees from a steel girder and laughing at the circles of rocks and frill of shallow water a hundred feet or so below. I wondered what would happen if I slipped. If I plummeted to earth as the civet cat had once done. If I was no more. Would my parents be sorry? But it was a fleeting thought. There were too many beautiful things to live for.

One came along in a matter of days when I found that Olivia Newton-John was appearing at the Las Vegas–style resort of Sun City in Bophuthatswana, an independent state within South Africa. A lot of artists boycotted Sun City, which was seen as the playground of many of the debauched white architects of the Apartheid regime, but Olivia was not one of them and I was still at an age where pop-star worship took precedence over politics. A bus tour was going, and I planned to be on it. Money was tight and it took a few weeks of pleading, but eventually I was allowed to go, and I took my scrapbooks and sat outside my idol's hotel door until a security guard agreed to deliver them and Olivia autographed them all the way through and made comments like "You have a fantastic collection of photos!" I wanted so badly to meet her but in the end had to be satisfied with her signature and being allowed, at fifteen, to travel on my own to another country to stay in a hotel where perma-tanned, glassy-eyed grown-ups nodded over slot machines at breakfast, just so I could see Olivia in concert. Although Mom, who couldn't stand the idea of missing out on a trip, spoiled it slightly by popping up at Sun City in the middle of it all.

I came home to find that it was not only the dinner table that had become a war zone. Between Mindy the deranged cow, the mad Brahman bull, the snakes, and the ostriches, the game park required careful negotiation. It was a certainty that somebody was going to be trampled or bitten at some stage, and sure enough, Dad and Lisa were charged by Cheeky down at the water hole. They had no chance of outrunning him, so Dad just scooped up Lisa and tossed her into a thorn tree, yelling: "Grab something and hang on for dear life."

Then he scrambled up after her and tried to beat the ostrich off with a stick.

Their cries attracted the attention of Mom, who came out into the game park and tried to distract Cheeky by screeching, cooing, and waving her arms. He ran at her with the speed of a champion race bird, gray-pink legs flying like knives, but she was close enough to the gate to get away. Next he turned his attention to Goat, who'd been watching these antics with interest. Crazed, he literally pounded Goat into the ground. But Goat played dead and, despite being a bit battered and bemused, was basically unharmed.

In the meantime, Dad had lost his temper with Lisa for crying.

"Like it isn't normal to cry when you're eight years old and you've been chased by an ostrich," she said drily later.

But in one way or another he was always saving us.

Soon afterward, Cheeky chased his last victim. He was pursuing the game park caretaker, when—some might say karmically—he stepped into a hole and broke a leg. He had to be destroyed. Ostriches have pocked, leathery skin, which is prized by people who like that kind of thing, so a short while after his last temper tantrum, Cheeky was a belt holding up Dad's trousers. He, like the crocodile, stretched to a handbag, but not one Mom had any intention of carrying.

Sometimes, though, it felt like it was raining death. As if there was no way to get through a week or even a day without someone or something meeting a peculiarly African fate. In rapid succession, Goat disappeared (stolen, we established later, for a compound cooking pot), Bacon was killed by the fox terriers, and our old thoroughbred mare Queenie's newborn foal—which, after a series of miscarriages, she loved as intensely as any human mother would have done and mourned just as bitterly—was killed by a ridgeback we'd acquired just a week earlier from the SPCA. The woman from the SPCA was outraged when Dad took him back, but foal murdering aside, he was a good dog, and she quickly found another home for him.

After that, we went through a phase when it seemed like every time we left the house, the fox terriers killed one of our cats, or one of the other dogs was run over by a game park visitor's car or died of biliary, a tick disease, or was bitten by a snake, or a cobra was found under the dining room table and beheaded. Only the fox terriers were indestructible.

Then one morning Luka didn't come to work. I'd taught Luka to ride so that he could exercise some of the horses when I was at school, and he'd learned in the space of an hour. The rising trot, cantering, and the riding aids were all effortless for him. I'd puzzled over it for days afterward. Was he a natural? Could he have been teaching himself secretly? Could he have learned to ride in a previous job? But Luka was a man of few words and just smiled evasively when I tried to question him about it, so I'd never really got to the bottom of it.

"Luka *ari kupi?*" I asked Gatsi when Luka didn't appear, but no one seemed to know where he was or what he was doing. Then a somber deputation arrived to talk to Dad. He sped away to the compound, where a crowd was gathered around Luka's hut. African custom would not allow Dad to enter the house of the death, but somebody handed him the cause: a plastic bottle of Cooper's cattle dip, administered by Luka's own hand. Diluted, it looked like skimmed milk, but the harsh, sulfuric smell of it was unmistakable. Like Peter's wife back at Giant Estate, he had been driven to suicide by a domestic crisis. Like her, he'd used cattle dip and died a slow, excruciating death.

It was hard not to feel that almost everything in Africa ended in tragedy.

But these things, although important in my world at Rainbow's End, were of pinhead significance compared with the whispers about what was going on in Matabeleland and the Midlands. For the first couple of years after Independence, there'd been simmering hostility and several violent skirmishes between rival groups of ex-guerrillas, always along tribal lines. Mugabe's former fighters, men whose allegiances were to ZANU (Zimbabwe African National Union), the political wing of

ZANLA, were all Shona speakers from the northern part of the country. Supporters of Joshua Nkomo's ZAPU (Zimbabwe African People's Union), ex–ZIPRA fighters, were mostly Ndebele speakers from Southern Zimbabwe. In 1981 and 1982, the tensions between the two groups twice erupted into pitched battles, the first of which led to three hundred deaths and the air force and the Rhodesian African Rifles (RAR) being called in. South African tanks massed at the border.

Then came the news that Nkomo, known affectionately among the Ndebele people as Umdala Wethu, "Our Old Man," had been accused, along with several other ZAPU leaders, of plotting a coup. They were "relieved of their duties" and Nkomo's passport confiscated and his movements restricted to Bulawayo following the discovery of arms caches on ZAPU properties. In response to the "unrest" that followed, Mugabe sent in his Shona army, Fifth Brigade, to rout out the "dissidents" of Matabeleland and the Midlands.

Early in 1983, tales of acts so barbaric and depraved as to be inhuman began to filter out of Matabeleland, the heartland of the minority Ndebele people. These stories traveled almost on the wind because to repeat them was to risk inviting the same brutality to one's own door. They concerned the North Korea–trained soldiers of Fifth Brigade, also known as Gukurahundi (a Shona term for the storm that sweeps away the chaff before the spring rains). These soldiers were loyal only to the prime minister and operated under the command of Colonel Perence Shiri, known as the "Black Jesus." One of the methods they were said to use to bring "about peace very, very quickly" was to force Ndebele villagers to dig mass graves and climb in before being shot or buried alive. They also sliced open the wombs of pregnant women to reveal "dissident" fetuses and watched as the women bled to death; gang-raped girls and women and then hacked at their genitals until they bled to death; threw villagers down mine shafts or starved them in detention camps; made them have sex with dogs or pigs; ordered fathers to rape their daughters; made survivors eat their loved ones; burned villagers alive in their huts; or made them stand in a line, facing the same direction, and killed them with a single bullet.

None of these things were reported in the state-controlled media, and it would be years before we knew the scale of the genocide. Unofficial estimates put the number of dead in that period at between 10,000 and 30,000, as many as perished in the whole "Liberation Struggle." But it was only the beginning of a campaign of intimidation, torture, murder, and displacement of innocent civilians that continues to this day and, at the time of writing, is thought to involve hundreds of thousands of Ndebele people, plus anyone else thought to oppose Mugabe's rule. The only "official" report into Mugabe's mission to cleanse the area of dissidents was the 1997 Catholic Commission for Justice and Peace inquiry, which concluded that there were 2,000 confirmed and 4,000 "almost certain" deaths in Matabeleland and the Midlands between 1980 and 1989, "at least" 10,000 detentions, and "not less than" 7,000 beaten and tortured. The authors of the report conceded that the true figures were probably many times higher. None of the governments that had sponsored Mugabe's ascent to power condemned him in any meaningful way, and the Matabele didn't rise up because Nkomo, their political and spiritual leader for generations, still believed in a democratic solution. He believed it even when he went into self-imposed exile in 1983, and so he said little and protested even less about the torture and massacring of his people.

It was the Deafening Silence all over again.

Once more we were on our own. Once more we were united in perhaps the only language Zimbabweans knew how to be united in: the language of grief.

The fear that had gone away was back again. It wasn't constant, the way it had been during the War, and it was no longer a fear of the unknown. At sixteen, I was afraid when Mugabe's motorcade went by with its siren-blasting, blue-light-flashing motorcycle outriders, bodyguard and decoy cars, and gray truckloads of soldiers just dying for an excuse to use their machine guns, because when that happened we had to get off the road as quickly as we could—even if it meant crashing the car into a ditch—in case they thought we were a threat and chopped us down in a blizzard of machine-gun fire. Which they would, and had done to others before. I was afraid, too, that we might inadvertently drive past Mugabe's residence during its dusk-to-dawn curfew and be similarly annihilated, like other unfortunates we'd heard about. Suspicious accidents and unexplained deaths were also on the increase, with potential political rivals turning up in car trunks. Josiah Tongogara, the immensely popular Shona guerrilla commander who'd been at the Lancaster House talks and was seen as a moderating, pro-Ndebele influence and likely leadership candidate, had been the first to go, dying mysteriously in a Mozambican car wreck on Christmas Day 1979, before Mugabe ever took power.

But most of all I was afraid of the Central Intelligence Organization (CIO), Zimbabwe's secret police—also North Korean trained. It was said that they infiltrated social clubs and bars and put taps on telephone lines and paid domestic workers to listen at doors, and that anyone caught saying anything negative about the government or so much as doodling on a picture of Mugabe could be arrested and thrown into the STD (sexually transmitted disease)- and lice-infested cells of Chikurubi Prison. That was if they were lucky. A lot of times they just disappeared. There was talk of a crocodile farm.

The day the CIO came to Rainbow's End, Dad recognized their trademark white Land Rover and ordered Mom to stay inside. Five men climbed out and surrounded him in the yard. For more than an hour they fired questions at him until Dad, who could stare into the barrel of a gun without flinching, who didn't turn a hair at grenades falling at his feet or putting snakes into sacks in the dark or firefights on dam walls, shook like a child with fear. *Perspired* with it. He answered their questions fervently and with increasing desperation. "Yes, sir. No, sir. No ways, sir. Never, sir. I *promise* you, sir. You can check with anyone, sir."

And Mom watched fearfully from the front door, not understanding entirely what they were there for but knowing what it could mean.

They accused Dad of collecting arms and ammunition from a farmer in Selous. They knew he'd done it because the cook who worked for the farmer had witnessed it. What worried Dad was that the men seemed very sure of their facts, and he knew that if his memory didn't improve, they'd take him somewhere where it would. They kept going on about boxes of guns and stun grenades. They even described the boxes—two cardboard grocery boxes.

That's when Mom stepped forward and said: "You're not talking about the dahlia bulbs we were given, are you?" And she showed them the boxes.

"Your mom saved my life that day," Dad would say afterward. "She really did."

So sometimes it felt like we were at war again. Only the ground rules had changed.

But the ordinary people of Zimbabwe were as gentle as Inyanga rain. I saw it in the careless joy of the children who attended the farm school at Wicklow Estate; in the teasing of the mushroom sellers, who persuaded us to take home wild mushrooms the size of dinner plates and two or three times the thickness of steaks, which were delicious grilled with cheese; in the boisterous crowds who packed the beer garden of the Hartley Hotel to see Thomas Mapfumo & the Blacks Unlimited; and I saw it in Daniel, who'd replaced the retiring Medicine.

Daniel was sweetly, entertainingly hopeless, to the point of being comical, but he immediately became one of my favorite people, and I, for some reason, became one of his. Everything I did or said made him dissolve into laughter, and when he wasn't laughing, he was trying his hardest not to laugh. Sometimes when I went home to Rainbow's End, I looked forward to seeing Daniel more than I did my own parents, even though our conversations were restricted largely to small talk about animals and family:

> Me: *Kunjani*, Daniel? (How are you, Daniel?)
> Daniel: Ah, *yena mushi stelek. Yena mushi.* (Ah, very good. Good.)
> Me: *Zonke, yena* right? (Everything's all right?)
> Daniel: Ah, *yena* square. (It's square.)
> Me: *Kunjani lo picannin gawena?* (How are your children?)
> Daniel: *Yena mushi.* (They're good.)
> Me: *Kunjani lo shamwari gamina?* (How's my friend [Star]?)
> Daniel: Ah, *yena mafuta stelek.* (He's very fat.)

It was in these small ways that I reconnected with the Africans of my country and learned, in tiny degrees, to love them and love their culture.

In less tiny increments I began to feel a nagging sense of alienation. The whites who left the remembered paradise of Rhodesia generally found it so difficult to adjust to the harsh realities of life in the real world that they'd earned themselves the derisory nickname "The Whenwes." As in "*When we* were in Rhodesia, the Lion beer never stopped flowing and the sun never stopped shining, et cetera, et cetera." They wandered the world like restless spirits, unable to relinquish the Good Old Days, unable to fit into their chosen countries, unable to fit in back home. There was even a comic book about their woes.

But I was in a different limbo. It was getting harder and harder for me to live with what I now knew to be the reality of our former lives. I felt caught between two worlds: an African world that, because of the past, I might never truly be part of, and my own world, to which I found it increasingly hard to belong. I didn't want a life of eternal sunshine. I didn't want to be waited on and made cups of tea. Blacks, whites, and Asians were integrating, forming wonderful, rewarding friendships, and healing one another more quickly and more whole-heartedly than non-Zimbabweans would ever have believed possible, but decades of social conditioning meant that casual, offhand racism from people from all walks of life was a constant. So was the happy-go-lucky, make-a-plan attitude of Zimbabweans of all races, which was admirable in many ways because it allowed people to function and even to be content under the most unendurable circumstances. I went along with it to a certain extent, but as I grew older, I found it more and more disturbing for its denial of what lay beneath.

With the War over, secrets were surfacing daily about atrocities committed by the Rhodesian government and security forces, particu-larly by the Selous Scouts, who'd "specialized" in convincing guerrillas to change sides by any means necessary, and some of whom were implicated in an ivory poaching scandal in the Gonarezhou National Park toward the end of the War.

Michelle Swanepoel has a clear recollection of seeing two hairy, bearded men swagger into the bar at Hartley Club holding the top half of a skull and start swigging Lion beer from it.

She tugged at Swannie's arm. "Dad, do you know those men are drinking beer out of a human head?"

"Yes, sweetheart," replied her father. They're Selous Scouts."

Evil deeds had also been carried out by men we knew, one of whom was suspected of involvement in a massacre. Back in the seventies, when Mom was still a happy innocent, she'd unknowingly helped him flee the country. She'd had no idea that he was wanted by the Military Police, only that he was in some sort of trouble, which he assured her would be resolved if he went sightseeing in Europe for a few months. It was not until years later that she learned the truth of what she'd done. What *he'd* done.

So where did all this leave me? Was my love of the land any less valid because of the actions of my forefathers, my government, my father, or even, in my ignorance, myself? In Britain and the United States, people were accepted as British or American from the moment of their birth or the day they were granted citizenship; yet in Zimbabwe black people were Africans, Indians were Indians, and whites were regularly labeled Europeans.

My family had been in Africa for four generations.

Why wasn't I African? Why?

But despite these unanswerable questions, life went on, as it always does. Lisa left Chegutu Primary for Lilfordia, an even more draconian institution where, at eight years old, she was made to run two miles every morning before breakfast even though she fainted daily. She was also locked away for the entire term.

I was considerably better off. At the beginning of 1983, Merina and I had persuaded our parents that the food and other conditions in the school hostel had become intolerable—which to some extent they had, but really we were just sick of bells and rules—and we moved in with Sophie, a glamorous blond Greek divorcée who'd been accustomed to cooking for three large sons and made Greek-family-size pans of moussaka every evening and sliced them in half for just the two of us. Sophie had one spare room with a double bed, which Merina and I agreed to share on the proviso that nobody at school ever found out about it. She also had a twenty-something son, who was always trying to spy on us in the bath, and a suave fifty-something man friend who was a photographer for the Sunday *Mail*.

"How do we get to be famous?" I asked Mr. Grey. "How do we get into the newspaper?"

Mr. Grey said it was easy. Even criminals did it. He agreed to take black-and-white head shots for us so that we'd have them for our portfolios when we got our big break. He escorted us into the photography studio of the newspaper, and we posed like shy pop stars and came away with a stack of professional photos. In the pictures I look serious and innocent and not in the least pop-staresque, probably because, in response to all the deaths and turmoil in my life, I'd recently become a born-again Christian.

Jean had first tried to interest us in the idea of going to church in the middle of the previous year, but it was some months before we gave in. I still loved the Anglican cathedral for its architecture and atmosphere, but the hymns and sermons bored me, and the blank faces of many churchgoers bothered me. But Immanuel was not like any church I'd ever known. It was a nondenominational, evangelical church with a talented band, catchy songs of worship, and fantastic fire-and-brimstone sermons about the Twelve Horsemen of the Apocalypse and the Second Coming and other soul-stirring subjects. During the service, the spirit of God would sweep through the church like a whirlwind through a field of corn, and people would be struck down and talk in tongues and undergo dramatic conversions.

In mid-February I was officially Born Again in a baptism ceremony at Immanuel, which Mom was upset about because, she said, I'd already been christened in a proper church. During the baptism, I was plunged backward into an icy pool and my white gown spread out around me like the broad petals of an arum lily. I felt closer to God but not quite as charitably toward the pastor, whom I felt should have heated the water first.

It was while I was doing my bit to "go forth and make disciples" afterward that I discovered that Dad, whose soul I felt was in need of urgent rescue, was an atheist.

I couldn't understand how I could not have known such a vital fact about him, and I couldn't take it in that it was true.

"So you really think we die and we go in the ground and that's it?"

"*Ja*, I do. Once you've snuffed it, that's it."

"But surely there were times in the War when you thought you might die that you maybe prayed a little or at least hoped there might be a God."

"No, my friend, I didn't. What kind of God would allow the suffering we have in this world?"

At the height of our churchgoing phase, Merina and I spent a lot of Sundays and the occasional Saturday night with Jean and her warmly eccentric mother, Margot. Margot was a reformed Bohemian who had taken to Christianity with the zeal of a recent convert. She drove a sporty blue Alpha, which never started in the morning, and cooked up an alarming line in boiled chicken, usually on the pink side, gluey spaghetti Bolognese, and scrambled eggs swimming in urine-colored juice. Then she found in the toaster a dead rat that clearly had been toasted many, many times, and that finished us off.

Because Merina and I had our hearts set on becoming pop singers,

Margot forced us to listen to Jim Bakker tapes, in which the U.S. tele-vangelist bemoaned the evils of pop music and devil-promoting bands like Queen and AC/DC, and detailed the subliminal satanic messages contained in songs like "Another One Bites the Dust," which you could hear if you played the records backward. We tried it for ourselves, and sure enough, a spooky voice advised us: "It's fun to smoke marijuana." According to Jim Bakker, even angelic Olivia corrupted the innocent with her lyrics about there being nothing left to talk about "'less it's horizontally." These sessions always ended in terrible rows, after which Merina and I would lie awake plotting to hitchhike back to Sophie's house at the crack of dawn because, as much as we loved Jesus, we also loved rock music and boys.

On one of these lost weekends, we were sitting on Margot's brick porch sucking the nectar from orange honeysuckle flowers when I looked up and saw a blond head and set of rugby-player shoulders encircled by a halo of sunlight and outlined against the sky. A beauti-ful boy stepped forward and stood laughing, holding my gaze in a teasing, frankly sexual way among the discarded blossoms at our feet. His name was Troy. He was a friend of Jean's brother Richard, big for his age and, at an age when it matters, two years younger than I was.

The first time he kissed me was on the road outside Roosevelt after I'd eaten the pink center out of a Charons' chocolate bar. When he leaned toward me, his blazer moved and the sweaty boy smell of him came out, and I put my palms on his chest and felt his pecs ride up under the thin cotton of his gray Churchill school shirt. He had a con-fident, sensual mouth, curling up at the edges. His kiss was soft, salty, and ice-creamy.

"You taste like chocolate and strawberries," he murmured.

And so, for the first time, I had a proper boyfriend. On weekends when I didn't go home to Rainbow's End, we'd lock ourselves in Mar-got's spare bedroom and kiss until we felt drugged while she hammered at the door and ranted about heavy petting. Twice we made the trip to church and then, just as everyone was getting out of the car, announced that we weren't going in after all. We'd spend the time kissing and gig-gling and writing "I Love You" in the fog of our breath on the windows while the songs of Immanuel floated out to us.

At Roosevelt we caused a small scandal because he was so young, and within a few months there was talk of him and some other girl, but by then the sudden evaporation of his interest was the least of my concerns. For it was at that time, when I was the most attracted to a boy I'd ever been, that I began to have dreams about girls—vivid, erotic dreams in which I was not just kissing them, I was making love to them. I told no one, least of all Merina, with whom I was still sharing a bed, although each time I woke I was sure she could view them on my face in full Technicolor. But I dismissed them out of hand as figments of my imagination or unfortunate by-products of the power of suggestion. Either way, it was just one more thing to process and not something I was prepared to deal with then.

Even so, the continual shifting of the foundations beneath my feet was starting to wear me down. One weekend as I was riding Star across the triangular yellow plain that separated the lands from the house, I suddenly became conscious of looking at the view as if through a wide-angle lens; at the red-brick barns, the distant silver gums, the game park, and our thatched home tucked among the msasas and jacarandas, its once-gold roof darkened with time. And I had the overwhelming sensation that I was living in a house of cards, with everything about to collapse.

8

Nothing was stable anymore, nothing was sure. On sleepless nights at Rainbow's End, I put my head under the pillow and listened to the blood pound in my ears like an African drum.

After a spitting cobra in the kitchen sink shot a stream of venom into Madala's only seeing eye (his response was hampered because his other eye was still bandaged from a glaucoma operation), I began to get a phobia about snakes. Near-imperceptible rustles in the thatch sent me into a fever of terror, and on several occasions I convinced myself that a thread of green boomslang was dangling above my bed in the darkness, ready to inflict a fatal bite. I had recurring dreams in which I'd be walking through the bush, or maybe driving, and I'd see a snake and stop to look at it. Only then would I realize that I was surrounded by snakes of every species. They'd be draped over branches or coiled upon rocks or at my feet, and I'd know that I would never escape without being bitten. I never was, but the terror was no less intense. It didn't help that in daylight the nightmares constantly threatened to become reality. Twenty-six pythons made their way into our chicken run before we stopped counting, and I almost stepped on a night adder trying to get through the lounge door. Only the whisper of its scales as it slid up the glass and flopped back down again saved me.

It seemed to me that, even for a farm in Africa, *even* for a farm on a river with resident poultry, an unnatural number of snakes were hell-bent on getting into the house.

• • •

One March afternoon in 1983 I was up in my room writing a song when Mom, who rarely rushed anywhere, came hurtling up the stairs. Her face was as colorless as the walls and her hands were in bird claws, the way they sometimes went in hospital. She was trembling like she hadn't trembled since the War, and she was breathless and slightly incoherent, but it was impossible to misunderstand the last part of what she said, which was "Carl B is on his way over. Anything could happen. You've got to get away from here."

So I ran. I ran the way I'd run a thousand times before, past the still, dry weir and the sentrylike acacias on the river's edge, and through the autumn bush; slipping and scrambling up and down the dead-leaf-piled gullies. I ran until I doubled over with a stitch that cut like a switch-blade and started retching bile, because it had happened again: Dad had had another affair. Another name had been added to the long, long list of women who had pursued him or been pursued by him, who had driven us from town to town. Another husband was coming to beat him up, just like the one at the double-story.

But, of course, there hadn't been a man yet who was a match for him, and so apart from a tussle and a lot of heated words ("Sticks and stones can break my bones but words kill"), Dad was left unscathed, and the only thing he'd had to do in return was promise he wouldn't see her, Betty B, again. His tennis partner. The woman with the maroon-brown tan, henna-red hair, and nasal voice. The woman whose farm fire he had gone to fight, almost wrecking our brand-new car by driving like a man possessed over a plowed land at some ungodly hour—while Mom shrieked and the engine screamed—to raise the alarm and beat away the blaze, so that both Mr. and Mrs. B had thought him worthy of a medal.

Mr. B had since revised his opinion.

When I went back to school, Mom kept me abreast of developments.

Yes, it was over between them.

No, it wasn't quite over, but Dad was planning to go and have a long talk to Betty B about it being well and truly over.

Yes, it was officially over.

No, it wasn't over after all: six weeks on, she'd seen them together at a cattle sale and been devastated yet again. Not to mention embarrassed in front of the entire farming community.

So she'd rung Carl, the husband, and organized an intervention. The four of them had met at the Bs' farmhouse. And while she was sitting there listening to a series of half-truths and sordid revelations that made all four parties look stupid, a garish orange china ashtray had somehow come into her hands, and when she couldn't stand it anymore, when the other three were sparring over semantics and appeared to have forgotten her, she'd stood up, walked casually over to Betty, and smashed the ashtray over her head, almost giving her a concussion.

So now it really was over. But then again, so was their marriage.

On the other end of the phone, or holed up with Mom in her bedroom while Merina paced outside, I listened to all of this and attempted to empathize, sympathize, and advise, and with every word I felt my soul and everything I'd ever trusted in, had faith in, or depended upon, being stripped away to nothing, until in the end, when I set that against the War and Rhodesia and the collapse of all we'd believed in, that was what I was left with: *Nothing*. The small gains I had made seemed infinitesimal.

In June, Mom took her clothes and a few essentials and moved out of Rainbow's End. It was winter then, and at school I went the entire term without wearing a sweater, as if I were paying a penance of some kind. I felt bereft without my little sister, from whom I always seemed to be apart. Now, when we most needed each other, we were separated by the razor-wire walls of distance, of boarding school, of an ocean or two of unspoken hurt.

Dad drank more and more heavily. It was almost as if he'd decided he was a terrible person, so he'd just give up and do what was expected of him. One weekend Merina came home with me and Dad took us to some disco at the Chegutu Club, where there was tinsel and shiny red tassels everywhere and lots of overly made-up farmers' wives and farmers with awkward feet and a DJ with a turntable playing things like "Winner Takes It All." I spent a lot of time sitting alone at a table with a club special and a plate of chips 'n' dip while Dad made merry on the other side of the room and Merina danced and kissed a farm boy, who immediately declared undying love.

Eventually the farm boy left and Merina was weary and wanted to go home to bed, but Dad kept having one more beer. By the time he was ready to leave, I was seething. I was also sick with dread. Dad was rubber-legged as he led us under the ghostly floodlights to the car. Merina, whose own parents had an entirely healthy relationship with alcohol, who knew nothing about the police roadblock incident, and who had heard only the bare bones of the story of my parents' separation, was tired but still relatively cheerful after her encounter with the farm boy and mystified as to why I was in such a black mood. She kept tickling me to try to make me laugh. "Smile, Pookie!" she said. "Smile!"

As soon as we were in the car, she went quiet. Negotiating the wide, silent streets of Chegutu was relatively straightforward, but the strip road was another story. The headlights arced like prison searchlights through the pale grass as we veered along, first on one side of the road and then the other, until we ended up heading for a tree at ninety kilometers per hour and Merina's hands bit into my shoulders as she shouted from the back: "Do something!"

"Dad!" I screamed, wrenching at the wheel.

He snatched it back, laughing a little, cursing a little, and then a minute later the same thing happened again. And again. And as we became progressively more afraid for our lives and I tried, surreptitiously, to hold a corner of the steering wheel, an impotent fury gripped me, because this time it was not just about me but about my best friend, for whom I felt responsible.

The next morning, when I emerged wan and aggrieved from the bedroom, Dad said from behind a smoke screen of Madison: "Are you sulking, are you?"

"No," I lied.

"Well then, why are you sniveling?"

I didn't answer. I *couldn't*. I just muttered something about being tired and fed up, which he took as disrespect, and as I exited the house as loudly and rudely as I could without actually drawing Dad's attention to the fact that that was what I was doing, I thought I heard him say: "You're not too old for a hiding."

Later, though, he came to say sorry.

In the August school holidays, I wrote a song called "Grey Weather," which reflected my state of mind, and posted it to my friend Colleen, who I knew would understand it. I enclosed one of Mr. Grey's photos and signed it because I thought that if I acted out the small details of my dreams, the big ones would become real. But I could feel the walls closing in on me. Girls at school who'd once fantasized about becoming dancers or stand-up comedians now talked about doing typing courses so that they had "something to fall back on." Some wanted to go overseas for a year and go fruit picking or get temp work as a rite of passage before settling down in Harare in an office job or marrying a farmer and having babies and everything else I didn't want. And yet, when it came right down to it, what was it that I actually wanted? Fame? Which was ephemeral and never happened to people like me and anyway what would I be famous for? And yet still it burned away at me, a desperate, unnamed yearning to go somewhere, to be something, to make my own way in the world.

When it all gets too much, Star calms me. I lie on the ground like a starfish and allow myself to fall into the infinite sky, into the skidding froth of cloud, into the warm, washing sun, and Star grazes around the outline of my body or pushes me to try to get at the grass underneath me or explores my face with a velvet muzzle peppered with prickles or just stands over me like a sleepy sentinel, eyelashes flat against his rough, black cheek, lower lip drooping.

My last term at school was a hedonistic whirl of forgetting, of sweltering, bikini-clad days at Mermaid's Pool or dances where I kissed the smoky lips of boys I'd only just met and tried to forget about the girl dreams and everything else. Now that the end was in sight and freedom from parental constraints and the regimental demands of school beckoned, my spirits had lifted. Merina and I did almost no work. After school we'd walk back to Sophie's house, eat a small mountain of sandwiches, sleep for two hours, walk to the shops and buy something salty (biltong or Willards chips), something sweet (a Choc 99 ice cream), and something sour (a packet of sherbet with a licorice straw or, if we were short of cash, a homemade mix of icing sugar and Eno antacid salts).

In between, we wondered why we had acne.

After dances or school debates, we'd go to Gremlins for hamburgers and milk shakes and then climb into the tinny Datsun Pulsars of barely licensed boys who'd race each other down Enterprise Avenue to a Police sound track. In the boy department, everything was effortless for Merina. At an impromptu party at Rainbow's End, which we organized after persuading Dad to go out for the evening, I spent my time topping up drinks and mopping up fruit punch while Merina kissed Bruce Campbell in the horse paddock.

I studied for most of my O levels the evening before, which worked fine for all subjects bar English literature and French. *Wuthering Heights* did not lend itself well to speed-reading, and my French oral exam involved a scenario in which I'd locked my keys in a car, which since I couldn't remember the words for "key," "car," or "lock," earned me a U for Uncertified to match the one I received for English literature.

In the middle of my exams, Mom phoned me to tell me that she and Dad were getting divorced. Aside from the timing, it was a relief. It was hard to muster the energy to say anything more than "Why didn't you do it years ago?"

She said: "We stayed together for the sake of you children, for you and Lisa."

I said gently: "But we never, ever wanted you to stay together if it meant that you were unhappy."

"You don't understand what it's like being a mother. I wanted to give you your dream. I wanted you both to grow up on a farm and have your horses and be with Jenny and the other animals. I wanted to give you Rainbow's End."

And I saw that, after all, there'd been a price.

Without it being said in so many words, it was clear it was over, Rainbow's End. There would be no custody battle. In spite of everything, she and Dad loved each other, and us, with all their hearts, and everyone wanted the best for everyone else. In November, Mom went down to Cape Town, where she'd always hoped to live again, and while she was there was rushed into hospital for an emergency operation. For years she'd been either traveling or in hospital, and now, ironically, she was both. She sent for my sister, who didn't have exams, and Lisa flew down on her own. I stayed behind and, a month shy of my seventeenth birthday, quit school. I was a year young for my class, and the idea of dropping out then, at sixteen, seemed rebellious. There were lots of tearful good-byes with friends in which we promised to keep in touch and then, with few exceptions, never communicated again.

Adrift in the sea of my fallen-apart world, I held fast to the only things I knew to hold on to: love, faith, my Ambition List, and the lessons I'd learned and sins I planned to atone for if it took me all of my life to do it.

9

The day I left school, Dad came to collect me in the truck. Merina and Jean were off to college to do typing courses and repeat O levels, and I felt a little alone with my dreams and my untuned guitar, but I also had the feeling that I'd been running along a cliff for the longest time with a hang glider and I was finally ready to fly.

At the Marimba Shopping Centre, on the outskirts of Harare, we stopped to pick up a few groceries. Dad ran into the Spar. I hung both arms out of the window to let the sun toast them, and a stream of people came by to sell their wares. There were rose sellers, half-naked picannins with ingenious wire toys, and women with skin like brown satin and golden baskets over their arms. With each there was a dialogue—"*Shamwari*, what about some buskets for your veggie-tables?"—and because it was so good-natured and done with such humor or heartrending appeal, it left me feeling happy and part of it all, part of Africa. Oliver Mtukudzi was playing on some distant radio, and I suddenly felt it was going to be okay. Everything.

That's when my father's ex-mistress, Betty B, stepped into my sight line. At least, I thought it was her. I wasn't really sure. She was walking across the car park laughing with a friend and her tennis tan was more maroon than ever and the sun was blazing down on her henna-tinted perm as if her head were on fire. Right at that moment, every scrap of the hurt, frustration, and helpless fury of the past few years coalesced in my chest into a single point of molten loathing and I wanted to rush over to her and scream: "Why did you have to destroy our family? *Our perfect life?*"

Even though I knew that, if our life had been so perfect, nothing and no one could have destroyed it.

But I didn't move. I just sat there with a paralyzing poison chugging through my veins, trying to figure out if it was her and, if it was, blaming her for seemingly everything but most of all for inadvertently being the cause of us leaving Rainbow's End. There was a jingle of keys. She lifted a hand in good-bye to her friend. She strolled over to her car—which, when I thought about it later, was only spitting distance from ours—and *still* I couldn't move. I told myself it was now or never. The taillights of her car flickered. She was reversing; she was cruising slowly to the entrance; she was stopping to check both ways; she was gone.

The truck door swung open, and the seat springs squeaked under Dad's weight. He tossed me a couple of chocolate bars and a packet of Willards chips, handed me a Coke, and said in his Happy Voice: "I bought you some things. Some *treats.*"

I kept it together until just past the Lion & Cheetah Park, and then the tears began to stream down my face. Dad reacted the way he always did. First with panicky concern—"What's wrong, my friend? Has something happened? Was it something I said?" And then, when I replied, No, not really, I was just sad about him and Mom—because I could hardly say that I was upset after seeing his ex-mistress glide, like a copper battleship, across the Marimba Shopping Centre car park, only I wasn't really sure it was her—with growing fury.

"Oh, for crying in a bucket." He looked at me with glacier eyes. "Why do you have to do that?" he snapped. "Why do you always have to spoil things?"

There was a hostile silence.

"It takes two people," he said finally. "Just remember that."

At Rainbow's End, Tiger jumped into my arms—a red blur of love—and that for some reason made me feel even worse. All I could think was: This wasn't how it was supposed to end. Not with Dad a cruel stranger and me so angry that I never wanted to see any of it—not him, not the farm, perhaps not even Africa—again. I threw my school things uncaringly in the back bedroom, and my tin trunk crashed loudly on the concrete floor. Then I took refuge from my father and the white afternoon heat in the shadows of a deserted stable. My red dog lay panting at my feet. A rage deeper and wider than I'd ever known boiled through me. And the more incensed I became, the more determined I was to leave it all behind and start over.

At some point Dad came into the straw- and horse-infused cool and started to talk, but the walls I'd put up were so high and thick that for a long time his voice was muffled. Only the odd word or phrase filtered through. Eventually I heard him say: "When you were little, Mom was forever sick—well, she couldn't have always been sick, it just seemed that way—and I used to take care of you. I used to dress you in your smart clothes and carry you across to Mrs. Robinson, your daymother (child minder); then when I came home from work, I'd bathe you and put you to bed." And some of the fight went out of me.

And even though I was still only partially listening, my mind began to fill in the blanks. When I was five and in an all-dark room and sorry for myself with measles at Pussy Willow cottage, Dad had brought me a nurse doll he told me would take care of me, a tall doll with brassy yellow hair and a red cross on the front of her uniform. I thought about that and how she'd made me smile, and about how he'd taught me to love horses and nature and deliver calves; about the magical failed fishing trip at Shamrock and how we used to pack our Army rat packs together; and about how strong and proud and brave he was, braver than anyone I'd ever known. Slowly the rage began to dissipate, because the thing I'd never doubted was how proud he was of me, even though almost everything he'd ever watched me do had been a disaster; how he had always been there for me in all the ways that mattered; and how, in one way or another, he was always saving us, Lisa and me.

In the midst of this, my eyes, which were doing everything possible to avoid his, happened to sweep in his direction, and it struck me that our hands were the same. His were red-brown and strong, scarred from multiple clashes with bulls and guns and lethal chemicals, and mine were light gold and smooth, but they were the same shape. We both had a habit of holding them as if we were about to take up the reins of a horse. And there was something about that simple thought, the realization of our mutual flesh and bone, that made me remember he was human, and that, more than anything, lit the first glimmer of forgiveness in my heart. He was stubborn and he was flawed, but he'd done the best he could with what he had. At any hour, on any day, he would have taken a bullet for us.

He'd have done the same for Rhodesia, and I knew that he'd do it again for Zimbabwe, because although he'd believed with every fiber of his being in Ian Smith's war, for him it was never about the politics but about the feeling that had poured through him the day he crossed the Great Green Greasy Limpopo on the train, aged eighteen and bound for basic training: "this incredible sense of being free." It was about every rock, every tree, every grain of soil. Every Kariba sunset and every fall of rain. He was born to love the land, and maybe his transgressions were just that. Maybe he'd had to be the way he was to get through. To survive war and all its false promises, life and all its disappointments.

In war and sometimes in marriage, you start out on the right side, then history moves on and you're on the wrong side.

But in life, as in law, ignorance is no excuse, and in that I saw that I, too, was culpable. We'd been sold a dream that was especially seductive because it came with a whole lifestyle. It was an exclusive club. It even had its own language. But I should have been capable of seeing beyond that. Should have known that any club that relies for its existence on the denial of the needs and feelings of others is not a club to which any just person should want to belong. The beautiful, gentle people of Zimbabwe, I had appreciated them too late. I'd been cheated out of knowing them, and cheated myself out of it, too.

And now we had Mugabe, with his mad eyes and murderous motorcade and the CIO and stories of what happened if you took a wrong turn at State House, and the genocide and so many dead for nothing. Now someone else had been sold a dream, and look how they had been repaid. And I didn't know what the answer was, but it wasn't that, it wasn't living in fear.

Yet in spite of everything, the indomitable spirit of the people of Zimbabwe was filled with optimism. They refused to be crushed. They were still hopeful, still *certain*, that Mugabe and the wider world would do the right thing by them. But my head was full of immigrant dreams. I wanted to live somewhere where people were born free and could speak the truth openly, not somewhere where I'd be swapping one set of lies for another. Or maybe that, too, was an illusion. Maybe the only truth anywhere was your own.

In the meantime, Rainbow's End was to be sold, and new homes would have to be found for all our wild animals, including our beloved giraffe. Within months, little of our former life, our corner of heaven, would remain. Tom Beattie would buy the farm, and in years to come, Douglas, my old playmate, would cover Rainbow's End in a miracle of fragrant orange groves, but in the immediate aftermath of our leaving, a temporary manager fell asleep with a smoldering cigarette and the thatch created an inferno.

It was, Lisa said, as if the house burned down and took our history with it.

We went for a last ride. Soon Mom and Lisa would be arriving to pack up, and Dad and the horses and dogs would be moving to Wicklow Estate, to the house at Shumavale where the Forresters had lived before that one fateful night at Rainbow's End.

I stood at the field gate and called Star, and when he came I buried my face in his black mane and pressed my lips against the silken hollows behind his nostrils. He shoved me hard, not understanding, impatient to get out on the road and get running, but I wanted to imprint every detail on my mind—not just of the tensile sheen of his muscles or the way his eyes crinkled at the corners with kindness but of the house and farm beyond him.

Wherever life took me, I wanted always to remember the majesty of the storms and the smell of the fertile, wet earth afterward. I wanted to be able to close my eyes and see the giraffe slouch toward the sunset like a celestial horse, or the dawn tint the early morning mist on the river, or breathe in the hessian and tobacco in the grading sheds, or eat *sadza* and Lion beer gravy or fresh-caught bream *braaied* on a plow disk. I wanted forever to hear the haunting cry of the fish eagles, the ancient rhythms of the compound drums, the harmonies of the women returning from the lands, the sound of doves in the evening.

Dad and I saddled the horses and rode past the barns. It was late afternoon, but the air was already smoky with cooking fires. When we reached the cotton lands, we started to race. I pushed Star faster and faster, and his ears pinned flat against his head and flecks of white foam collected on his neck like crests on a midnight ocean. Dad and Cassandra dropped behind. Soon all that was left was the peculiar stillness and silence of galloping and a sense of trying to outrun the past. But the past can never be outrun. So I prayed instead that the moment would never end. That on some airborne stride we wouldn't come down but would stay forever suspended between the earth and sky.

Back at the house I helped Dad pull off his cowboy boots, and I sprawled on the couch while he went into the bar and fixed us pint glasses of Mazoe orange and soda clunking with ice—beloved rituals that would be no more. There was the crackle of static on vinyl, and the whiskey-warm tones of Don Williams filled the room with a song that, for the rest of my life, would remind me of my father. *So what do you do with good ole boys like me?*

In the morning, I'd climb the stairs to my room and begin to remove all traces of myself. The contents of my vet box would be divided between the dustbin and Dad, who could use some of them on his next farm. My paintings, rosettes, song lyrics, and favorite books would be packed away into my school trunk. With the posters taken down, the room would start to echo the way the house did the day we first came to look at it. And even though I'd have the door thrown open to the summer breeze and the thrill of birdsong, a coldness would creep in, and I'd lean against my bunk and shiver a little and think about the time that Kim saw the ghost. I'd wonder to myself what he or she had made of us.

Within a week or so I'd be gone. I'd spend a couple of months in Cape Town with my mother and sister before realizing that in order to find what I was searching for, I would have to go out into the world alone. At seventeen, I'd board a plane to England. I'd spend a year working as a veterinary nurse under the low, gray claustrophobic skies of Berkshire before returning to the citrus light of Zimbabwe and enrolling, grudgingly and under pressure from my mother to get an actual qualification, in a journalism course at the mostly black Harare Polytechnic. And there, in the unlikeliest of places, I'd begin to find myself.

At college I was surrounded by people like Arthur, who'd been sent to college by the PAC (Pan African Congress) and whose chest was a latticework of scars inflicted, so it was whispered, by South Africa's Apartheid regime; by Kingsley, who'd been sent by the ANC (African National Congress); by pompous Claudius, who'd been sent by the Army; by smart, funny Fanwell; by our beaming, roly-poly political science lecturer Dr. Zondo; by our earnest, dry-humored reporting lecturer Nyahunzvi; by our huge African law lecturer, whose sessions always began with him lighting a cigar, reclining in a chair with his feet on the desk, and telling deadpan jokes until we were crying with laughter; and by my friends—Reyhana, a Moslem girl whose mother made the best samosas in Zimbabwe; Irene, a cheerful, free-spirited part-Australian; and Emelia, the niece of heroic revolutionary Ndabaningi Sithole, who started the political party ZANU in 1963, was jailed for ten years after it was banned by Ian Smith's government, and later became part of Zimbabwe-Rhodesia's transitional black-white government and a respected political author.

Most of our other lecturers either resigned midyear or never showed up at all, and there was no budget for equipment like cameras or film, so we spent most of our time talking life, love, and politics in the sunshine or eating *sadza* and goat curry on spurious rural reporting assignments. I remember laughing more than I'd ever laughed before.

Shortly afterward Maud would come on holiday with Mom, Lisa, and me to Malawi. By that time, her uncle was the mayor of Blantyre, so while we stayed in cut-price holiday villas on the lake, she was whisked away in a limousine to stay in the mayoral mansion. When it came time to leave, she was enjoying herself so much she decided to stay on longer.

As for me, I was still consumed by the same yearnings and still driven by the same need to escape Zimbabwe in order to come to terms with the past, so in 1987 I was on a plane bound for London, and this time I knew I wouldn't be back, except when an even stronger yearning for the sounds, scents, and tastes of Africa tugged at my soul.

Twenty-two years after leaving Rainbow's End, I'd go to see Camilla to ask her for the story that we'd never really known the truth of and to ask her permission to tell it. We'd sit together on the veranda of the home she shared with Billy, looking down from a hilltop at a sky blue thread of Lake Chivero and the tops of the trees, woven together like green lace, and there, caressed by a breeze, she'd talk me through it, moment by moment, and it was the saddest story I'd ever heard. I wept with the pain of it. I cried for Bruce, for Ben, for her, and for Billy, for the pointlessness of war and the lessons history never seems to teach us, but Camilla's eyes stayed dry. She'd long since made her peace with it. The cook who'd fled out of cowardice or fear on the night of the Rainbow's End attack still worked for her.

"The important thing is not to hate," she told me. That was what had kept her sane. That and her faith in God and the love of good friends and meeting Billy, who having lost his wife and daughter in almost identical circumstances, understood what she'd been through. They'd healed each other, Camilla and Billy and their respective children, Nigel, Julie, and Victoria. They'd tried, and for the most part succeeded, to build a loving, successful future for themselves. But over the years, it had become abundantly clear that the devastation of January 9, 1978, hadn't ended on that night. Not for the Forresters, not for the other family whose sons had been killed and wounded, and not for those whom the tragedy subsequently touched: the farmers and soldiers who came to their rescue; Camilla's brother and his wife, who cleaned up the bloody rooms; and us, the family who moved in after them.

"The ripple effect," Camilla said, "the clearing up of smashed-up lives, it goes on and on forever."

Within a year of our meeting, the simple, peaceful home where I'd visited her, the home that she and Billy had built and in which they'd lived for more than a decade, had become, amid the anarchy and insanity that followed Mugabe's failed program of land reform, as dangerous as at any time during the Rhodesian War. A Norton family living on a nearby homestead were beaten and almost murdered by a gang who bypassed the alarms by coming through the roof like a television SWAT team. Another Norton farmer was killed for refusing to give up his land. Camilla and Billy felt that they had little choice but to move on and try to rebuild their lives once again before the life they had left was taken from them by force.

These things, though, were still to come. For now, it was all about good-bye.

When Dad and I had finished our drinks, we took the dogs down to the water. The evening bush was alive and vital, timeless in its capacity to keep on keeping on, to survive the vagaries of nature, the whims of men. The river, high with the summer rains—though not as high as usual because of their scarcity—flowed on unstoppably.

I sat there feeling as if my heart would break, just shatter and scatter its shards, like seeds, on the soil of Africa. There was too much to say and no way to say it.

"We had a good time here, Dad, didn't we? We've loved it here" was all I could manage, and my voice was ragged with tears.

He never took his eyes from the river. "I've had the time of my life, my friend, the time of my life," he said, and his words, too, were weighted with regret, with love, with unbearable sadness. And he meant them.

That night, perhaps because we were alone, we went to the Etheridges' for dinner. After the meal I excused myself and went outside. The sky was crazy with stars. I lay down on the riverbank and looked up at them, and I could feel the pulsing energy of the earth beneath the cold grass. The swish of water and musical *pshh* of fish jumping washed over me like a balm. Beyond the river bend, just out of sight but no less of a force, a dark presence, was Rainbow's End. I tried, and failed, to make sense of everything. What had it all been about?

Up on the rise, the Etheridges' house glowed with a soft luminescence and the faint sound of laughter and tinkle of glass floated down to me. I envied them their sureness. Their sense of place. They knew that they'd be staying in Africa and that their sons would be staying on after them. The only thing I knew for certain was that I was no longer sure where I belonged.

And as I lay gazing up at the blue-black heavens and imagining, as usual, that I was falling into them, I saw a shooting star. It was only momentary—a curving shower of light—and there was no one to witness it but the dogs, but I made a wish anyway, even though I felt, because of the lack of witnesses, a bit self-conscious doing it.

I wished that somehow, some way, I'd return to Rainbow's End. And I understood then that all I had to do was be patient.

glossary

Ag	Ach, ah.
babotie	Curried mince dish with a thin layer of egg.
badza	Hoe.
bakkie	A small pickup truck or van.
bas	Boss.
Basopa!	"Look out! Beware!"
bemba	Homemade, hand-beaten, and sharpened scythe.
biltong	Marinated, air-dried lean meat, made from beef or game.
boerewors	Spiced sausage traditionally cooked at *braais* (literally "Boers' sausage").
boma	Temporary, fenced enclosure.
boomslang	Tree snake.

braai   Barbecue.

bundu   Bush country (see also bush).

bush   The countryside, the African savanna (southern African idiom).

bushveld   *Veld* made up largely of woodland.

Chibuku   A brand of beer.

Chilapalapa   A simplistic form of Nguni (Zulu, Xhosa, Ndebele, and related languages) amalgamated with snippets of English, Dutch, and Afrikaans, which evolved out of the need to create a common language that could be quickly learned by an ever-changing migrant workforce. Also known as Fanagalo and Kitchen Kaffir.

Chimurenga   A term widely used by Zimbabwe's Shona majority to describe their struggles against oppression. The First Chimurenga refers to the 1896–1897 revolt against colonial rule, and the Second Chimurenga to Zimbabwe's war of independence.

dassie   Rock rabbit, hyrax.

doek   Cap or head scarf.

donnering   Killing.

duiker   Small African antelope with short backward-sloping horns.

Fanagalo   See Chilapalapa.

goggo   An insect, derived from the Khoikhoi word *xo-xon*, meaning "creeping things." The *g* is

	pronounced like the *ch* in the Scottish word *loch*.
Got	God.
granadilla	Passion fruit.
gukurahundi	A Shona term with several definitions along the lines of the "storm that sweeps away the chaff before the spring rains."
Hamba lapa	"Go there. Go away."
Hayikona, hayikona.	"No, don't, don't."
impala	A brown antelope with a white underbelly noted for its ability to make long, graceful leaps. The male has slender horns that grow in the shape of a lyre.
impis	Zulu warriors.
jongwe	Cockerel.
kaffir	African (derogatory).
kapenta	Dried minifish staple of African diet.
kaya	Lodging or hut.
koeksister	A syrup-drenched pastry, an Afrikaner delicacy.
kopje	A low hill or small, rocky outcrop.
kudu	The largest African antelope, with long, spiral horns.
Kunjani?	"How are you?"
kutundu	Belongings.

Lekker!	Fantastic!
lobola	A marriage dowry usually paid in cattle.
madala	Old man.
mielie-meal	Corn, maize.
munt	African (derogatory).
muntu	A person, a human being.
muputahayi	Unleavened African bread made from *mielie-meal.*
mush	Nice, delicious (slang—pronounced "moosh," as in "It's moosh in the bush").
ntsimbi	Iron, steel implement or gong, bell.
numnah	Felt or sheepskin cloth placed under a saddle to prevent chafing.
nxa	Expletive, expression of displeasure.
nyoka	Snake.
okes	Blokes (slang).
pawpaw	Papaya.
picannin	Small; child.
quagga	Extinct southern-African wild ass. Less fully striped than the zebra.
sadza	Porridge made from maize or *mielie-meal.*
shamwari	Friend.
shateen	The wilderness.

shumba	A lion, or slang for beer (Lion beer is a common Rhodesian brand).
sjambok	A whip, traditionally made of rhinoceros hide.
skelem	Rascal.
sponspek	Honeydew melon.
stoepas	Identity papers.
takkies	White plimsolls or sneakers.
tsotsi	A young hooligan or scoundrel.
umbanje	Marijuana.
umdala wethu	"Our old man."
veld	Open, unforested, or thinly forested grassland.
veldskoens	Fawn-colored, rough suede shoes.
vlei	Low-lying ground where a shallow lake forms in the wet season.
Voortrekkers	Dutch farmers from the Cape who took part in the Great Trek to the Transvaal in the nineteenth century.
Wena mampara, wena	"You useless person, you."
wildebeest	Gnu.
Yena file?	"Is he dead?"
Yena penga stelek	"He's very mad."

ACRONYMS

ANC	African National Congress
CID	Criminal Investigation Department
CIO	Central Intelligence Organization
FRELIMO	Front for the Liberation of Mozambique
PATU	Police Antiterrorist Unit
RAR	Rhodesian African Rifles
RENAMO	Mozambique National Resistance
RLI	Rhodesian Light Infantry
UDI	Unilateral Declaration of Independence
ZANLA	Zimbabwe African National Liberation Army
ZANU	Zimbabwe African National Union
ZANU-PF	Zimbabwe African National Union Patriotic Front
ZAPU	Zimbabwe African People's Union
ZIPRA	Zimbabwe People's Revolutionary Army

acknowledgments

Although it's true that writers spend an unnatural amount of time alone, staring at blank sheets of paper, very few books happen without the help of an extensive network of people. This particular book would not have happened at all without the extraordinary kindness of Clive Priddle, the editor of my biography of Steve Earle and one of my very favorite people, and Catherine Clarke, my agent. Between them, they changed my life.

I'm indebted to Clive, who, when I was fresh out of confidence and ready to give up on writing and get a real job, gently persuaded me not to and put me in touch with Catherine, who is, for me, the perfect agent. Writing this book has been one of the hardest, most rewarding, most terrifying, most beautiful experiences of my life, but I couldn't have made it through a day of it without the unwavering faith and support of Catherine. Thanks for every amazing thing you've done for me—and there have been too many to list—and, most of all, for always, always being there when I need you. You're the best. The absolute best.

In the United States, Beth Wareham, Nan Graham, and Susan Moldow at Scribner; in the UK, Tom Weldon, Simon Prosser, and Judy Moir at Hamish Hamilton; and in Holland, Sander Knol at De Boekerij took a huge leap of faith by signing me on not a huge amount of evidence and, from the very beginning, blew me away with their incredible belief in my book. So, too, did Emma Parry at Fletcher & Parry, who was responsible for getting the book to Beth and Nan in the first place and who, like Catherine, is an ace agent in every way.

Thanks also to the wonderful translation agents at Andrew Nurnberg Associates and to James Kellow, Sarah Day, Jill Vogel, and everyone else behind the scenes at Scribner and Penguin, but especially to Judy, my editor at Hamish Hamilton, who apart from being a gifted editor and one of the nicest people in publishing is a Zimbabwean! I'm holding out for my *sadza* and gravy supper in Edinburgh!

A big thank-you to Beth Wareham for being a "pussycat of an editor" and for being so irrepressibly enthusiastic and embracing me and my pet stories so wholeheartedly! Yours and Nan's faith in me helped so much when I sat down to a blank page each morning. I'm so happy that it was my proposal you decided to read on the subway that day!

Nerrilee Weir and Tracey Cox collectively saved my sanity by allowing me to gatecrash their lunch and making me laugh and diverting me over the course of several weeks with the most entertaining, stimulating, and memorable conversations and emails. Thanks. I owe you both, and I plan to make sure you collect!

Writing can be the most outrageously solitary profession, and sometimes a phone call is the only thing that lies between an author and total despair. It also reminds you that somewhere out there, people are going to movies, reading newspapers in the park, watching *Prison Break*, and doing other things that you did once and might, on some unimaginably far-off day, do again. I feel incredibly fortunate to have amazing friends who were prepared to listen, uncomplainingly, while I whined about how I felt like I was climbing Everest and I'd only just left Base Camp, for the best part of seven months! Thanks to Merina who supported me through one of the toughest times in my life; Jane, one of the most caring people I know; Liz (Thanks for always being there and for the unbelievable food! Cheers, Caroline!); Bev (Thanks for listening); Will (Thanks for mentoring me for all these years!); Jean (Thanks for the lessons in faith); Chris, Reyhana, and the Santin family, Carole, Don, and Kellie, who were there at the beginning. Thanks also to Martin and Emelia, who have accepted me and my flawed past with so much love and forgiveness and trust, and who encouraged me to write the truth and, in the midst of the telling of it, did me the huge honor of making me godmother (with Reyhana) to their firstborn son, Matis Sandile Sithole Matarise. Thanks. It means the world to me.

In Zimbabwe, Richard and Catherine Etheridge entertained me for hours over coffee and delicious homemade biscuits with very funny and unbelievably detailed anecdotes. I'm also grateful to Sue, Thomas, and Douglas Beattie for their willingness to be part of my book; and to Lee Walters and Juliet Keevil for the great afternoon of catch-up!

Thanks to Canadian singer Jann Arden, whose wonderful music and hilarious London show provided the perfect celebration for the completion of this book.

There is no way for me adequately to express my love and gratitude to my parents and my sister, Lisa, who put their lives in my hands and allowed me to tell the whole story, knowing what it would mean. Thanks for the beautiful times and, most of all, for Rainbow's End.

A special thank-you to Miss Zeederberg, my English teacher at Roosevelt High School in Harare, Zimbabwe, for giving me the courage to become a writer. You made me believe in the power of words, and I never forgot yours.

Lastly, and most important, thanks to Camilla and Billy, two of the bravest and most extraordinary people I've ever known, for entrusting me with your story. I hope that my words, though inadequate, go some way toward honoring the gentle, beautiful people who lost their lives in Norton and at Rainbow's End.